Movies and
the Meaning of Life

Movies and the Meaning of Life

Philosophers Take On Hollywood

KIMBERLY A. BLESSING
and
PAUL J. TUDICO

OPEN COURT
Chicago and La Salle, Illinois

To order books from Open Court, call toll-free 1-800-815-2280, or visit our website at www.opencourtbooks.com.

Open Court Publishing Company is a division of Carus Publishing Company.

Library of Congress Cataloging-in-Publication Data

Movies and the meaning of life : philosophers take on hollywood / [edited by] Kimberly A. Blessing and Paul J. Tudico.
    p. cm.
  Includes bibliographical references and index.
  ISBN-13: 978-0-8126-9575-5 (isbn 13 - trade paper : alk. paper)
  ISBN-10: 0-8126-9575-5 (isbn 10 - trade paper : alk. paper)
  1. Motion pictures--Philosophy. I. Blessing, Kimberly Ann. II. Tudico, Paul J.
  PN1995.M665 2005
  791.43'684—dc22

                            2004030778

*To our family and friends
who make our lives meaningful*

Contents

Take Five: How Should I Live My Life?

You Mean So Much to Us

Thanks to our authors for their talents and patience; given such a broad topic, we were delighted by the diversity of approaches to the question and enthusiasm with which you engaged the project. We are also grateful to Bill Irwin for making this project possible, and for his helpful editorial feedback and advice. We thank David Ramsay Steele at Open Court for supporting our project, from beginning to end.

Various friends and colleagues have provided useful comments on drafts of essays: David Baggett, John Zavodny, Tony Sciglitano, Abigail Myers, and Justin Donhauser. Special thanks are due to Brennan Hanagan, for his professionalism and efficiency, and Walter Ott for his help on the index.

Kimberly would like to thank her very dear friend Paul for being "the big picture guy"—at the end of the day, if the devil is in the details, you are a saint! Thanks to my students who participated in the pilot for "Movies and The Meaning of Life"— your questions and comments helped to shape my ideas for this book, and more importantly, my thinking about the meaning of life. Thanks to my former friends and colleagues at Siena Heights University, especially Brother Frank Rotsaert C.S.C., Mark Schersten, Dan McVeigh, Jun Tsuji, Mike Clinton, Claudia Blanchard, and Peter and Kim Barr (and the girls)—I miss the collegiality and the cocktails. Thanks to George Hole at Buffalo State College who has been supportive of the project from the beginning. I have been blessed with good fortune, good family, and good friends: to my parents, Bob and Barb, to Kirsten, Brennan, Jack and Harry, and to my friends, especially Michelle, Paul, and Tony—thank you for your generosity and love. And finally to Tim, the most generous and loving—we'll always have Wilkes-Barre.

Paul would like to thank Kimberly for her patience on this project and her friendship throughout the years. A big thanks goes out to all those thoughtful students who suffered through my sections of "Philosophy as Conversation." There are too many to name (but you know who you are). I would also like to thank my colleagues in the Department of Philosophy and Humanities at East Tennessee State University, and Marie Graves for her ability to make sure everything happens that needs to happen. Good philosophy is very often done with good friends and I have had the pleasure of sharing discussions of this project and others with Steven Fesmire, Rebecca Hanrahan, John Hardwig, Heather Keith, Hugh LaFollette, Anna McGalliard, Walter Ott, David Reisman, Jim Spence, James Stacey Taylor, Hamish Thompson, and John Zavodny. Finally, I have the luxury of being surrounded by a supportive family, and my deepest thanks go to my mother and father, Claire and Jack Tudico, and my sisters, Karen, Maryellen, and Maria.

So . . . Why "The Meaning of Life"?

As sure as you're reading this page, you've probably asked yourself: "What's it all about?" "Who am I?" "Why am I here?" Maybe it was a bad break-up, losing a job, the death of a loved one, being confronted with a tough moral dilemma, or simply getting philosophical over a late-night beer (or two) with friends that prompted your query. These and similar questions are related to the larger one: "What is the meaning of life?" There is probably no other question that people more commonly associate with philosophy. It's a grand question, but it's also a great question because it forces us to reflect on our values, beliefs, and worldviews. The question "What is the meaning of life?" is related to the age-old question posed by the ancient Greek philosopher Socrates, "How should I live?" We'll come clean. We've not yet solved the riddle of existence.

Yet the twentieth-century existentialist philosopher Albert Camus says that "the meaning of life is the most urgent of questions." At the same time, American filmmaker Woody Allen wonders: "How is it possible to find meaning in a finite world, given my waist and shirt size?" So we might be in a bit of a bind. One response might be that life has no meaning, which is a view supported by *nihilists*, from the Latin *nihil*, meaning "nothing." Suffice it to say, if the nihilist is right, we're out a book deal. So instead we might think that the meaning of life is found in the grand scheme of things, that is, the meaning or purpose of life is found in *discovering* our place in the world or cosmos. This view contrasts with a third alternative, which suggests that we need to *create* meaning in our lives through the choices and projects that we find important.

So . . . Why Movies?

The old fashioned approach towards finding the meaning of life involves traveling to a far-off land, climbing a distant mountain, and consulting a bearded old wise man. We're suggesting a cheaper and easier method: to look at the question through popular movies. Movies pervade our culture. Who hasn't filled an uncomfortable silence with: "So have you seen any good movies lately?" Everyone, even philosophers, likes talking about movies, and we think that we've assembled a pretty good list of titles. Some are Hollywood blockbusters, others are smaller independent movies, and some are cult classics. Instead of asking our contributors to simply wax philosophical on their favorite flick, we asked them to focus in on what their movie says about the meaning of life.

In order for a life to be meaningful, we might think about who we are, whether or not we are happy, whether or not the projects we pursue are worthwhile, and how our relationships with others contribute to a meaningful life. Additionally, we may wonder if God's existence is necessary in order for our lives to be meaningful, to what extent we have control over who we are and how we live our lives, and whether or not truth, beauty, and moral goodness are necessary for a life to be meaningful.

To help the reader navigate these waters, we've divided up the book into five sections. "Take One: Are You For Real?" looks at Jim Carey in *The Truman Show*, the ultimate in reality-TV. *Contact*, starring Oscar-winning actress Jodie Foster, is based on astronomer Carl Sagan's 1985 science-fiction novel. And Richard Linklater's independent film *Waking Life*, which opened only days after September 11th, is an animated odyssey through life and dreams. Essays in this section examine in general questions about how the search for truth relates to our search for meaning.

"Take Two: Who Am I?" includes the cult favorite, *Fight Club* with Ed Norton and Brad Pitt. *Being John Malkovich*, written by Charlie Kaufman (who also wrote *Eternal Sunshine of the Spotless Mind* and *Adaptation*), stars John Cusack and Cameron Diaz. Kimberly Pierce's *Boys Don't Cry* is a movie based on the 1993 murder of Teena Brandon; the film stars Hilary Swank who won an Academy Award for Best Actress. The final movie is Christopher Nolan's epistemological thriller *Memento*, starring Guy Pierce. All of the essays in this section take up questions having to do with personal identity, or questions about ourselves as persons; for example, what it takes for one person to persist from one time to another, and what makes you the person you are.

"Take Three: Am I Alone?" begins with one of Woody Allen's all-time great movies, *Crimes and Misdemeanors*. Then we look at *Shadowlands*, directed by Richard Attenborough, which tells the story of the love affair between the Christian apologist C.S. Lewis (played by Anthony Hopkins) and Joy Grisham. And Kevin Smith's *Chasing Amy*, starring Ben Affleck and Joey Lauren Adams, takes a look at the confusing world of modern relationships. The essays in this section consider whether or not God is necessary for meaning, and how our relationships with others, including our relationship with God, contribute to the meaningfulness of our lives.

"Take Four: What Do I Want Out of Life?" includes *American Beauty*, winner of the 1999 Academy Award for Best Picture, staring Kevin Spacey and Annette Bening, who portray characters caught up in the *ennui* of American suburban life. Roberto Benigni's *Life Is Beautiful* tells the story of one family's love in the midst of the horror of a Jewish Concentration Camp; it won Benigni the 1998 Oscar for Best Actor and Best Foreign Film. *The Shawshank Redemption,* based on a short story by Stephen King, stars Tim Robbins and Morgan Freeman who play prison inmates in search of hope and redemption. Finally, Uma Thurman stars in Quentin Tarantino's *Kill Bill, Volumes I and II,* the violent tale of one woman's quest for revenge. These essays all take up various specific values and ideals that make up a meaningful life.

Finally, "Take Five: How Should I Live My Life?" includes *Pleasantville*, a comedy directed by Gary Ross (who wrote *Seabiscuit*, *Big*, and *Dave*), starring Toby McGuire and Reese Witherspoon, two modern-day teenagers transported back to the black and white land of a 1950s TV show. The blockbuster mega-hits, *Spider-Man 1 and 2* follow the growing pains of the Marvel Comics superhero. *Minority Report* has Tom Cruise as a futuristic cop who attempts to stops crimes before they even happen. Quentin Tarantino's cult classic *Pulp Fiction,* stars John Travolta and Samuel L. Jackson who play modern-day thugs attempting to navigate the murky moral waters of the contemporary world. And to conclude, we've included a movie that has got to be on everyone's list of all time great comedies, *Groundhog Day* starring Bill Murray—by putting this essay at the end, we're hoping you'll be tempted to read the book all over again. The essays in this final section raise the connection between meaning and morality, and consider the extent to which being morally good is necessary for living a meaningful life.

So . . . Why This Book?

The essays in this book don't need to be read in any particular order, but it's probably a good idea to see the movie before reading the corresponding essay. We'd suggest skimming the Table of Contents, and starting with one of your favorite movies. We hope you'll also discover other movies that might be added to your list of favorites. But most of all, we hope you'll discover a little philosophy—that's the bait and switch that we've shamelessly employed. To help you to think more philosophically about these issues related to the meaning of life, we have come up with questions for reflection, as well as suggestions for further reading at the end of each essay. But it's not homework, so feel free to blow it off. You won't hurt our feelings.

Philosophy begins by asking a question. The twentieth-century philosopher Bertrand Russell adds that "philosophy, if it cannot answer so many questions as we could wish, has at least the power of asking questions which increase the interest of the world, and show the strangeness and wonder lying just below the surface even in the commonest things of daily life." We hope that these essays we've brought together will help readers to both ask questions and wonder about the meaning of life.

At the very least, we hope that watching these movies and reading these essays will better equip you for those late night discussions.

Take One

Are You for Real?

1

Deceit and Doubt: The Search for Truth in *The Truman Show* and Descartes's *Meditations*

KIMBERLY A. BLESSING

> You'll be surprised how fast, how easy it is for someone to steal your and my mind. You don't think so? We never like to think in terms of being dumb enough to let someone put something over on us in a very deceitful and tricky way . . .One of the best ways to safeguard yourself from being deceived is always to form the habit of looking at things for yourself, listening to things for yourself, thinking for yourself, before you try to come to any judgment.
>
> — MALCOLM X, *At the Audobon* (1965)

> And let him deceive me as much as he can, he will never bring it about that I am nothing as long as I think I am something... *I am. I exist...* What am I? A thing that thinks."
>
> — DESCARTES, *Meditations on First Philosophy* (1642)

Who am I? Why am I here? What's it all about? What is the meaning of life? Imbedded in these questions is the assumption that the life being considered really is *my* life. In other words, the life I am living, the activities I engage in, the friendships I nurture, the beliefs I form (about art, politics, morality, religion, life, death, the afterlife), the things that I value, all of these things involve me. *I* am central to the story-line. *I* am so to speak the star of the show.

But what if I were to find out that the life I am living had been scripted? What if I'm simply starring in a play of my life,

3

and I don't know it? How do I know that I'm not being tricked into thinking that the events of my life are actually happening, and the result of my choices, when in fact it's all an illusion? Would this life still be a meaningful life?

In Peter Weir's movie about the ultimate "reality" TV show *The Truman Show,* we are introduced to a powerful television producer who undertakes to build the largest television studio ever created in order to film an entire human life "recorded on an intricate network of hidden cameras, and broadcast live and unedited twenty-four hours a day, seven days a week to an audience around the globe." Christof (Ed Harris), the show's creator, adopts Truman as an infant, the first child legally adopted by a corporation. Truman Burbank (Jim Carrey) seems relatively content to live out a clichéd happy existence on the idyllic island of Seahaven. Until, that is, Truman narrowly escapes being crushed by a movie-camera light that comes crashing down from "the heavens." This event, followed by other similar events, suggests to Truman that something is not right. Sitting on the beach, watching the sunset with his best friend Marlon (Noah Emmerich), and sharing what appears to be a moment of genuine male-bonding, Truman begins to wonder.

> **TRUMAN:** Maybe I'm being set up for something. You ever think about that, Marlon? That your whole life has been building towards something?
> **Marlon:** Nnnnn-no.

Little does Truman know, that instead of God, or some higher power, initiating a plan for Truman's life, he's being deceived by Christof into thinking that the life that he is living is one that he has chosen for himself.

Both television and movie viewers alike know that Truman is being duped. The drama comes from wondering, "How will it end?"—a slogan captured on buttons, T-shirts, and posters purchased by fans of the TV show. We all wonder when Truman will find out, if ever. And what will happen when, and if, he does? Christof thinks that Truman will simply "accept the reality of the world with which we're presented." Christof has himself convinced that he is actually helping Truman by sheltering him from the real world, which he refers to as a "sick place." Christof wants for his son what any loving father wants: a "normal" life.

Though he admits that Truman's world is "in some respects counterfeit," he assures us that "there's nothing *fake* about Truman himself. No scripts, no cue cards . . . It isn't always Shakespeare but it's *genuine*. It's a life." But what kind of life could this be?

Lights, Camera, Action! *Cogito ergo Sum*

Almost four hundred years before the making of *The Truman Show*, French philosopher and mathematician, René Descartes (1596–1650) locks himself away in a *poêl* (that's French for a stove-heated room) and begins to think. Instead of constructing the world's largest television studio (Guttenberg had only recently invented the printing press), Descartes imagines that the entire world external to him is a grand illusion cooked up by some clever and malicious demon. "I will suppose . . . some malicious demon of the utmost power and cunning has employed all of his energies in order to deceive me."[1] Should such a demon exist, even the most simple and universal truths like '2 + 3 = 5' and 'squares have four sides' would have to be called into question. By the end of the first of his six *Meditations on First Philosophy*, Descartes is forced to conclude that

> the sky, the air, the earth, colors, shapes, sounds and all external things are merely the delusions of dreams which he has devised to ensnare my judgment. I shall consider myself as not having hands or eyes, or flesh, or blood or senses, but as falsely believing that I have all these things. (p. 15)

One can't help identifying the character of Christof with Descartes's deceiving demon, both of them master tricksters. Whereas Descartes's malicious demon deceives for the sake of deceiving, Christof deceives for the sake of something greater— television ratings! He makes it so that nothing in Truman's world is real: not his childhood, not his job, not his marriage. Everyone, including his adoring television viewing audience, is

---

[1] René Descartes, *The Philosophical Writings of Descartes*, Volume II, translated and edited by J. Cottingham, R. Stoothoff, and D. Murdoch (Cambridge: Cambridge University Press, 1984), p. 15.

complicit in the lie: his perky, impeccably coiffed wife Meryl (Laura Linney), a capable actress making a killing on well-timed product placements, his best friend Marlon, whose friendship with Truman comes across as perhaps the most genuine of any of his relationships, even his own mother (Holland Taylor), who guilt-trips Truman over the "accidental" death of his father. (Christof actually had Truman's father "die" in a boating accident, once the actor tried to let Truman in on the ruse.) Christof even goes so far to manufacture Truman's fears, like his fear of water, which is used to keep him from escaping the island-set of Seahaven.

The Truman Show depicts the difficulty in maintaining such an intricate and elaborate falsehood. Things go wrong: camera lights fall from the sky, actors don't follow their cues, and stages and sound sets are eventually exposed. It will take the entire movie for Truman to discover the extent to which he is being deceived. When he does put it all together, Truman bravely confronts Christof. Contrary to Christof's prediction, Truman resolutely rejects the world that his adoptive father has so carefully constructed for him.

In Descartes's *Meditations*, Descartes was both producer and star of his own show. Some people might see genius, others lunacy, at forcing himself to maintain such hyperbolic doubts, against his own will.[2] The subsequent drama that unfolds in the *Meditations* has to do with wondering how Descartes will beat the demon at his own game. Like Truman, Descartes comes to realize that there is at least one thing about which he can't be deceived. Truman points out that Christof could never get the camera inside of his head. For Descartes, the Evil Demon can never make him doubt his existence as a thinking thing: "and let him deceive me as much as he can, he will never bring it about that I am nothing as long as I think that I am something . . . *I am. I exist*, is necessarily true . . ." (p. 17).

---

[2] "I am like a prisoner who is enjoying an imaginary freedom while asleep; he dreads being woken up and goes on with the pleasant illusion as long as he can. In the same way, I happily slide back into my old opinions and dread being shaken out of them, for fear that my peaceful sleep may be followed by hard labour when I wake, and that I shall have to toil not in the light, but amid the inexorable darkness of the problems I have now raised," First Meditation (Descartes, p. 15).

So What's the Problem?

The Cartesian version of *The Truman Show*, in which Descartes uses the Evil Demon to ponder the possibility that everything in his world is counterfeit, raises what has come to be known as *The Problem of the External World*: Can I know [with certainty] that there does exist a world independent of my perceptions or ideas of the world? This problem was first raised by the ancient school of philosophers known as the Skeptics, who questioned whether certain knowledge was possible.

Pyrrho of Elis (around 365–275 B.C.), the father of Pyrrhonian, or extreme, skepticism was perhaps the archetype of the non-committal male. He believed that the nature of things is beyond our grasp; as a result none of our beliefs (or experiences) are either true or false. We ought to therefore suspend judgment (skeptical *epoché*) with respect to such questions. By declining to give our assent or dissent from any proposition, including the proposition 'knowledge is not possible,' Pyrrho thought we could achieve *ataraxia*, a state of "unperturbedness," or untroubled mental calm.[3] Bobby McFerrin's famous song, "Don't Worry, Be Happy" comes to mind.

Around the same time (300 B.C.), a more moderate version of skepticism was *en vogue* at Plato's Academy. These Academic Skeptics took literally Socrates's claim "All that I know is that I know nothing," and agreed with the Pyrrhonians that absolutely certain knowledge was not possible. Instead of advocating the suspense of judgment—which could lead to some real practical problems for everyday living—they advocated a theory of probabilism: the best information we can gain is only probable and should be judged by probabilities or persuasiveness.[4] I can't know with certainty that the sky is not falling, but it's pretty unlikely.

Unlike the Pyrrhonists, Descartes does not advocate skepticism as a way of life; instead his doubt is *methodological*. He believes that by *acting* like a Skeptic—*pretending* that we are being deceived by an Evil Demon (or that we are dreaming, or

---

[3] There are no written records of Pyrrho's own words, but his teachings, as well as those of other ancient Skeptics, come down to us through *Outlines of Pyrrhonism* by Sextus Empiricus (around A.D. 150–250).

[4] In the early middle ages, Saint Augustine (A.D. 354–430) wrote a critique of Academic Skepticism, which was accepted as a definitive rejection of this school of philosophy for almost a thousand years.

insane)—we can *answer* the Skeptic's challenge that certain knowledge is not possible. We must imagine that we, like Truman, could be the victims of some cosmic joke: maybe the world isn't as we know it to be. This novel approach for arriving at truth, or *Cartesian Method*, consists in using doubt to arrive at certainty. For Descartes, resolution of such self-imposed doubts is found in the one thing that he cannot doubt, namely his own existence. This gives rise to the famous Cartesian axiom "I think therefore I am," (in Latin, *Cogito ergo sum*), which has also been captured (sometimes distorted) on buttons, billboards, and t-shirts.

Of course we know that *The Truman Show* is merely a fictional story. Likewise for Descartes there really is no evil demon. Sometimes students remark that the whole scenario seems too implausible—this guy (maybe all philosophers) has too much time on his hands. But seventeenth-century Europe was experiencing tremendous social, political, religious, and cultural change that was spurred on in part by the great intellectual revolutions of the day. All of this made the Skeptic's claim that 'certain knowledge is not possible' seem more compelling, and skepticism was *en vogue* once again.

In our own day, the challenge that is presented in Descartes' *Meditations* is equally gripping: What, if anything, can be known with certainty? And if I can't be sure of what is real, or whether or not I can know what is true, then how can I really be said to care about being in control of my life? For it seems that in order for a life—*my* life—to be meaningful, *I'd* have to exercise control over it: where I go to college, what I chose for a major or career, where I live, who I marry, which friends I spend my time with, where I go on vacation, which activities I pursue in my leisure time. It's pretty hard to think of *my* life being meaningful if I'm a mere puppet, or actor, playing out a role scripted by someone else. Put another way, before we can even begin to figure out the meaning of life, either of "life" in general or our own particular lives, hadn't we better be sure that the lives we are living are truly ours?

Who Cares, As Long As I'm Happy?

But what of another kind of skeptic who might suggest that none of this really matters, as long as I'm happy? Prior to knowing that he's being duped, Truman was living a seemingly idyllic life: he had a good job, a nice house with a white picket fence, friendly neighbors, a good job, a beautiful wife, a caring best friend, a loving mother. And these seem to be the things that we all want. But could Truman's life really be considered meaningful if he were to remain ignorant of the truth that he is merely a character starring in his own TV-show?

To show that the truth about his life *does* matter, let's look at Truman's real and apparent love interests, comparing his relationship with his made-for-TV-wife Meryl, and Truman's true love Sylvia (Natascha McElhone), the former actress named Lauren, who was ousted from the show when she tried to reveal the truth to Truman. When Truman begins to figure out that he's being deceived, he confronts Meryl. Instead of expressing any concern for Truman's welfare, all she cares about is her career: "How can anyone expect me to carry on under these conditions? This is . . . *unprofessional*." It seems that if Meryl really loved Truman, she'd want to help Truman figure out the truth, and perhaps empathize with his well-placed anger at having been lied to.

In the following exchange between Sylvia / Lauren and Christof, Sylvia / Lauren expresses her indignation at what he is doing to the man she loves.

SYLVIA: I'd just like to say one thing: You're a liar and a manipulator and what you've done to Truman is sick . . . What right do you have to take a baby an-an-and turn his life into some kind of mockery? Don't you ever feel guilty?

CHRISTOF: I have given Truman a chance to live a normal life. The world. The place you live in is the sick place. Seahaven is the way the world should be.

SYLVIA: He's not a performer, he's a prisoner. Look at him. Look at what you've done to him.

CHRISTOF: He can leave at any time. If it was more than just a vague ambition, if he was absolutely determined to discover the truth, there is no way we could prevent him from leaving. What distresses you really, caller, is that ultimately, Truman prefers his "cell," as you call it.

SYLVIA: That's where you're wrong. You're so wrong. And he'll prove you wrong.

Sylvia / Lauren, the only person in Truman's life who truly cares for him, ends up being right. When given the chance, Truman does leave the safe haven of Seahaven.

We care about the truth because truth is integrally tied to our happiness. What I want when I'm in love is to actually *be* in love; the goodness of love comes from *being* in love, not the mere *appearance* of being in love. Instead of being a mere feeling, happiness is concerned with a relationship between the subject claiming to be happy and the object of that person's interests. But that object has to be real.

There's Nothing Like the Real Thing, Baby

To strengthen this point, we might look to contemporary philosopher Robert Nozick and his famous experience machine, introduced in his *Anarchy, State, and Utopia*.[5] Nozick devised this thought experiment to argue against the utilitarian philosophy of Jeremy Bentham, which relies upon *hedonism*, or the view that equates pleasure with goodness. Nozick's machine is a very sophisticated network of electrodes that can be used to stimulate our nervous system. While plugged into this machine, we could imagine that any kind of experience we enjoy having (going to the movies, eating pizza, kissing Tom Cruise) could be simulated by the machine. Nozick then asks: "Should you plug into the machine for life?" Who-cares-as-long-as-I'm-happy-guy would probably answer "yes." Nozick, and I think most of us (including Descartes and Truman), would probably answer "no." As Nozick claims: "We want to do certain things, and not just have the experience of doing them" (p. 43).

If we carry this idea through to *The Truman Show*, we might imagine that a more clever producer might have consulted with the neurophysiologists who made Nozick's experience machine. Not only could they script Truman's life, but they could also program into him the experience of liking his job, loving his wife, enjoying beers with his friend Marlon. But something would still

---

[5] New York: Basic Books, 1974, pp. 42–45. For the discussion of Nozick's experience machine, I've borrowed heavily from the discussion of it found in Gerold J. Erion and Barry Smith, "Skeptics, Morality, and The Matrix," in *The Matrix and Philosophy: Welcome To the Desert of The Real* (Chicago: Open Court, 2002), pp. 25–27.

be missing. As Christof admits, the world he has created, like the world generated by Descartes's deceiving demon, *is* counterfeit. And no one would prefer a counterfeit hundred dollar bill to the real one. Even *Coca-Cola* realized, there's nothing like the real thing, baby. Given the option, Truman chooses the genuine relationship with Sylvia / Lauren to his staged marriage to Meryl. He constructs a picture of Sylvia / Lauren out of magazine photos, and sets out on a seaward journey to the ends of the earth in order to find her. The fact that he is willing to risk life and limb to find her suggests his commitment to *true* love. Moreover, it's doubtful that Truman would go back to Seahaven, even if even if Sylvia / Lauren could be somehow brainwashed into rejoining the cast of the show.

It should be emphasized that the point of Nozick's experience machine is not for us to imagine that there could exist a machine so sophisticated that it could actually succeed at deceiving us into thinking that we're having an experience when we are not. Instead, Nozick uses this thought experiment to show us that it's not the *appearance* of meaningful action (or a meaningful life) that matters, it's the genuine, meaningful action (or life) that does. "We learn that something matters to us in addition to experience by imagining an experience machine *and then realizing that we would not use it*" (emphasis added, p. 44). Nozick's point is that, *given the choice*, most of us would opt for the real thing rather than the mere experience of it.

How's It Going to End?

In the following exchange that takes place between Christof and Truman towards the end of the movie, Truman finally realizes that he is unwittingly the star of his own show.

CHRISTOF: Truman, you can speak. I can hear you.
TRUMAN: Who are you?
CHRISTOF: I am the Creator [pause] of a television show that gives hope, and joy and inspiration to millions.
TRUMAN: Then who am I?
CHRISTOF: You're the star.
TRUMAN: Was nothing real?
CHRISTOF: *You* were real. That's what made you so good to watch. Listen to *Me* Truman, there's no more truth out

there than there is in the world *I* created for you. The same lies. The same deceit. But in *my* world you have nothing to fear. I know you better than you know yourself.

TRUMAN: You *never* had a camera in my head.

CHRISTOF: You're afraid. That's why you can't leave. [Caressing the screen.] It's okay, Truman. I understand. I have been watching you your whole life. I was watching when you were born. I was watching when you took your first step. I watched you on your first day of school. The episode when you lost your first tooth. You can't leave, Truman. You belong here. With me.

Manipulating his fear of water that he created in Truman, Christof cues a storm at sea like the one that was used to kill Truman's father. In his boat the *Santa Maria*, Truman clutches his picture of Sylvia / Lauren.

CHRISTOF: Give me some lightning . . . Again! Hit 'im again!

MOSES: For God's sake, Chris! The whole world is watching! We can't let him die in front of a live audience!

CHRISTOF: He was born in front of a live audience!

Television and movie viewers anxiously watch Truman navigate the increasingly dangerous waters.

TRUMAN: Is that the best you can do!? You're gunner haft' KILL ME! (*sings*) What shall we do with the drunken sailor? What shall we do with the drunken sailor? What shall we do with the drunken sailor, early in the morning? . . .

CHRISTOF: Increase the wind. Increase the wind . . . Capsize him . . . Tip him over . . . DO IT . . . DO IT!

To the relief of everyone in the production studio, except Christof, the storm is cued to subside. Through the exaggerated viewpoint of the camera lens, we see Truman hanging limp over the side of the boat unsure if he is dead or alive. Slowly he comes to, and crawls along the side of the boat to hoist the sail. As the sun reappears and the winds pick up the sail, the *Santa Maria* runs abruptly into a wall of the set. Truman stands at the bow and pounds the imaginary sky. Leaving the boat, he walks across the set's water and comes upon a set of stairs that lead off of the sound-stage. He ascends and approaches the door marked "exit." In response to Christof's demand that he say something "live to the whole world," he turns around and responds: "In case I don't see ya', good afternoon, good evening and goodnight. Hahaha! Yeah!" He then bows deeply and exits the stage.

Audiences cheer as Truman exits the studio. We cheer because we, like Truman, realize that reality, even if unknown, must be preferred to some counterfeit version of it. Like Truman, Descartes was lost at sea: "So serious are the doubts into which I have been thrown as a result of yesterday's meditation [referring to the Evil Demon] that I can neither put them out of my mind nor see any way of resolving them. It feels as if I have fallen unexpectedly into a deep whirlpool which tumbles me around so that I can neither stand on the bottom nor swim to the top" (p. 16). As we do with Truman, we feel empowered when Descartes boldly pronounces that nothing or no one, however powerful, can render him nothing as long as he *thinks* that he is something. For some of us, the book is better than the movie!

The Cartesian Challenge

In *The Truman Show*, Weir portrays Truman as an unusually adventurous boy with a vivid imagination, who as an adult plays make-believe in the bathroom mirror before leaving for work. In a flashback to his childhood, we see the young Truman in the classroom.

> **Truman:** I'd like to be an explorer. Like the great Magellan.
> **Teacher:** (*a bit too quickly and pulling down a map of the world*) Oh, you're too late. There's really nothing left to explore.

This spirit of adventure is further reflected in Truman's recurring desire (which seems to be of his own making) to travel to Fiji, where one "can't get any further away before you start coming back." If we recall the early scene in which Truman sits on the beach with his friend Marlon, wondering if he is not a part of something bigger, Truman appears restless. And this restlessness seems evident long before Truman figures out that his entire life has been scripted. Christof sees this in Truman, which is why he goes to such great lengths to manufacture ways to keep him on the island, such as creating in him a fear of water, bridges, and barking dogs.

Descartes too was restless as a boy: "From my childhood I have been nourished upon letters . . . But as soon as I completed the course of study at the end of which one is normally admitted into the ranks of the learned, I completely changed my opinion. For I found myself beset with . . . many doubts and errors . . ." (Descartes, Volume I, p. 113). Reflecting back upon his years at university (having attended one of the most celebrated schools in all of Europe) Descartes recounts that as soon as he was old enough to emerge from the control of his teachers, he abandoned the study of letters and "firmly resolved to seek no knowledge other than that which could be found in myself or else in the great book of the world" (Descartes, Volume I, p. 118).

Once both Truman and Descartes were old enough to think and ask questions, they began to suspect that something was not right. At the very least, they seemed to realize that at some point in our lives, we need to take some time away from it all to ask the big, and sometimes scary questions about our lives, our selves, and the world in which we live. Descartes thinks that few of us would ultimately take the "Cartesian Challenge"—push doubt to its absolute limit. In a Prefatory letter to the *Meditations*, Descartes writes the following.

> I do not expect any popular approval, or indeed any wide audience. On the contrary I would not urge anyone to read this book except those who are able and willing to meditate seriously with me, and to withdraw their minds from the senses and from all preconceived opinions. Such readers, as I well know, are few and far between. (Descartes, Volume II, p. 8)

Maybe Descartes is right. Perhaps more of us than would like to admit are content to simply live a life that is somehow dictated to us, by society, media, advertising, culture, family, or fad. It's not that these lives are then fake, ignoble, unreal, or disingenuous, but they are not truly ours. For this to happen we must, as Descartes does, take stock of our lives: set aside some time to withdraw from our daily routines, leave behind the comforts of reality as we know it, and venture into the unknown. It's when we find ourselves teetering on the brink of uncertainty, like Truman hanging over the edge of the boat, that we come to know who we truly are, and for Descartes, *that* we truly are. It's here that we find ourselves. It's here that we find truth. It's here that we begin to find meaning for our lives.

Postscript

Malcom X is right: no one wants to think that they're dumb enough to be duped into thinking that something is true when it isn't. A dear friend of mine, Brother Frank Rotsaert, C.S.C., used to challenge his students: "Do you know why you have to learn to think for yourself? Because if you don't, then someone else is going to think for you."

Few of us have the imagination to dream up something like the Evil Demon hypothesis, much less sit down to write a work like the *Meditations*. Maybe more of us could write a screenplay comparable to *The Truman Show*. But surely all of us could pick up Descartes's *Meditations*, or pop in *The Truman Show* DVD, or any of the other movies discussed in this volume, and begin to ask some questions. Maybe we'll be forced to entertain some of our deepest doubts about who we are and where our lives are headed. The word 'skeptic' means "inquirer," one who carefully observes, examines, or considers. If Descartes is right, and I think he is, it's in *acting* like a skeptic that we'll find a little certainty. Or at least a little peace of mind.

TO THINK ABOUT

1. Christof believes we would rather live in a safe cell than seek freedom in the unknown world. Do you agree or disagree?

2. In what ways is Christof like God? In what ways is he different? Is there an analogy between Truman's rebellion against Christof and our own possible relation to some cosmic design or purpose?

3. Relating back to the Malcolm X quotation, what are some ways in which we can be deceived about who we are, where our lives are headed?

4. Can a life be meaningful if it's fake or counterfeit? Can "you" be real, while the life you are living is not?

TO READ NEXT

Augustine. *Against the Academicians and The Teacher*. Indianapolis: Hackett, 1995.

Cottingham, John. *Descartes*. Oxford: Blackwell, 1986.

Cottingham, John. *On The Meaning of Life*. London: Routledge, 2002.

Sextus Empiricus. *Outlines of Scepticism*. Edited by Julia Annas and Jonathan Barnes. Cambridge: Cambridge University Press, 2000.

2

Our Place in the Cosmos: Faith and Belief in *Contact*

HEATHER KEITH and STEVEN FESMIRE

> Some of [the experimental method's] obvious elements are willingness to hold belief in suspense, ability to doubt until evidence is obtained; willingness to go where evidence points instead of putting first a personally preferred conclusion; ability to hold ideas in solution and use them as hypotheses to be tested instead of as dogmas to be asserted; and (possibly the most distinctive of all) enjoyment of new fields for inquiry and of new problems.
>
> —JOHN DEWEY (American philosopher, 1859–1952), *Freedom and Culture*

It's a hot, windy evening in the middle of the desert. You're sitting alone at the base of an imposingly large satellite dish—a telescope for detecting radio waves from insanely distant objects like quasars and pulsars. Only it turns out that you're not exactly alone. Your laptop is plugged into the dish, and what before was static in your headphones forms itself into a distinct and haunting rhythm. The aliens are calling, and they want to talk to you. You feel a shiver down your spine, a blend of elation and terror. Elation, because you have spent your scientific career poised to hear some hint of order in the cosmic chaos, and your professional credibility hinges on this moment. Terror, because—well, they are aliens, after all. It's an awesome experience. But now anxiety presses itself upon you. What on earth will you do with this information? What can it possibly mean? How does it affect your place in the cosmos? How can you even be sure that what you are experiencing is real, not an illusion or hoax? How will others respond to you? Will they believe you? Why should they?

In *Contact*,[1] such is the experience of Dr. Ellie Arroway (Jodie Foster), a scientist working with S.E.T.I., the Search for Extra-Terrestrial Intelligence. Based on the 1985 science-fiction novel by the astronomer Carl Sagan,[2] *Contact* tells the story of what a first encounter between humans and intelligent extraterrestrial beings might be like. It also details the complexities of faith and belief in a world where religion and science often come into conflict—a favorite theme of Sagan's, and a major subject in the history of philosophy.

This chapter explores tangles of faith and belief through the lens of philosophy and the characters and concepts of *Contact*. We pay special attention to Sagan's mouthpiece Ellie Arroway, who embodies the practice of *doubting* as essential to living a life rich in insight and meaning. While this is far from the sole philosophic quandary raised by the film, it is perhaps the central one.

Making Contact

Perhaps, like us, you are a bit of a geek. Not of the stereotypical techno-crazed pocket-protector-wearing klutzy misfit variety, but simply someone more often transfixed by ideas than fashions and trends. Thinking matters more to you than what's on tonight at 8:00 or whether you're a Size 8. It's okay. You're not alone.

Here's some food for thought for us geeks wondering about meaning in life: We humans have been emitting radio waves, which travel at the speed of light (186,000 miles per second), for about one hundred years. So a sort of "shell" of radio waves extends a hundred light years in a sphere around Earth. This

---

[1] *Contact*, Directed by Robert Zemeckis, 2 hr. 30 min. Warner, 1997. Video-cassette.

[2] Carl Sagan, *Contact* (New York: Simon and Schuster, 1985), based on the story by Carl Sagan and Ann Druyan. Sagan gained national fame in the early 1980s as host of the PBS television series, *Cosmos*. He died in 1996. The last book he published before his death was *The Demon-Haunted World: Science as a Candle in the Dark* (New York: Random House, 1996).

shell is one-thousandth the distance across the Milky Way galaxy, one of hundreds of billions of galaxies. If intelligent beings were to emit powerful radio waves from the other side of our own galaxy, they and their planet might be long gone before we detected the signals. Or radio waves may have arrived while our distant ancestors were too busy being single-celled organisms in the primordial ooze. The most distant object visible to the unaided eye, our nearest neighbor the Andromeda galaxy, left its source around two and a half million years ago; anatomically modern humans, in comparison, evolved in Africa around 150,000 to 200,000 years ago.

It's humbling, but we historically educated geeks are used to being humbled. A few centuries ago our medieval European ancestors were safely ensconced as the central figures in the universe's drama of redemption. We're the end-all be-all of it all, they believed. Your great great grandparents were probably unchallenged in the belief that their species was specially created in an instant by a word from God. Your great grandparents' schooling probably did not include the notion that we live in one galaxy among many. Today, thanks to fellow geeks like Copernicus, Darwin, and Hubble, students today can contemplate their evolving primate lives circling a medium-sized star in a galaxy with hundreds of billions of similar stars in a cosmos with hundreds of billions of galaxies clustering across fifteen billion light years.

Now the story: Downtrodden by the loss of government funding for S.E.T.I., Ellie seeks financing in the private sector. Her passion finally persuades a corporate philanthropist, the eccentric and reclusive S.R. Hadden (John Hurt), to support her project at the Very Large Array radio telescope in New Mexico. Here, Ellie spends countless hours listening to static from space. At the last minute before her lease is revoked, she detects an encoded message emanating from the Vega star system, twenty-eight light years away. Disturbingly, the message includes a television image of Hitler at the opening of the 1936 Olympics in Berlin, the first television broadcast strong enough to be picked up in space. This prompts the President's Press Secretary (Angela Bassett) to exclaim, "Twenty million people died defeating that son of a bitch, and he's our first ambassador to outer space?" Apparently the message was an E.T. way of saying "hello, we heard you." Attached to this is a coded message that

Hadden helps Ellie to break: a blueprint for a machine that might take a passenger to meet the aliens.

In the midst of a predictable explosion of public attention, a conversation begins in various religious communities about the nature and consequences of such a discovery. From abductee fanatics to Christian fundamentalists to intergalactic Elvises, the public discourse seems to reflect more superstitious than scientific beliefs. While Ellie might want to ignore the religious buzz, it imposes itself on her world in the character of Palmer Joss (Matthew McConaughey), once her lover, and now a presidential advisor on religion and public affairs.

At first, Palmer is Ellie's foil. While she finds truth and meaning in scientific discovery based on hard evidence, his meaning comes via what he experiences as a personal relationship with God. Having read Palmer's book, Ellie quotes it back to him at a White House reception: "Ironically, the thing that people are most hungry for, meaning, is the one thing that science hasn't been able to give them." Ellie replies, "Come on, it's like you're saying science killed God . . . what if science simply revealed that He never existed in the first place?"

Ellie then introduces "Ockham's Razor," a principle made famous by the medieval philosopher William of Ockham (1285–1349) which holds that all things being equal, the simplest explanation tends to be the best. That is, the best explanation isn't an extravagant one, littered by unnecessary assumptions. Using Ockham's Razor, Ellie says: "So what's more likely, an all-powerful mysterious god created the universe and decided not to give any proof of his existence, or that he simply doesn't exist at all, and that we created him so that we wouldn't have to feel so small and alone?" While Palmer—ironically, like Ockham himself—can't imagine a meaningful existence without faith in God, Ellie finds meaning through scientific practice.

Even as a child, filled with grief after her father's fatal heart attack, Ellie seeks only natural explanations. In a misguided attempt to comfort Ellie, a priest tells her that all things happen for a reason. The death, he implies, is justified as part of a supernatural plan. Ellie agrees that things happen for a reason, but using Ockham's Razor she shaves away the supernatural assumptions: She laments that she didn't place her father's heart medicine in the more accessible downstairs bathroom.

Wise Fools

Is there some particular way of forming beliefs that makes a meaningful life more likely? Let's assume, perhaps wrongly, that there is some correlation between living a meaningful life and sincerely pursuing truth: if ignorance is bliss, then only the timid crave bliss. Yes, we humans are all turtles carrying comfortable shells, but we engage life fully and sensuously only when facing the joys and hazards outside our shells. Is there, then, a way of forming and evaluating beliefs that can best be trusted to reveal the way things *actually* work rather than merely confirming whatever we *wish* to be true? This question is an important theme for Ellie, and also for the philosopher Charles Sanders Peirce (1839–1914), an American regarded as the father of the philosophic tradition called Pragmatism.

Peirce (pronounced "purse," like a handbag) recognized that there is no psychological difference between believing a truth and believing a falsehood; whatever we believe, we believe is true until we have some reason to doubt it. As Socrates (Plato's teacher in ancient Athens) grasped 2,300 years before Peirce, we humans are a sophomoric bunch. A "sophomore" isn't merely an arbitrary and uninteresting designation for second-year college students. The word literally means "wise fool," someone who thinks she knows things she does not in fact know. What she mistakenly *thinks* she knows far exceeds the little she *actually* knows. To the degree that we are sophomoric, we mistake ignorance for knowledge, and we generally pay a price for this delusion. Avoiding this is one of the greatest challenges of human existence.

If only a bell would go off in our heads whenever we hit upon a true belief! Then we could escape the perils of ignorance. Our reputations would never again suffer from false claims of knowledge, our bodies would be spared the agony of false beliefs in our own abilities ("Sure, I drive better when I'm drunk," "Of course I can ski on the expert slope!"), and our social perspectives would finally be liberated from inherited prejudices about "our kind" and "their kind." An American philosopher and U.S. congressperson named Thomas Vernor Smith (1890–1964), influenced by Peirce, wisely observed that "much of the misery that men inflict upon one another is in the name of and because of their feeling so certain that they know things and that the other fellow does not."[3]

Fixing Beliefs

In an 1877 article titled "The Fixation of Belief," Peirce explores this human predicament. He describes ways in which people's beliefs become "fixed" (in the sense of "hardened," not "repaired"). We are all too aware of how people become "*set* in their ways" just as plaster becomes fixed or set. Peirce writes as though his descriptions are neutral, but he does not hold that all approaches are created equal. To the contrary, he implies that some ways of believing are more reliable than others. This may appear controversial, but consider his descriptions in turn. We'll discuss them alongside corresponding characters in *Contact.*

According to Peirce, one very popular approach to believing is the "method of tenacity," better known as the "ostrich mentality." We are all experts at using this method. People sidestep their rational capacities and stubbornly avoid situations that might provoke doubt. In Peirce's words: "When an ostrich buries its head in the sand as danger approaches, it very likely takes the happiest course. It hides the danger, and then calmly says there is no danger."[4] Many people are remarkably skilled at hiding from all that could challenge their beliefs. This is the method of a religious terrorist in *Contact.* He simply won't—or can't—tolerate the obvious upshot of a message from outer space: the universe *doesn't* revolve around humanity! So he denies access to the evidence by setting off a bomb in the heart of the machine. He and many others are killed in the massive explosion (a required element for all science-fiction films!), including David Drumlin (Tom Skerrit), the scientist who edged out Ellie in the bid to represent humanity to the ETs. This is indeed a dangerous and deadly method of believing.

A second approach, the "method of authority," is to hold beliefs because institutionalized authority declares them to be

---

[3] Thomas Vernor Smith, *Creative Sceptics: In Defense of The Liberal Temper* (Chicago: Willitt, Clark, and Co., 1934), p. 7.

[4] Charles Sanders Peirce, "The Fixation of Belief" in *Philosophical Writings of Charles Sanders Peirce,* edited by Justus Buchler (New York: Dover, 1955), p. 12.

true. Since new discoveries can challenge traditional beliefs, this approach often works hand-in-hand with the ostrich mentality. Those who took a literalist view of scripture were infuriated by Copernicus's 1543 *On the Revolution of Heavenly Bodies,* which proposes a Sun-centered rather than Earth-centered universe. Martin Luther quoted Joshua 10:12–14 in the Bible, in which Joshua commands the sun to stand still in the heavens. Luther reasoned that if the sun stood still, then it must first have been moving. Therefore, the sun is in motion rather than the earth. On the basis of scriptural authority, Copernicus was thus refuted, and human beings could for a few more years believe they were the literal center of the cosmos.

It is precisely this de-centering of humanity by science that leads some today to reject evolutionary biology in favor of an interpretation of religious authority. Some feel an almost primal need for humans to be the central figures on the Divine stage. In *Contact,* authority-driven fear sets the social environment within which the religious terrorist destroys the machine. Peirce evaluates the method of authority with biting sarcasm: "If it is their highest impulse to be intellectual slaves, then slaves they ought to remain."[5]

According to the eighteenth-century German philosopher Immanuel Kant, the problem with those who follow the method of authority is not "lack of intelligence, but lack of determination and courage to use that intelligence without another's guidance. Sapere aude! Dare to know! Have the courage to use your own intelligence."[6] Recognizing the dangers of methods such as tenacity and authority, Peirce, like the philosopher John Dewey in the epigraph to this chapter, turns to science for a model of experimental, community-engaged, and error-correcting thinking. As Ellie sees it, religious believers like Palmer follow tenacious and authority-influenced methods when developing what she regards as their unquestioned and unanalyzed faith. Meanwhile, she exemplifies an approach to "fixing" her beliefs through constant questioning,

---

[5] Peirce, p. 14.

[6] Immanuel Kant, "What Is Enlightenment?" in Marvin Perry, *et. al.*, eds., *Sources of Western Tradition* (Boston: Houghton Mifflin, 1999), pp. 54–55. Kant replaces the method of authority with an *a priori* approach that, according to Peirce, is not much better than what it replaces.

probing experimentation, and hard evidence: the method of science. Ellie, Sagan, and Peirce believe this method to be best suited to the quest for truth.[7]

Science and the Meaning of Life

The philosopher Bertrand Russell wrote in 1903 that science reveals us alone in a hostile and purposeless universe, our loves and beliefs "the outcome of accidental collocations of atoms."[8] We must, says Russell, revolt in active defiance of this meaningless void. Like Russell, Ellie does not believe science supports traditional religious beliefs about a divine cosmic plan. But in contrast with Russell's pessimism, science gives meaning to Ellie's life. By opening the doors to contemplation of the sublime vastness of the universe ("billions and billions of stars surrounded by billions and billions of galaxies," as Sagan was reputed to say), science reveals that we Earthlings may be far from alone in the universe. If not, as *Contact* tirelessly repeats, "It'd be an awful waste of space."

Yet science is not just about *conclusions*; it is a way of living and thinking that embraces intellectual suspense and constant questioning. Suspense is endured gladly in films, novels, and magic. It is not always welcomed, much less enjoyed for its own sake, in matters of real world beliefs—particularly religious, moral, and political ones. To Ellie, a scientific turn of mind spells an end to the dogmatism and fanaticism that mark the idea that beliefs can be declared true without worldly testing. Consider the feeling of absolute certainty that drove the Inquisition and that today drives terrorism, genocide, and nationalism. To whatever extent a belief is held scientifically, it is tentative and hypothetical. Through testing, we ask the world to answer back, and the answer we hear is always open to ongoing questioning.

This suggests a sort of faith that differs from the authority-driven variety. Ellie's scientific faith embraces doubt and suspense as an ally, not an adversary. She passionately wants to be

---

[7] For more on science, pragmatism, and meaning, see Steven Fesmire, *John Dewey and Moral Imagination* (Bloomington: Indiana University Press, 2003), Chapter 2.

[8] Bertrand Russell, "A Free Man's Worship," in *Why I Am Not A Christian* (London: Allen and Unwin, 1957), p. 107.

the passenger transported to Vega by the machine, and she appears before a committee formed to make that decision. Seemingly betraying her, Palmer thwarts her chances by asking her if she believes in God. While it happens not to be of any great importance to Palmer (who, out of romantic interests, wants Ellie to stay on Earth), other members of the committee and the general public are put off by her answer: "As a scientist, I rely on empirical evidence, and in this matter I don't believe that there is data either way." Since, one member of the committee falsely asserts, "ninety-five percent of the world's population believes in a supreme being in one form or another,"[9] the committee chooses Ellie's former boss and professional competitor, David Drumlin. He disingenuously seals the deal by saying what the committee wants to hear about "our most cherished beliefs."

When the machine is sabotaged (killing Drumlin), Ellie's dreams of cosmic contact seem destined to remain unfulfilled. However, the mischievous and ingenious S.R. Hadden arranges for Ellie to travel on a secret, second machine that has been built in Japan. The massive machine's arms spin to create a highly charged vortex. Her pod is dropped into the energy field. The moviegoer shares her experience, which she describes as a trip through some kind of wormhole. Ellie apparently arrives on a planet that resembles a picture of Pensacola, Florida that she drew as a child. An alien greets her in the comforting form of her late, beloved father. Contact made, culminating in promises for future small steps in developing an Earth-extraterrestrial relationship, Ellie travels safely home after an eighteen-hour adventure. A baffled mission control, relieved that she was not injured, struggles to detect the source of what seems to them an obvious malfunction: her spacecraft appears to have fallen unimpeded through the machine straight into the water below. Only a few Earth seconds have elapsed.

This makes it difficult for even Ellie's friends and colleagues to believe that she traveled light years away. In a government hearing dominated by National Security Advisor Michael Kitz (James Woods), Ellie is forced to scrutinize what she fervently believes to have been a non-subjective (that is, not a movie

---

[9] It should be underscored that this is a deeply misleading statistic, particularly in light of atheistic perspectives in Asia.

projection of her own mind) experience—the most awe-inspir-
ing and meaningful one of her life. Was Ellie's adventure distin-
guishable from thousands of so-called "abduction" experiences,
in which people faithfully and whole-heartedly believe they
have been kidnapped and experimented on by aliens? She
appears to have no evidence to prove that her experience was
more than a vivid hallucination or nightmare. Yet Ellie has faith
in her experience. Is her faith any different than the religious
terrorist's absolute faith in the objective moral rightness of his
suicide bombing?

In fact, one very important capacity sets Ellie's interpretation
of her experience apart from the beliefs of abductees and religious fanatics: *doubt*. Rather than being mortally offended by
others' lack of faith in her experience, she encourages doubt as
the most reliable path to knowledge. In Sagan's own words:
"Surely it's unfair of me to be offended at not being believed; or
to criticize you for being stodgy and unimaginative—merely
because you rendered the Scottish verdict of 'not proved.'"[10]

The "Beacon of the Wise"

We're prone to think the opposite of belief is disbelief—that, for
example, the opposite of belief in God is atheism. While accurate as far as formal logic goes, this captures nothing of any relevance to how we think. The psychological opposite of belief is
doubt, uncertainty about what to believe. To doubt that we're
alone in the universe is not to assert its opposite. Ellie's doubt
reveals her readiness to re-open her mind to other interpreta-
tions; this is what it means to have an open, rather than an
empty, mind. She is not indifferent or slacking, nor is she merely
putting on an act of doubting; she is simply unwilling to make
claims that outstrip her knowledge. Peirce describes this scientific spirit: it "requires a man to be at all times ready to dump
his whole cartload of beliefs the moment experience is against
them. The desire to learn forbids him to be perfectly cocksure
that he knows already."[11]

---

[10] Sagan, *The Demon-Haunted World*, p. 172.
[11] In Smith, p. 232.

Freedom from doubt is often purchased by those with low tolerance for bewilderment, but the price is high: such fear has always been a prelude to atrocities. The terrorist attack in *Contact* disturbingly illustrates this all-too-familiar point. Doubt is the key to learning and growth; it is essential to any passage from ignorance to knowledge. Insofar as one does not doubt one does not *grow*. For organic life, this is equivalent to death or dying. Ellie doubts her way to a meaningful and value-rich life marked by humility and tolerance.

In this spirit, the great philosopher (and ancient geek!) Socrates is reported to have said "the unexamined life is not worth living."[12] In 399 B.C.E., Socrates was put on trial by his fellow citizens for "corrupting the young," but he in fact aided young and old by showing that those who claimed to have wisdom often did not. Unlike those he daily questioned in the Athenian marketplace, Socrates was wise enough to recognize his own ignorance. Unlike his accusers, Socrates was not afraid of examining beliefs, and he encouraged such activity in others. He described himself as a "gadfly." Just as a horsefly buzzing around your hammock makes it impossible to doze, Socrates pestered his fellow citizens whenever they were sleepwalking through life. He wouldn't let them intellectually doze, resting on whatever beliefs they happened to have picked up. While most of his neighbors mistook their unexamined beliefs for knowledge, Socrates creatively disturbed himself and others.

In contrast, because of David Drumlin's willingness to say whatever he thinks will get him aboard the machine (without opening himself up to self-examination and doubt), he gives up his integrity. J.D. Salinger's Holden Caulfield would have called Drumlin a "phony." Two thousand, four hundred years ago, the unexamined beliefs of Socrates's accusers had disastrous consequences: he was executed by the state. Drumlin's life was also unjustly taken as a result of fanaticism, but he left little legacy of integrity and humility.[13]

Although Ellie's life is not on the line, her professional credibility and integrity are. In the end, it is intellectual humility that gives weight to Ellie's beliefs. Her openness to self-examination

---

[12] Plato, "Apology" in *Five Dialogues* (Indianapolis: Hackett, 1981), p. 41.

[13] Drumlin's character is much more nuanced in Sagan's novel, from which the movie is loosely adapted.

validates her experience—both to herself and to the audience—
and nurtures her scientific and personal growth. As a scientist,
Ellie must both trust her experience (as empirical data) and
doubt it at the same time. Unfortunately, she—like us—is surrounded by people who are uncomfortable with doubt.
Impatient, they have no tolerance for ambiguity. Fearful of
being bewildered, they clamor for ironclad certainty. This fear
drives Kitz to persecute Ellie. Like those who put Socrates on
trial, Kitz probably believes that's what the public desires. Ellie,
however, responds to Kitz's arrogance by expressing her own
doubts rather than countering his abuse with statements of
unquestioned truth. There is a vital lesson in *Contact* for our
post-9/11 world. Again in the words of Thomas Vernor Smith:
"The world may flee from doubt in fear; but the world will come
back to the method of doubt in sanity."[14] "Modest doubt,"
Shakespeare adds, "is call'd the beacon of the wise."[15]

In the hearing, Kitz ridicules Ellie's claim that she traveled in
the machine through a wormhole. He hypothesizes that either
she is lying or that she is the victim of a malicious scheme of
Hadden's. When Kitz asks Ellie if she expects him to take her
word on faith, she replies in a way that embodies experimental
thinking and open-mindedness:

> **ELLIE:** Is it possible that it didn't happen? Yes. As a scientist,
> I must concede that, I must volunteer that.
> **KITZ:** Wait a minute, let me get this straight. You admit that
> you have absolutely no physical evidence to back up your
> story?
> **ELLIE:** Yes.
> **KITZ:** You admit that you very well may have hallucinated
> this whole thing?
> **ELLIE:** Yes.
> **KITZ:** You admit that if you were in our position you would
> respond with exactly the same degree of incredulity and
> skepticism?
> **ELLIE:** Yes.

---

[14] Smith, *Creative Sceptics*, p. 233.
[15] William Shakespeare, *Troilus and Cressida*, Act. II, Scene II, in *The Complete
Works of William Shakespeare*, edited by William Aldis Wright (New York:
Garden City Press, 1936), p. 830.

But when asked why she doesn't withdraw her testimony in this case, Ellie responds:

ELLIE: Because I can't! I had an experience . . . I can't prove it, I can't even explain it . . . but everything that I know as a human being, everything that I am tells me that it was real. I was given something wonderful, something that changed me forever. A vision of the universe that tells us undeniably how tiny and insignificant, and how rare and precious we all are. A vision that tells us that we belong to something that is greater than ourselves, that we are not, that none of us are alone. I wish I could share that. I wish that everyone, even for one moment, could feel that awe and humility and hope.

"I Don't Know" (Or Does She?)

Though Ellie has faith in her own experience, she tempers it with a healthy dose of doubt. This moves Palmer, who himself evinces a new temperament of openness. When asked what he thinks is true, he replies, "As a person of faith, I'm bound by a different covenant than Dr. Arroway. But our goal is one and the same—the pursuit of truth. I for one believe her." This openness to experience is a hallmark of Peirce's method of science.

Unlike Palmer, the moviegoer doesn't have to decide whether to trust Ellie's experience. We can consider her claim skeptically, at least until the end of the film when we eavesdrop on a conversation between Kitz and the Press Secretary regarding video taken during Ellie's "trip." The video shows only static. But it shows *eighteen hours* of it. Although we may still be able to come up with reasons to be skeptical, this is substantial evidence for Ellie's claim. Has director Robert Zemeckis made our experience of *Contact* more, or less, meaningful? Would having to wrestle with doubt about the reality within the film be a more meaningful, provoking, and fitting way to end Ellie's story?

Rejecting blind faith, even in her own experience, Ellie finds meaning in examining her beliefs by embracing and encouraging doubt wherever possible. The end of the film finds Ellie giving a school tour of the Very Large Array. When a child asks Ellie if there are aliens, she replies with the skepticism and humility of an experimental thinker:

> **CHILD:** Are there other people out there in the universe?
> **ELLIE:** That's a good question. What do you think?
> **CHILD:** I don't know.
> **ELLIE:** That's a good answer. A skeptic, huh? The most important thing is that you all keep searching for your own answers.[16]

---

[16] For viewing *Contact* and offering suggestions and insights, thanks to Tatiana Abatemarco, Joshua Bakelaar, Daniel Guentchev, Elizabeth Howe, Charlotte Norris, David Rasmussen, and Alisha Rogers.

TO THINK ABOUT

1. Should we approach all aspects of our lives with Ellie's skepticism? Moral beliefs? Political beliefs? Religious beliefs? Scientific beliefs?

2. By including hard-to-dispute evidence of Ellie's ET encounter (the eighteen hours of static), has director Robert Zemeckis made our experience of *Contact* more, or less, meaningful? Would having to wrestle with doubt about the reality within the film be a more meaningful, provoking, and fitting way to end Ellie's story?

3. Some people have claimed that science has its own area of expertise and explanation, while religion occupies another. Neither account can give us the entire view of the nature of the universe. Do you think *Contact* supports such a position?

TO READ NEXT

John Dewey. *Democracy and Education*, Volume 8 of *The Collected Works of John Dewey: The Middle Works*, edited by Jo Ann Boydston. Carbondale: Southern Illinois University Press, 1985 [1916].

William James. *Pragmatism*. Indianapolis: Hackett. 1997 [1907].

Charles Sanders Peirce. The Fixation of Belief. In Justus Buchler, ed., *Philosophical Writings of Charles Sanders Peirce* (New York: Dover, 1955).

Plato. Apology. In *Five Dialogues* (Indianapolis: Hackett, 2002).

Carl Sagan, *The Demon Haunted World: Science as a Candle in the Dark*. New York: Random House, 1996.

Michael Shermer. *Why People Believe Weird Things*. Second edition. New York: Owl Books, 2002.

3

The On-Going Wow: *Waking Life* and the Waltz between Detachment and Immersion

KEVIN STOEHR

It's a "total kitchen sink movie."[1] That's how director Richard Linklater (*Slacker, Dazed and Confused, Before Sunrise, The Newton Boys, School of Rock*) describes *Waking Life* (2001)—a mind-whirling medley of computer-animated portraits and fragmented glimpses of characters that pontificate upon or simply exemplify various aspects of human life. At times the movie (like life itself) becomes too much—*too* mind-boggling and eclectic. Some critics loved the movie, lauding it as "visionary," "stunning," "exhilarating," "transporting," "groundbreaking," "liberating," "beautiful," and "wondrous," while others absolutely hated it, criticizing it as "pretentious," "wearying," "yawn-inducing," and "disappointingly dull."[2]

It's true that the movie doesn't invite much emotional engagement in the lives of its many characters—even in the life of its main protagonist, Wiley Wiggins (voiced by the actor of the same name). But what it does do well is to provide much intellectual engagement, especially for the philosophically curious. Simply put, it's a roller-coaster ride of the mind and senses,

---

[1] See the director's commentary to the movie on the DVD version of the film (Twentieth Century Fox Home Entertainment, 2002, Special Features). During the initial scene with the two children, Linklater comments in reference to their "fortune teller" toy: "I like the idea of a certain randomness and a certain fate that . . . is in the whole movie . . ."

[2] Excerpts of critics' reviews of this film can be found at www.rottentomatoes.com under the keyword "Waking Life."

if not the heart. Its daring dips and climbs provide a great opportunity for the movie viewer to ponder whether or not life's overall meaning can lead to any definite answers. The movie tells us that *life itself* is brimming with answers to such questions. Better stated, life itself is *the* answer. The meaning of life is, then, *a life of meaning*—an existence composed of truly significant choices and actions. And yet the contexts for these decisions and acts are a matter of mere chance rather than of some pre-determined order established by God or Nature.

This view shares much in common with an *existentialist* approach to questions about the meaning of life. Though varied and wide-ranging, existentialism is often characterized by the following idea: each individual's existence is an activity of creating order and meaning from chance events. *Waking Life* reflects an intentional randomness that is supposed to mirror that of life itself. It's this randomness that challenges us to create meaningful structures and patterns in order to make sense of the fluctuating details of our individual lives. The disjointed and fragmented nature of this film calls the viewer to uncover his or her own "overarching" message. But such a message must be pieced together provisionally, like an open-ended life story. And this challenge—for the viewer to create his or her own pattern of ideas in the face of the on-going flux of random experiences—is itself a type of message. It's a message that stresses an individual's capacity for creating his or her very own *self* or *life* through the on-going creation of *personal meaning and order.*

Jazzing It Up or Tuning Out

When we try to answer questions about the overall meaning of our lives, we seem to arrive immediately at a fork in the road: immersion or detachment. If we take the path of *immersion*, we engage actively in life, with full enthusiasm and participation, in order to grasp life's overall meaning. If we really want to know what baseball is all about, it would be better to learn the game as a player rather than as a spectator. The problem with this route, however, is that our immersion in life would provide a very personal, subjective, and therefore one-sided kind of "knowledge."

Taking the path of *detachment*, we become as *removed* as possible from the detailed and moving landscape of life, and so gain a less biased view of the terrain. Detached thinking permits us to understand and evaluate our existence with some degree of impartiality and objectivity since we can't genuinely come to *know* or *judge* the entire stream of life while swimming amidst its fluctuating waves and changing currents. However, detached *thinking* tends to lead to detached *living*. And that can't be good.

Waking Life evokes not merely the idea, but also the *feeling*, of detached existence, and prompts us to reflect on the tension between immersion-in-life and detachment-from-life. The unique visual styles and animation disorient the viewer right from the very start.[3] A sense of unfamiliarity and dislocation—even *disembodiment*—is felt at the very outset of the film, when the viewer becomes puzzled.[4] We see a boy and girl playing with a paper toy (a "fortune teller") that dispenses cryptic messages by chance. The camera wavers and waltzes arbitrarily, with no stable or unified point of orientation, as if from the perspective of a dreaming and disembodied mind. Colors change and shapes shift with no rhyme or reason. Is this a dream that is unfolding? ("Dream is Destiny")[5]

Following the same scene, after choosing (seemingly arbitrarily) the message "Dream is destiny," the boy strolls outside his home, beneath a night sky. We see his eyes positioned to create the appearance of being detached from his face, merely hovering before it—like something we might see in a dream. He is staring skywards at what appears to be a slow-moving comet.

---

[3] One aspect of the film's visuals that intensifies the feeling of disorientation is the arbitrary blending of ultra-realistic animation and clumsy cartoon art, a mystifying mixture of styles that is especially evident in the scene in which Wiley boards the "boat-car."

[4] Contemporary philosopher Hubert Dreyfus makes an intriguing case that the growing use of the Internet in recent years has led to an overall sense of detachment and de-situated existence that he calls "disembodied presence." See Dreyfus, *On the Internet*, in the *Thinking in Action* series (London and New York: Routledge, 2001). Contemporary environmental philosopher David Abram makes a similar argument that our growing detachment from Nature has led to an overall feeling of disconnection and disembodiment in his *The Spell of the Sensuous* (New York: Vintage, 1996).

[5] For references to particular film scenes in this essay, I have provided (in quotation marks and parentheses) the titles that correspond to individual movie segments (as listed under the Scene Selection feature on the DVD version of *Waking Life*.)

He begins to levitate: yet another symbol of not being situated, located, or "grounded." He grabs a car door handle, trying to keep himself anchored. Likewise, the viewer begins to feel un-situated and un-grounded, removed from the familiar waking world. Will this type of detachment lead to some sort of liberation or transcendence? Or will this detachment serve simply to numb the senses while emptying the mind of its thoughts?

The scene then switches to a young man (Wiley Wiggins) sleeping and then waking up on a train. Was he merely dreaming of the levitating boy? Was the boy a figment of his unconscious imagination? Is that why the initial scene was so surreal? Or was this a vivid unconscious memory of a past experience, embellished by mind play? Are these two introductory scenes completely unrelated? At this point, we may find ourselves slightly confused. Confusion often evokes a sense of dislocation, which in turn breeds a feeling of detached presence—it's as if our minds are no longer rooted in our bodies and lack a definite place in the world. The opening credits begin to roll.

We switch to a music group rehearsing informally. Again, the animated style distances us as the dancing camera de-centers us with its haphazard motion. The musicians improvise, smiling to one another in amusement and creative release. The accordion-playing conductor of the group encourages them: "Rock out. Rock 'n' roll . . . Dig in . . ." He encourages, in other words, active engagement or immersion in the music. But as the music soon ceases, he advises them: "Try it a little more subdued . . . Just try it and see what you think . . . I want it to sound rich and maybe almost a little wavy due to being slightly out of tune . . . slightly detached." Like the music, *Waking Life* (maybe even life itself) feels improvised. Its rich and wavy images convey an overall style that is "detached" and "out of tune."[6] How then can we find meaning amidst this randomness and sense of dislocation?

Vessels, Values, and Voluntary Voyages

Waking Life frequently implies (and a few of its characters even preach) that life only gains authentic or genuine meaning when we actively create meaning for ourselves in the occasion of the

---

[6] All quotations are taken faithfully from the movie's spoken dialogue in the DVD version of *Waking Life*, rather than from a written screenplay.

present moment—rather than when we passively receive meaning from elsewhere (Society, God, Nature, and so forth). The meaning of life does not simply arrive at our doorsteps as a pre-packaged gift, so to speak. It's in the "doing" or "living" of life that meaning arises, and this "doing" includes thinking as well as acting, theory as well as practice. Take the scene in which we witness a roving gang of young men who, while engaged in abstractions and complaining about various ideologies, confess to being "all theory" and "no action." Immediately, they point to an old man who has climbed a telephone pole for no real reason—"all action" and "no theory." ("Society is a Fraud")

Indicating the importance of both dimensions of our lives, the movie's various scenes come together to suggest that the activity of self-creation requires the exercise of our free will, the cultivation of our individuality, and the integration of the conscious and unconscious aspects of our selves. We must appreciate the present moment as an on-going creative opportunity for positive self-transformation. Thus we overcome negative attitudes such as resentment, indignation, and general life-denial, which are exhibited by a few of the characters in the film, including the "protestor" who lights himself on fire and the red-faced prisoner who rages viciously against those who put him behind bars. We also learn that a proper understanding of the meaning of life entails an awareness of the unity and interconnectedness of everything that exists, which conditions and gives context to the present moment.

These key lessons of *Waking Life* begin to take shape, one at a time, after Wiley has departed from the train station. Once outside the station, Wiley watches an unusual "boat-car" approach ("Anchors Aweigh"). In the waves of pulsating shapes and colors, along with the arbitrary camera motion, the viewer feels a tad amphibious, not quite bound to solid ground, which makes a boat-car seem quite fitting. It pulls up in front of Wiley, and the driver proclaims: "Don't miss the boat." Wiley climbs aboard, alongside another young man (animated director Linklater) sitting in the back seat. They listen as the driver expounds upon the need to maintain a "go-with-the-flow attitude" and then embarks upon a wild mini-lecture littered with nautical references and various other metaphors. Our philosophically minded driver announces that he has learned to accept each experience as it occurs in its respective moment, whether he understands that experience or not. He tells Wiley that each individual is born with his or her own box of crayons, with which to color the canvas of his or her respective "world." The driver-philosopher advises Wiley to "keep things on an even keel" and to "remain in a state of constant departure while always arriving." (Whatever that means!)

Again we return to a main theme, which can be drawn from the crayon metaphor: Life as a creative activity. Each individual must create his or her very own "self" and "world" by seizing the moment and taking advantage of creative opportunities afforded by changing situations and conditions. Our lives are not somehow pre-given or pre-determined. Instead, they are dynamic products of our choices and actions (both past and present) that are undertaken in the encounter with random happenings. Notice how Wiley makes a "chance" exit from the boat-car, "determined" by the other passenger's whimsical advice to disembark from the vehicle at a particular point along the way. Yet the location and timing of Wiley's exit from the car is ultimately a product of his *personal choice* to leave at that particular time and place. Wiley appears to exit the vehicle because of the passenger's seemingly capricious suggestion to get out at a certain location, but also because of his own decision to heed the young man's advice. Upon leaving the boat-car, Wiley is told that *choice and chance* will determine the rest of his life.

Strolling along, Wiley stoops to pick up a piece of paper lying in the street, which tells him to look to his right. So he glances up to see a fast-approaching car bearing down on him. We assume that he has been struck. But has he been killed? The scene then switches to Wiley in bed, waking up. Was all of this—the children at the beginning of the film, the train trip, the stroll through the train station, the boat-car "voyage," the car accident—but a dream? Are all of these episodes simply stages of Wiley's larger dream-odyssey? Even if they are dream-scenes, are they not somehow *real?* For just as with experiences in ordinary waking life, they are experiences that are capable of teaching Wiley a lesson.

With questions again left unanswered we find ourselves accompanying Wiley as he attends a class on Existentialism ("Life Lessons"). The teacher—an animated version of real-life philosophy professor Robert C. Solomon—tells his students that Existentialism is not really about anguish and despair, as it is sometimes taken to be, but rather about the exuberance of being alive. He declares that people today are "losing the real virtues of living life passionately, the sense of taking responsibility for who you are, the ability to make something of yourself, feeling good about life." In other words, humans are becoming too detached and passive. We need to become more actively engaged in life. Wiley accompanies Professor Solomon after class as they stroll through campus and eventually sit in a cafe. Solomon continues lecturing in a non-Socratic fashion (almost as if speaking only to himself), making mention of existentialist philosopher Jean-Paul Sartre whose works teach us that our lives are built on individual choices and that we must accept responsibility for their consequences. Persons should not view themselves as hapless victims of external forces, advises Solomon. He tells Wiley that "what you do makes a difference," which again emphasizes the movie's main theme regarding self-creation and individual choice.

But choices and decisions require the *freedom* to choose. Otherwise, we would be mere robots, programmed or determined to do what others (perhaps higher powers or authorities) wish. In a later scene (directly after the episode in which the prisoner rages against being caged), we're introduced to a bespectacled man—animated version of real-life philosophy professor David Sosa—who lectures Wiley on the problem of human freedom ("Free Will and Physics"), or what is sometimes referred to as the problem of free will, which involves our capacity to choose freely. Sosa points out that this problem has been around "since before Aristotle"[7]: Are humans really free, or do we only think that we are? Sosa poses the question that confronted Medieval theologians such as Augustine (354–430) and Aquinas (1225–1274): How can we really be free if God can foresee through a providential plan, and thereby determine, everything that will happen to us? Whether we are speaking of the determining forces of God or the physical laws of Nature, if human actions are pre-determined, this excludes the idea that humans possess free will.

Wiley's new acquaintance goes on to explain that humans cannot do without freedom. First of all, freedom is crucial to our

---

[7] Greek philosopher (384 B.C.–322 B.C.), student of Plato and tutor to Alexander the Great.

sense of *individuality*: "Who you are is mostly a matter of the free choices that you make," Sosa explains. Freedom is also essential in upholding any notion of *moral responsibility*: "You can only be held responsible—you can only be found guilty or you can only be admired or respected—for things you did of your own free will." Sosa concludes that freedom is central to the idea of a choice-making and responsibility-taking individual. Neither science nor religion can refute this: "We have to find room in our contemporary worldview for persons, with all that that entails. Not just bodies, but persons. And that means trying to solve the problem of freedom, finding room for choice and responsibility, and trying to understand individuality." In other words, to be a human *person*, a genuine *individual*, one must have the capacity to make free choices.

From this discourse on human freedom, we turn to a scene in which a man is driving down a city street, angrily shouting into a hand-held microphone that broadcasts his message through car-top speakers. The driver is engaged in his own fight for personal freedom, taking a vocal and vehement stand against any system of authority that forces him to surrender his "sovereignty" and "liberty." He warns that it is time to begin challenging the "corporate slave-state," but such a revolt depends upon individual choice. "It's up to each and every one of us to turn loose just some of the greed, the hatred, the envy, and yes, the insecurities, because that is the central mode of control." If such a "revolution" is successful, freedom will guarantee a new era of morality and passion. Without such freedom and creative spirit, life would hold very little value or meaning. How we choose to live is ultimately up to each of us.

Noise about Narrative

One way in which we can exercise our freedom for the purpose of creating meaning *in* our lives and *for* our lives is to confront the lack of continuity and coherence in our daily existence. On the one hand, we wander aimlessly through arbitrary trials and tribulations that seem meaningless; on the other hand, we weave together the fragments of our lives into unified "stories" or "narratives" that tell us who we really are. The theme of creating a life-story, one in which each individual serves triple duty as author, narrator and main character, is prominent in *Waking Life*. We learn that we should create our personal narratives in ways that successfully integrate our various instincts, desires, wishes, passions, ideas, beliefs, values, etc. Such a narrative gives each of us a sense of meaning, order, personal identity, and authenticity—the ability to be true to our own convictions.

Yet tying together the otherwise separate moments of one's on-going life requires an understanding of passing time. This theme is picked up in the scene in which two young women discuss a paradox involving personal identity: How can I look upon a photo of myself as a baby and look at myself today and call both persons "me," when I have changed so substantially (biologically, mentally, and emotionally) over the intervening years? ("The Aging Paradox") In response, the speaker suggests that we need to create stories or narratives (even "fictions") about ourselves in order to connect these different "selves." An on-going *story* about one character (me), changing and experiencing new things over time, provides the sense that there is an underlying identity or unity that weaves together the different versions of "my-self" (along with the countless moments of my life).

Narrative, as the pre-condition for gaining self-knowledge and a sense of identity, arises in at least two other episodes. One of these involves a parody on evolution in which a monkey narrates a short documentary film ("Noise and Silence") that offers an ambiguous and overly simple story of humankind, a kind of *collective* narrative that integrates various moments of the history of our species. We then switch to a scene in which a young woman asks a young man seated at the next table what he is writing. "A novel," he replies. "What's the story?" she asks. The novelist answers: "There's no story. It's just people, gestures, moments, bits of rapture, fleeting emotions . . . In short, the greatest stories ever told." "Are *you* in the story?" she inquires. "I don't *think* so," he responds a bit hesitantly, musing over the question. "But then I'm kind of reading it and then writing it" ("What's the Story?"). Similarly, Wiley dreams up characters who narrate or who reflect on the need for narrative. At the very least, he is in search of his own story, one that might grant him a sense of consistency, continuity, location, orientation, and situated existence—thus returning him to the regular order and stability of "waking life."

Flabbergasted Moments

Waking Life connects themes of freedom and individual choice and self-creation with the importance of the present moment, which involves a kind of cosmic consciousness or holistic awareness of the interconnectedness and unity of all existence. The present instant or "now" in which I always reside moment to moment is, so to speak, a gathering place of personal possibilities. In the moment I can choose a future course of action among various alternatives. There are always possibilities from which to choose freely in the present instant, despite the fact that there are also always certain limits and conditions that life imposes upon me.

In refusing to take for granted the value of the creative opportunity that each moment affords, I also learn to appreciate the very fact that I exist (rather than not exist), and that there is a world around me (rather than *nothing at all.*) In other words, I come to affirm the fact that *life is a meaningful condition for the very reason that life is the opportunity for creating meaning.* To affirm life is to affirm our capacity to make the world a meaningful place. In "We Are the Authors," Wiley walks along a cabled bridge with a curly-haired man in a shirt and blazer. His new acquaintance celebrates the significance of the present moment as well as the principle of self-creation: "The on-going Wow is happening right now. We are all co-authors of this dancing exuberance . . . We are the authors of ourselves . . . Life is a matter of a miracle that is collected over time by moments flabbergasted to be in each other's presence . . ."

Emphasis on the value of the living moment is connected with a need for some type of awareness of "the whole" in what is perhaps the briefest and most tranquil segment of the entire movie ("Free Will and Physics"). Here we find Wiley listening to the words of an elderly, sage-like gentleman: "The quest is to be liberated from the negative, which is really our own will to nothingness. And once having said yes to the instant, the affirmation is contagious. It bursts into a chain of affirmations that knows no limit. To say yes to one instant is to say yes to all of existence."

Wiley then turns his attention to a young man who speaks of the unity of the mind as well as of the moment ("Free Will and Physics"). He lectures Wiley on experiences that he describes as "liminal," "edge-zone," or "frontier"-like. These experiences, "where the mind is most vulnerable," sometimes provoke a "breakthrough to that common something that holds them together," much as this entire film attempts to present a random series of "liminal" cinematic experiences that compel the viewer to search for unifying lessons and motifs. The speaker stresses the idea of a universal mind that is expressed in terms of each single mind. He does not think that a person's communion with the universal mind is incompatible with personal individuality. In fact, as he suggests, knowing one's self more fully as a unique individual leads, paradoxically, to the awareness of a *transpersonal unity* that underlies everything: "You can see [that] a radical subjectivity, radical attunement to individuality, uniqueness, to that which the mind is . . . opens itself to a vast objectivity. So the story is a story of the cosmos . . ." This meditation on cosmic unity recalls an earlier scene involving a bedroom dialogue between animated versions of actors Ethan Hawke and Julie Delpy, who starred in Linklater's earlier film *Before Sunrise* (1995). In discussing reincarnation, they are led to the notion of a *collective* or *universal* "self" that underlies and shapes all of our conscious activities in ordinary waking life[8] ("Death and Reality").

What are we to take from all of this? The ever-present moment is the "arena" of an individual choice that leads not only to *self*-creation, but also to the creation of meaning that we bestow upon *all that exists* (i.e., "the world"). Each person's "world" or "cosmos" is like a film that is viewed, scene-by-scene, by the creator of that movie. In other words, life is like a cinematic narrative that is constructed by each of us, that is narrated by each of us, and that stars each of us as the main character. Even though each of us is creating our own narrative, when we compare our views and experiences with each other, we come to realize that we are all drawing upon common and interconnected themes—the Cosmic Wow!

Smelling the Coffee

Waking Life intentionally blurs the line typically drawn between the ordinary world of waking consciousness and the extraordinary dream world of the unconscious. The problem that

---

[8] The notion of a collective, universal, transpersonal self or psyche can be related to the Hindu notion of Brahman as well as to the modern psychological idea of a Collective Unconscious (as proposed by Carl Gustav Jung).

arises when we can't tell the difference between these two worlds is known by philosophers as the Dream Argument: If one cannot distinguish between dreams and reality, how can one truly know what is real?

This is an old skeptical puzzle, which dates back to the Ancients, and was made famous by the father of modern philosophy, René Descartes (1596–1650). In his *Meditations on First Philosophy*, he famously hypothesized through his method of radical doubt that the-world-as-we-know-it may simply be the illusory product of a dreaming mind. Though certainly not intended, this dissolution of the distinction between "internal" mind and "external" reality may, in fact, reflect the existential insight that the world is never given to us in a completely objective or universal way, with all of its shapes, lines, colors, and connections neatly drawn and organized ahead of time. In other words, "reality" is always subject-related and mind-dependent, which is to say that the world is always filtered through the personal perception and creative reflection of a "subject" or "self." And only in this way can order and meaning be bestowed upon all that exists.

Leaving the theater (or living room), we may happen to believe that Wiley was indeed struck by a vehicle toward the beginning of the film, and that he has been subsequently experiencing some strange post-mortal reality. Or we may think that the automobile accident, like everything else in the movie, is simply a part of Wiley's dream-state. Either way, we're compelled to realize that, just as all of these characters would not exist apart from Wiley's dreaming or experiencing mind, our worldly existence would have no genuine or authentic meaning if we did not choose to *create* such meaning *for ourselves*. It's this lesson that inspires us to become more actively engaged in life. Like Wiley, we need to "wake up" and become much more than mere passive and detached spectators.[9]

---

[9] Friedrich Nietzsche refers to a passive, detached, life-negating attitude—one that rejects conventional beliefs or values and replaces them with nothing else—as "passive" or "pathological" *nihilism*. He refers to its active, life-affirming counterpart as an attitude of "active" or "healthy" nihilism, a form of creative individuality or "master-morality." See, for example, Sections 22 and 23 of the collection of Nietzsche's unpublished writings, *The Will to Power*. In Section 28, a similar distinction is made between "complete" and "incomplete" nihilism.

To Think About

1. Is there a way of proving that you are awake rather than having a vivid, detailed dream about being awake?

2. Do you believe that human life is always a matter of *chance* or is life governed by some *divine plan* (providence)? If the latter, can you still account for human choice and free will?

3. Do you believe that, at the deepest levels of the unconscious, we are all interconnected, as parts of some *universal-cosmic mind or spirit*? If so, how could we possible prove or demonstrate that? If not, how could we *disprove* it?

4. Think back to when you were an infant or a very young child. How is it that you can call yourself *the same person* as this infant or child, especially when you have changed physically, intellectually, and emotionally? Is there *anything* that has remained the same?

TO READ NEXT

Boethius. *The Consolations of Philosophy*. New York: Penguin, 2000. See especially Book Five on the problem of freedom and the notion of the Eternal Now.

Hubert L. Dreyfus. *On the Internet*. London: Routledge, 2001.

Herman Hesse. *Siddhartha*. New York: Bantam, 1982.

Hermann Hesse. *Steppenwolf*. New York: Picador, 2002.

Carl Gustav Jung. *Memories, Dreams, Reflections*. New York: Vintage, 1989.

Friedrich Nietzsche. *The Portable Nietzsche*. New York: Penguin, 1977.

Take Two

Who Am I?

4

I Am Jack's Wasted Life: *Fight Club* and Personal Identity

JOHN ZAVODNY

If you can wake up at a different place.
If you can wake up in a different time.
Why can't you wake up as a different person?[1]

Space Monkeys

When did *you* figure out that Brad Pitt and Edward Norton were sort of tag-teaming at playing Tyler Durden?[2]

Be honest.

Brad Pitt's character really lays it out while he and Edward Norton's character are in the hotel room after Norton has followed Tyler Durden's boarding passes all over North America:

> You were looking for a way to change your life. You could not do this on your own. All the ways you wish you could be . . . that's me. I look like you want to look, I fuck like you want to fuck, I am smart, capable, and most importantly, I am free in all the ways that you are not.

---

[1] Chuck Palahniuk, *Fight Club* (New York: Henry Holt, 1996), p 157. I will cite the Palahniuk novel sparingly when it explains or reinforces themes from the movie. When I cite the book, I will include a page reference. Any citation without a reference is from the 1999 David Fincher film.

[2] I hate it when people talk about movies before I've seen them; I presume that anyone reading this has seen *Fight Club* any number of times (greater than zero). If you haven't, then forget that first sentence, go rent the movie and get back to this chapter later.

Was it then? Did you get it then?

Or did you figure it out just before that when Ed Norton's character and Marla are on the phone and she finally calls him by name—by the name "Tyler Durden?"

Be honest.

Maybe it was a little earlier when the tall, bruised bartender in the head brace halo called Edward Norton's character "Mr. Durden" and told him that it was him who gave the bartender the acid kiss on his right hand.

Norton says that the earliest point at which the honest viewer can claim to understand that "something weird is going on here,"[3] is when the Brad Pitt character is in the basement (think subconscious) feeding lines to Edward Norton's narrator during the last kitchen conversation with Marla.

Is this when *you* figured out that Edward Norton's character had suffered some sort of mental breakdown and instead of sleeping was out blackening his own eyes, blowing up his own apartment, developing a strange relationship with Marla, training "space monkeys" and traipsing around the country planning the destruction of civilization—all under the name of "Tyler Durden"?

Honestly?

First of all, let's get past all this "Edward Norton's character" and "Brad Pitt's character"—past the simple (and philosophically uninteresting) confusion regarding the characters' *names*.

"Who *Are* You? Cornelius, Rupert, Travis— *Any* of the Stupid Names You Give Each Night?"

Apparently, Edward Norton's character is officially called "The Narrator" but let's adopt the less stuffy convention of calling him "Jack"—as in "I am *Jack's* Raging Bile Duct."[4] We'll call Brad Pitt's character "Tyler Durden," because Pitt is always (although not only) *Tyler Durden*. Helena Bonham Carter simply plays Marla Singer.

Jack, his plight, misadventures, self-destructive tendencies, trippy *alter ego* and ultimate (if not altogether healthy) self-

---

[3] *Fight Club* DVD audio commentary track

[4] In the book it's not "I am *Jack's* Cold Sweat," but "I am *Joe's* Cold Sweat." For the sake of continuity, when I quote the book, I will substitute "Jack" for "Joe."

renewal, all provide a vehicle for thinking philosophically about what it means to live a meaningful (or not so meaningful) life. Through Jack we encounter basic human questions like "Why am I here?" "Does life have purpose?" "Does it matter if it doesn't?" "How do culture and history help make me who I am?" "Who am I?" for that matter, and "How can I be so sure?" Jack's "progress" will lead us around the edges of all these questions and thick into a couple of alternatives for how to think about the central question of personal identity, what makes me, well, *me?*

Through all the black eyes and bruised egos, commentary and complications, *Fight Club* reveals a pretty clear and simple moral message: something like *Be true to yourself or who knows what might happen.* This moral message includes a (possibly negotiable) commitment to a general theory of personal identity—one I will call *romantic authenticity* (more on that later).

Over the next several pages, I will try to show that Jack's early and satirical identification with his belongings is a ridiculous version of a somewhat more interesting theory of identity. I will then try to see whether a little more creativity and effort early on might have helped Jack avoid such a messy crisis. All along the way, I will try and offer a philosophically provocative reading of the film *Fight Club*.

"I Am Jack's Wasted Life"

The basic motivation for all the chaos in *Fight Club* is that our narrator Jack is in existential crisis. A human life and its attendant accomplishments lack permanence and, according to Jack's existential logic, without permanence meaning is doubtful. In the book, when Bob is holding him at the support group for survivors of testicular cancer ("Remaining Men Together"), Jack finds release by letting go of the illusion of permanence: "Crying is right at hand in the smothering dark, closed inside someone else, when you see how everything you can ever accomplish will end up as trash" (p. 17).

Much later, in a parallel "self-help" moment in the bar basement Fight Club, when engaged in a very different kind of embrace, Jack echoes the sentiment he expressed in Bob's more straight-forwardly nurturing clutch:

Number three pounds until his fist is raw.
Until I'm crying.
How everything you ever love will reject you or die.
Everything you ever create will be thrown away.
Everything you're proud of will end up as trash. (p. 201).

Jack's frustrated attempt to find, make or see meaning in life, apparently coupled with his inability to cope with awkward feelings of attraction for the confusing Marla Singer,[5] manifests itself in his oddly optimistic hipster *alter ego*, Tyler Durden. But the meaninglessness is not limited to Jack's Tiny Life; he projects meaninglessness onto all human endeavors. Jack is constantly reminding himself and Tyler is constantly reminding the worker bees of Project Mayhem (dubbed "Space Monkeys" for their willingness to follow orders to their peril or death) that "everything you ever accomplish will end up as trash."

Like So Many Others, I Had Become a Slave to the IKEA Nesting Instinct

Jack's uninterestingly pointless existence is the result of his failed attempt to *buy* and *assemble* an off-the-rack identity that works for him ("I'd flip through catalogues and wonder, what kind of dining set defines me as a person?") Apparently it was not for lack of effort, or even a failure to acquire the proper belongings. After Tyler blows up Jack's apartment, but before he knows Tyler did it, Jack confides, "I had it all. I had a stereo that was very decent, a wardrobe that was getting very respectable. I was close to being complete."[6] In case there was any worry that Jack did not completely identify with his belongings, reassurance comes in his phone conversation with the detective assigned to his case.

---

[5] "I know why Tyler had occurred. Tyler loved Marla. From the first night I met her, Tyler or some part of me had needed a way to be with Marla" (p. 198). Also note that Jack first calls and hangs up on Marla when his apartment is destroyed. Only then does he dial Tyler.

[6] In the book, Jack summarizes his impetus for change by saying "I was too complete. I was too perfect. I wanted a way out of my tiny life" (p. 173).

Look, nobody takes this more seriously than me. That condo was my life, okay? I loved every stick of furniture in that place. That was not just a bunch of stuff that got destroyed—IT WAS *ME!*[7]

Tyler understands consumer identity perfectly, but reacts to Jack's attachment to and identification with his stuff with condescension and incredulity.

> **TYLER:** What are we then?
>
> **JACK:** We're, uh you know, consumers.
>
> **TYLER:** Right, we're consumers. *We're by-products of a life-style obsession.* Murder, crime, poverty, these things don't concern me. What concerns me are celebrity magazines, television with five hundred channels, some guy's name on my underwear. Rogaine, Viagra, Olestra . . .
>
> **JACK:** . . . Martha Stewart.
>
> **TYLER:** Fuck Martha Stewart. Martha is polishing the brass on the *Titanic*. Everything's going down man. So fuck off with your sofa units and Strinne green stripe patterns. I say, *Never be complete.* I say, *Stop being perfect.* I say, *Let's evolve. Let the chips fall where they may* (my emphasis).

This idea that identity is the objective manifestation of an individual's consumption patterns is pursued and rejected throughout the movie. How many times in the movie do we hear Tyler's litany of *what you are not?*

> You are not your job; you're not how much money you have in the bank. You're not the car you drive. You are not the contents of your wallet. You're not your fucking khakis.

Eventually, under Tyler's hypnotic spell, Jack agrees that he is not his "glass dishes with tiny bubbles and imperfections, proof that they were crafted by the honest, simple people of . . . wherever" and decides that he has failed his consumption-based bid at meaning and identity. Or, more importantly, *his consumerism*

---

[7] Jack is clearly mocking his own prior position regarding possessions at this point, and does a nice job of articulating the consumerist identity position as he once held it.

has failed *Jack*. Consumerism has failed to make him into the sort of person that he might live with for a lifetime.

But if Jack is not his "Rizlampa wire lamps with environmentally-friendly unbleached paper," then who is he? *If this chapter were a movie, this would be a good place for a single-frame flash of Tyler Durden, maybe peddling away at Jack's Hovetrekke home exer-bike, or placing bathtub dynamite on Jack's condo floor.*

Self-Improvement Is Masturbation. Now Self-*Destruction* . . . ?

In film as in life, the notion that people have to be broken in order to be rebuilt is widespread. From *Full Metal Jacket* boot camp to sexual-preference reassignment in *But I'm a Cheerleader*, from moral re-education in *A Clockwork Orange* to respect for authority in *Cool Hand Luke*—film has taught us that selves are amazingly resilient things and must be relentlessly quashed, if lasting personality change is to be achieved.

Jack's failure to create a meaningful and satisfying identity by selecting life-style elements from the *Fürni* catalog motivated a dramatic change. That dramatic change came in the hyper-stylized nitro-wielding form of Tyler Durden. Early in the story, Tyler takes matters into his own hands by preparing the demolition of Jack's condo, but eventually it becomes important for Jack to manage his own self-destruction, or in the lingo of the film it is important that Jack want to "hit bottom." At one point Tyler compliments Marla by saying, "at least she is trying to hit bottom."

In a pivotal moment Tyler sloppily kisses the back of Jack's hand and allows the saliva to act as catalyst for a flake lye chemical burn. The acid kiss works on several levels. Aside from giving Jack a ubiquitous reminder of Tyler's presence, it encourages him to pay attention both to his immediate experience ("This is your pain. This is your burning hand. It's right here!") and to his bigger existential crisis ("First, you have to know—not fear—*know*, that someday you're going to die.") The kiss also provides a turning point where Jack must begin to take responsibility for his own self-destruction and subsequent growth.[8]

---

[8] The theme of taking responsibility is echoed at least twice more in the film, when Tyler reminds Jack that he determines his own level of involvement and

When Jack lets go and agrees that "it's only after we've lost everything that we're free to do anything," Tyler releases Jack's arm, allows Jack to control his own melt-down and permits Jack to focus on his current situation (burning flesh.) It's only when Jack accepts control and responsibility that Tyler neutralizes the reaction with vinegar; as long as Jack resists "hitting bottom" Tyler maintains the upper-hand.

The car wreck is very similar in structure and meaning to the acid kiss and reinforces the paired themes of letting-go/hitting-bottom. Tyler is driving recklessly and Jack is squirming.[9] Tyler takes his hands off the wheel altogether and encourages Jack to do the same. "Hitting bottom isn't a weekend retreat. It isn't a goddamned seminar. Stop trying to control everything and just let go . . . LET GO!" They wreck. Tyler announces, "We just had a near life experience." So, okay, once you've hit bottom, where do you go from there? *[Insert subliminal Tyler Durden number 2 here.]*

Is This about You and Me?

Fight Club is at heart a basically *Romantic* film. I don't mean to say that *Fight Club* is *boy-meets-girl-meets-boy-meets-chemical-burn* romantic, although there is obviously some of that. I'm talking Romantic in the nineteen-*century-Transcendentalist-back-to-nature-self-reliance-Ralph-Waldo-Emerson-meets-Henry-David-Thoreau* sense of Romantic.[10]

The Romantics' legacy in America is a transcendental spiritualism that encourages personal renewal by getting in touch with *nature*—nature as in animals and wilderness, yes, but also conscious nature as spirit manifested in one's own distinct and inherent *personal human* nature. Emerson celebrates the nature and spirit of humanity this way:

---

at the very end when a disgusted Tyler tells Jack straightforwardly to take some responsibility.

[9] This scene is very subtle from a film continuity point of view. Although Brad Pitt drives, Edward Norton both gets into the car and is removed from the car from the driver's door. Pahlaniuk avoids the problem in the book by having a different character "the mechanic" drive and parrot Tyler's words and ideas.

[10] While there are probably some comparisons to be made between the film and eighteenth-century European Romanticism, in the manner of William Blake, I will focus my limited attention on American Romanticism.

O rich and various Man! Thou palace of sight and sound, carrying in thy senses the morning and the night and the City of God; in thy heart, the bower of love and the realms of right and wrong. An individual man is a fruit which it cost all the foregoing ages to form and ripen.[11]

Contemporary adaptations of Romanticism inspire us to reconnect both to the natural world around and to our own more authentic, better, inner, purer, stronger, hidden nature within. Romanticism questions technological solutions to sociological, environmental, and political problems. It does so at least in part because technology (computers, television, automobiles, air-travel) mediates and interprets the otherwise raw, authentic, pure moments of lived experience. Technology tells you what's important. Technology tells you what to think. Technology gets between you and your life ("This is the best moment of your life, and you're off somewhere missing it.") Tyler Durden is the modern day, anti-technology, primal urge, moment-idealizing, Romantic hero—he is technological man's own self-reliant fantasy of himself come to Technicolor life.

Tyler plays the Romantic hero first by helping Jack get in touch with his own more primal urges and inclinations, then by articulating a broader Romantic vision of a post-apocalyptic America where technology does not mediate individual experience. Operating from an implied theory of personal identity that I'll call the "Romantic authenticity view," Tyler takes it as a matter of simple self-knowledge that one should know how one will react in a fight. This is somehow basic. This is required for an authentic knowledge of oneself. Fight Club begins in *Lou's* parking lot as an exploration of Jack's previously untested physical limits.

Tyler: I've never been in a fight. You?
Jack: No, but that's a good thing.
Tyler: No it is not. How much can you know about yourself if you've never been in a fight? I don't want to die without any scars. So come on hit me before I lose my nerve.

---

[11] Ralph Waldo Emerson, "The Method of Nature," in *The American Transcendentalists: Their Prose and Poetry* (New York: Doubleday, 1957), p. 58.

Self-knowledge gained through a little unmediated animal aggression is Romantic indeed.

Having successfully challenged Jack's very sense of self-preservation, Tyler proceeds without discrimination to remove the boundaries—economic, social, hygienic—that Jack has worked very hard to perfect, but that imprison him and stifle his development ("I say, let's evolve. Let the chips fall where they may.") Through Tyler, and in keeping with the Romantic authenticity view of personal identity, Jack jettisons the sexual, political, economic, moral, and legal boundaries that have kept his more basic nature in check until this point.

Since Fight Club began as a way for Jack to better understand himself, it only makes sense that its development mirrors Jack's own personal growth. As Jack begins to outgrow his own odd new self-help movement, Fight Club "comes out of the basement" in the form of Project Mayhem. Tyler becomes increasingly independent and Jack becomes more and more like Tyler ("In the end, we all became what Tyler wanted us to be") and Tyler's aspirations outgrow the confines of Jack's small psyche. Tyler begins to imagine the anarchist social progress that provides the analogue to Jack's more individual evolution. Project Mayhem is Tyler's attempt to realize the financial and societal collapse that will clear the way for his neo-Romantic post-apocalyptic America.

After the car ride in which Tyler announces that Project Mayhem is "bigger than you and me," Tyler articulates his vision of a new America as a kind of dreamy farewell.

> In the world I see you're stalking elk through the damp forest canyons around the ruins of Rockefeller Center. You'll wear leather clothes that will last you the rest of your life. You'll climb the wrist thick kudzu vines that wrap the Sears tower. And when you look down you'll see tiny figures pounding corn, laying strips of venison on the empty carpool lane of some abandoned super highway.

Fight Club ends with Tyler dead (although a single-frame penis during the closing credits makes us wonder.) Dead or no, Project Mayhem seems quite functional and intent and capable of seeing Tyler's apocalyptic vision through to *Mad Max* reality.

No Wait. Back Up. Let Me Start Earlier

We have followed Jack from his original identification with belongings and the resulting existential crisis, through ideological self-destruction toward authentic romantic realization and into cultural destruction. Having outlined the wide-ranging philosophical structure of the film, we're now in a position to consider whether Jack might have failed before the movie ever began—whether he was forced to reject his original theory of personal identity and enact Tyler only due to a paucity of imagination. Maybe Jack's original ideas of personal identity didn't fail Jack. Maybe Jack failed his ideas.[12]

If you've bought my version of the story this far, it may seem that we have committed ourselves to a negative attitude toward Jack's original view of personal identity. First we dubbed Jack's original view of what makes a self "consumer identity"—a negatively-loaded categorization, no doubt. Then we allowed that Jack was as successful as he could have been at assembling a rich tapestry of belongings and at identifying completely with those belongings—which is to say that Jack did not fail his consumerism, his consumerism failed Jack. We even allowed that Jack's life was indeed meaningless and the person he had created insipid (I think we agreed to that, at least implicitly).

It might seem, then, that consistency requires that we do as Jack did and reject his original *consumer identity* view wholesale and embrace *the Romantic authenticity* view that Tyler epitomizes. It seems that we should either embrace the romantic authenticity view or provide another, possibly our own, understanding of what makes a self. Although rejecting both the consumerist position and the authenticity position and trying for another has some appeal, there is another option. Maybe Jack's attempt at self-creation just wasn't creative *enough*.

When a view, theory, perspective or argument is presented badly, just for the sake of forcing those judging the issue to

---

[12] Don't misunderstand me here. As a moviegoer, I'm glad Jack chose as he did. Even as a teacher of philosophy, I'm glad for his wonderfully provocative life. The movie is as entertaining a vehicle for thinking about personal identity and the meaning of life as any. In this section I'm trying to draw some philosophical life lessons from Jack's mistakes, so that you and I might avoid falling into the philosophical trap that Jack does. To do that, I have to criticize Jack as if he were my hapless friend.

choose the alternative, philosophers call that a "straw man" argument.[13] A straw man position is set up loosely, constructed of the poorest available materials and presented half-heartedly (kind of like a scarecrow; it only has to look vaguely like the real thing.) A straw man hints at the more carefully fleshed-out argument and stands long enough for the opposition to knock it down convincingly—kind of like a movie prop. Jack's original life—the life of consumption—is a straw man argument representing a small cluster of personal identity theories I'll classify as *life-as-art* theories of personal identity.[14] Think of life as the canvas on which a person is created as the product of choices from experience's rich palette of possibility.

Philosophers from the existentialists Friedrich Nietzsche and Jean-Paul Sartre, to today's post-modern philosophers Richard Rorty and Jacques Derrida have held some version of the life-as-art view.[15] These thinkers understand your identity as arising from what you do with your time—from the choices you make in life—the *least* interesting of which may be your purchases.

Tyler attacks some pretty inconsequential issues in his "*you are not your . . .*" speech. Who wouldn't agree that they are not their pants?[16] Would he get the same bleating worship if he bellowed *this* into a bullhorn?

---

[13] Being a highly conditioned college professor, I am sensitive to the gender-bias involved in calling the argumentative error under consideration a "straw *man*." Since the term is, if anything, an insult to men and since I'm one of those critters, I suspect I can get away with this slight.

[14] I'm not being critical of the wonderfully challenging novel or movie under consideration. Presumably, neither Palahniuk nor Fincher set out to thoroughly present, then offer a sound argument against any philosophical view of personhood or the meaningful life. But as we have taken it upon ourselves to treat *Fight Club* philosophically and somewhat seriously—in that mode, it is responsible to critique the arguments we have read in and into the work.

[15] The picture I paint in what follows is pretty much a Rortyan version of the life-as-art view, although he is really the last in line to articulate it.

[16] Next time you watch *Fight Club* listen for the space monkey in the background who expounds on Tyler's "you are not your . . ." speech. The monkey excitedly philosophizes, "When he was like, '*you are not your job*,' I was like, 'yeah," then he amplifies, "fuck yeah!'"

You are not *who you love.*
You are not *the place you call home.*
You are not *the difference that you make.*
You are not *your passion.*
You are not *what you create.*
You are not *your legacy.*

I doubt it. I think we agree that we are these things in some important way.

The portrait of a life is painted in great globs of color, a hundred choices at a time. And just as visual artists are expected to bend, break or invent new rules, people thinking of themselves as their medium are not judged according to a pre-existing set of external standards for success or by eternal expectations. People become part of a community by embracing some elements of society and individualize themselves by rejecting others. Freedom on this view is the recognition that there are no pre-existing standards to which we are *ultimately* accountable. Freedom is the admission that our first attitudes toward success and meaning in life are the product of our upbringing. And, most importantly, *freedom is the recognition that we can change our standards and attitudes toward success.*

All you need to do to construct a compelling argument for the life as art view is to consider examples of people who made better choices in creating their lives than Jack did—people who made a nice life for themselves. You know some interesting works of life, you must. You probably are one yourself. It really wouldn't take much to do better than Jack. Jack is the straw man of contemporary consumer society, a literary device devised to introduce the idealized romantic rebel, Tyler Durden.

But That's Just Me. I Could Be Wrong

So what about Jack on the life-as-art view? Do his Strinne green stripe pattern sofa and Rizlampa wire lamps count as an honest and concerted effort to construct a life? Jack seemed like a pretty suggestible, passive guy at the beginning of the movie. Identity creation may not require constant attention and creativity, but at the same time searching out rich life possibility may require more than counting on *[plug in the name of your favorite mail-order catalog here]* to sell your name to its competitors and then glossing their catalogs while on the toilet.

While the take home message of *Fight Club* seems to be, *Be true to yourself or everyone suffers*, we can easily tweak the message to make it, *Put forth a little effort in self-creation, or you'll end up with an off-the-rack identity*. But isn't that what's important about Jack?—he is a kind of off-the-rack everyman for this age. And maybe that's why the movie works. Likable and clever though he is, Jack is supposed to represent what is wrong with our culture. At this he is very, very good.

TO THINK ABOUT

1. How would you characterize the *psychological* relationship between Ed Norton's character and Brad Pitt's?

2. Is there a hero in *Fight Club*? If so who plays the hero? Brad Pitt? Ed Norton? Why? What makes a hero?

3. If you could turn loose your own inner "Tyler Durden," would you? Why or why not? Tell a story with your inner Tyler Durden as the main character—what would he or she do? Why? How is he or she different from you?

TO READ NEXT

Walter Truett Anderson. *The Truth about the Truth*. New York: Penguin Putnam, 1995.

Ralph Waldo Emerson. *Nature and Walking*. Boston: Beacon, 1991.

John Perry. *A Dialogue on Personal Identity*. Indianapolis: Hackett, 1978. For a brief and readable overview of personal identity issues read John Perry's "Third Night" dialogue.

Richard Rorty. *Contingency, Irony, and Solidarity*. Cambridge: Cambridge University Press, 1989. A thorough treatment of the "life-as-art" view.

5

It's my *Heeeeaaaad!*: Sex and Death in *Being John Malkovich*

WALTER OTT

> Hell hath no limits, nor is circumscrib'd
> In one selfe place, for where we are is hell,
> And where Hell is, must we ever be.
>
> — CHRISTOPHER MARLOWE, *Doctor Faustus*

Craig Schwartz (John Cusack) has discovered a portal into another person. For fifteen minutes, he can experience the world from inside John Malkovich: he sees what Malkovich sees, feels Malkovich's arms and legs move, and hears Malkovich's voice as if it were his own. When his time is up, Craig is rudely ejected on to the New Jersey Turnpike.

An expert puppeteer, Craig soon works out a technique to make the Malkovich body obey his will. What do he and the others he lets in on the secret want to do with this fascinating discovery? Maxine (Catherine Keener), his co-worker, decides they'll sell tickets for a 'ride' through Malkovich. Craig, like his wife Lotte (Cameron Diaz), wants to use Malkovich to make love to Maxine. And the sinister director of LesterCorp (Orson Bean), in whose building the portal exists, wants to live forever, using Malkovich and others like him as 'vessels'.

The dominant visual metaphor of *Being John Malkovich* (1999) is confinement: the chimp Elijah in his cage, the absurd dimensions of the "seven-and-a-halfth" floor of the Lester building, and the mask-like view from inside Malkovich's skull all seem designed to inspire claustrophobia. This is no accident.

The selfishness and self-absorption of the main characters is mirrored in the narrow limits of the world they inhabit. But the visual claustrophobia also reflects the traditional view of the self presupposed by the movie. On this view, associated with Descartes, the self is a unified subject that exists over time and is not necessarily tied to any particular body. This view underpins the desires and goals of the main characters: immortality makes no sense without it, nor does the project of copulating with someone using a third person's body.

Being John Malkovich presents us with a way of reflecting on our own predicament. Even though the events of the film are unlikely, many of us are committed to the Cartesian view that makes them possible. The movie's intriguing suggestion, I think, is that this metaphysical view is tied up with a range of destructive attitudes toward our own deaths, romantic love, and the meaning of life.

If the movie presents a despairing picture of human beings, it also, perhaps in spite of itself, suggests a way out. The goals of the main characters and the overwhelming importance they attach to them stand or fall with the particular view of the self as a non-physical *I* that can continue to exist apart from the body it now inhabits. Perhaps if we can see why this view is wrong, we can reason our way, as it were, out of our own heads.

What Are We?

When Malkovich discovers Craig's and Maxine's scheme, he's understandably upset: "It's my *heeeaaad!*" Think how differently the line reads with an emphasis on the possessive: "It's *my* head."[1] The complaint then would simply be that Craig and Maxine have trespassed on Malkovich's rights by appropriating the interior of his skull for their own benefit. But that wouldn't capture what really bothers Malkovich about his predicament: if there were a portal to, say, his left calf, things wouldn't be nearly so bad.

Why? What's so special about one's head? At least part of the answer must be that that's where our consciousness seems to

---

[1] As the line is written in Charlie Kaufman's script, available in many places on the web.

reside: it's the locus of our point of view on the world. When Craig goes through the portal, he sees the world as if from behind a Halloween mask. When Malkovich scratches his head, this is much louder from Craig's point of view than it would be to an outside observer; it is as if his own head were being scratched, and presumably he feels it as well, somewhere in the upper-right region of his 'tactile field'.

We might call this the 'homuncular' view of the self. It is as if each human body had another, much tinier human being inside it, a 'homunculus' somewhere in the skull, which both experiences the world through the body by receiving signals sent by the senses and controls the body's movements. Each of us is really a very tiny puppeteer, controlling the nerves and muscles of the body much as Craig controls what Lotte derisively calls his "dolls."[2]

In the world of the movie, of course, not everyone has a portal. Captain Mertin, the first discoverer of the portal, aims to live forever by moving from 'vessel to vessel'. Unfortunately, the vessels are hard to come by. Why this is the case is obscure, but Mertin claims it has something to do with the potential vessel's DNA. Most of us have become expert puppeteers in our own cases through childhood experience, becoming so adept that we don't realize we're doing it. So in these cases the homunculus is not a distinct person but ourselves. These selves must be non-material, since of course even by the movie's standards it would be crazy to think that there is literally a tiny duplicate of Craig inside Craig's body. What animates his body is Craig himself, the non-physical Ego. This is the view Gilbert Ryle stigmatized as "the ghost in the machine."

How does the movie commit itself to this Cartesian view? If the self is non-physical, there's no problem with supposing that more than one self animates a given body. When Craig (or anyone else) enters the vessel, the experiences they have remain their own, even while Malkovich himself has precisely the same

---

[2] There is an interesting parallel with some of the cruder understandings of Freudian psychoanalysis, which seem to suggest that 'man is . . . a dark cellar in which a maiden aunt and a sex-crazed monkey are locked in mortal combat, the affair being refereed by a rather nervous bank clerk' (D. Bannister, quoted in Ronald De Sousa, "Rational Homunculi," in *The Identities of Persons* edited by A.O. Rorty [Berkeley: University of California Press, 1976], 217).

experiences. The movie thus assumes that there can be two sets
of experiences inside the Malkovich vessel, one belonging to
Malkovich, and one to the intruding mind. To satisfy his lust for
Maxine, Craig enters the portal and through (or alongside?)
Malkovich has sex with her. But what makes it the case that
those experiences belong to Craig, rather than to Malkovich
alone? After all, if Maxine has the clap, it is Malkovich who will
suffer. The only way to attribute the conquest of Maxine to Craig
is to suppose a Cartesian ego, a non-physical self that can
inhabit bodies at different times. If we take it for granted that it
is Craig who has those experiences, we have already bought
into the Cartesian view.

To draw this out, let's consider some examples. Craig's goal
from the start is to seduce Maxine; when he learns she has nothing but scorn for him, he stumbles on the portal, and then,
seemingly, on another way to achieve his goal. But will occupying Malkovich help him? Consider these cases:

1. Craig, wearing a convincing Malkovich mask and walking
   on well-concealed stilts, dupes Maxine into having sex
   with him.
2. Craig builds a life-like robot and dupes Maxine into having sex with it.
3. Craig fantasizes about Maxine, while, unbeknownst to
   him, Maxine is having precisely the same fantasy about
   him, down to the last detail.

In which of these cases do we want to say Craig has succeeded? Case 1 is underhanded, to be sure, but successful; the
experiences are certainly Craig's. Case 2 would be much less
satisfying, but notice that it's not different in kind from the first
case, if we are all Cartesian homunculi: there's just an extra
step inserted here between the 'puppets' that Craig and Maxine
control. This is already an indication of the oddity of the
Cartesian view. Strictly speaking, we should have to say that
even in Case 1, Craig and Maxine have not had sex; their bodies have performed certain actions, but Craig and Maxine
themselves, the homunculi staring out through the windows of
their bodies' eyes, have not. This lets us see how the Cartesian
view distorts our ordinary picture of the world, in which it is
of course possible for persons and not just the bodies they

happen to control to have sex, and puts in its place a set of claims that might well lead us to Craig's "dance of despair and disillusionment." For we are all trapped inside a skull, and our skill at maneuvering the body we find ourselves in produces the persistent illusion that we *are* those bodies. (People manipulating robotic arms in order to deal with radioactive materials report that after a time those arms seem to be their own.) Pierre Gassendi, a contemporary of Descartes's, illustrated this distortion of our ordinary ways of speaking and thinking when he pointed out that Descartes must regard himself "not as a whole man but as an inner or hidden component" and goes on to call Descartes "Soul, or whatever name you want me to address you by . . ."[3]

So the only difference between Cases 1 and 2 is the connection between Craig, the Cartesian ego, and the body he controls. In one case, he controls a body that copulates with Maxine; in the other, he controls a body that controls another body that copulates with Maxine. But perhaps there is another way to account for the difference, one that does not involve the Cartesian self. Perhaps the difference lies in the very content of the experiences Craig has in Case 2: they will be from the point of view of the Craig body, not from the robot's point of view. He won't have the experience of Maxine's (or her robot's) body next to his, and he is (somehow) linked with the Craig body and not the others, at least for now. If we were to ask Craig after he is ejected from the portal why he thinks he has had sex with Maxine, he might advert to his memories: he can tell us all sorts of things that only someone who has had sex with her can tell us (although morally, perhaps, he should keep that information to himself.)

On this view, what makes these experiences Craig's is just that he is able to remember them: Lotte, Maxine, and Carrot Top did not have those experiences because they cannot remember them. This is a very popular view of personal identity, one devised by John Locke. But now we should consider Case 3. Recall that in Case 3, Craig fantasizes about Maxine while Maxine is having the identical fantasy about him. It seems pretty

---

[3] Fifth Set of Objections, in *The Philosophical Writings of Descartes* ed. J. Cottingham, R. Stoothoff, and D. Murdoch (Cambridge: Cambridge University Press, 1984), Volume II, p. 181.

clear that in this case, Craig would not be justified in carving a notch on his bedpost. And yet from the point of view of his experiences, everything is exactly as it would be in the case where he, 'inhabiting' Malkovich's body, seduces Maxine. After all, if the body plays no essential role in making us who we are, why shouldn't mere fantasy count as much as experiences had through another such body? The memory account will not work for Case 3, for Craig's memories of his fantasy are precisely the same as those he would have had he actually had sex with Maxine.

Perhaps the memory theorist has the resources to respond to this objection. To have a memory, she might say, it is not enough to be able to call to consciousness a particular set of experiences. Genuine memories require, at least, that the subject himself who seems to remember them really has experienced them. If we can draw this distinction between real and apparent memories, we can say that Case 3 doesn't really present any problems for the memory view, because Craig does not *really* remember having had sex with Maxine, even if his fantasy is so vivid that he comes to believe it really happened. Similarly, Craig-post-expulsion is the same person as Craig-in-Malkovich because he remembers, and not just seems to remember, having had sex with Maxine.

Unfortunately, we have now gone in a circle. We set out to explain why Craig's fantasies about Maxine, however vivid, don't count as a sexual conquest: even if he can call to mind the smell of Maxine's hair, her perfume, and the way she looked at him, those experiences, while his, are pure fantasy. We then suggested that the difference lies in his ability to actually remember those experiences and not merely to seem to remember them. But to draw this distinction we had to appeal to the very fact we are trying to explain, namely that they are had by one and the same subject, Craig.[4] The only account that allows us to make sense of the movie invokes the persistence of the Cartesian ego.

---

[4] Not everyone would agree that the account is circular; Sidney Shoemaker appeals to 'quasi-memories' to solve this problem. See Shoemaker's "Persons and their Pasts," *American Philosophical Quarterly* 7 (1970), pp. 269–285. For a rejection of quasi-memories, see Andy Hamilton, "A New Look at Personal Identity," *Philosophical Quarterly* 45 (1995), pp. 332–349.

Problems with the Self

Despite the popular perception of *Being John Malkovich* as a fantasy, its core assumption is widespread. For a true believer in the immaterial self, occupying a different body should seem no more implausible than, say, any of the events depicted in *Affliction* or *School of Rock*. One way to read the film is as a despairing look at the human condition; another, as a parody of a certain way of viewing that condition. As I've already hinted, I prefer the latter. But Charlie Kaufman's script itself suggests that the movie's presuppositions are incoherent by building in arbitrary features.

As far as I can make out, the metaphysical situation is supposed to be this: a homuncular Ego can occupy a different body for fifteen minutes at a time, after which the body originally inhabited by the Ego is ejected, Ego and all, on to the turnpike. The only exception is the vessel's forty-fourth birthday, when, at midnight, it is possible for an Ego to enter the vessel and remain there permanently, but only if it is powerful enough to squash the host's Ego back down into the subconscious, where it will remain as a passive observer. Once someone like Captain Mertin exhausts a body, he must find a new vessel and enter it at the precise time when it is 'ripe', or else face being 'absorbed', shunted off into the next available baby (or fetus?) where he will remain imprisoned, experiencing all that that body experiences but being utterly unable to exert any influence on how that body behaves.

There are other clues that the movie is to be taken as exaggerating the absurdity of what was already a difficult view to swallow. When Craig first goes in to the portal, he has a piece of wood with him; when he is ejected, he no longer has it. Where has it gone, he wonders? After he is permanently ejected from Malkovich, however, the board reappears. Why?

In one scene, Malkovich himself goes through the portal, body and Malkovich-ego and all. This should have no effect—the Malkovich-ego would now be inside the Malkovich-body, where it was all along. But of course since the Malkovich body has gone through the portal, there is now no body for the ego to inhabit. Thus by the movie's own logic, this should be impossible. But the Malkovich-ego finds himself in a restaurant full of Malkovich 'bodies' (they can't be real bodies, since there's only one of those) and then emerges intact onto the Turnpike, declaring that he has seen things "no man should ever see." Is this a clever metaphor for the egotistical self-absorption that seems to be one of the hazards of the acting profession or a confession of the movie's own absurdity? It can be both.

We can add to these a host of other questions. Captain Mertin/Dr. Lester decides to bring a few friends with him when he enters Malkovich. What happens to these friends? Why would they agree to this, if Mertin is to be 'captain' of the vessel? Presumably their situation would be no better than had they been 'absorbed'. Consider the penultimate scene, in which the Malkovich vessel, under the command of the Captain, offers Charlie Sheen immortal life along with himself and his crew in the body of Maxine's and Lotte's child. Kaufman gives us a subtle hint that the Malkovich homunculus is having at least some effect on what used to be his body when he has that body tell Sheen that they might invite Gary Sinise along for the ride. (The real Malkovich and Sinise worked together in the Steppenwolf theater in Chicago and starred in *Of Mice and Men*.)

This transparently silly metaphysical claptrap is, I think, designed to point up the absurdity of the Cartesian view. The view from inside the vessel is a nice illustration of the dangers of conceiving the self as a kind of ghostly denizen imprisoned inside a skull. Descartes himself said, "I am not in my body as a captain is in his ship,"[5] but it is notoriously hard to see how he can offer any other picture. (Perhaps it is no accident that Kaufman makes such use of nautical vocabulary.)

There are other problems waiting in the wings. To see this, all we need do is ask what precisely the connection is supposed to be between the homuncular Ego and its body. The self is non-physical and so cannot have a location in space. Only physical things are in space; the self is literally nowhere, in the same way the number 2 or the average taxpayer are nowhere. How can such a thing bring about changes in a body, which of course occupies a particular location at any one moment? The puppeteer and his puppet are connected by strings; the self-as-puppeteer can have nothing analogous on which to pull. The problem is not just how causation can take place when the

---

[5] See Descartes's *Meditation* VI.

cause is not in the same location as the effect; gravity, arguably, is one way in which there can be action at a distance. But the distance between physical and non-physical is of another order entirely. If the self were somewhere, we could entertain the idea that interacts with another spatially extended object. But it isn't, and so we can't.

Even if we lay this aside, consider what the view does to our knowledge of other people. Others are also ghostly homunculi, at best giving us signs of their thoughts and feelings by pulling their puppet's strings. How do we know they're in there? How do we know *who* is in there? Although dualists have tried many maneuvers to escape this, the conclusion seems to be that we are all imprisoned within our own bodies, at best inferring that there are other minds out there like our own. But any view that turns your best friend in to the object of an inference, however well-founded, is one that no one but a philosopher could take seriously.

Love

One way or another, the central goals of the main characters center around romantic relationships. Captain Mertin's own chief goal, apart from eternal life itself, is "to feel Floris's naked thighs next to mine—I want her to shiver in a spasm of ecstasy as I penetrate her . . ." Early in the movie, Craig fashions a Maxine puppet; in his love for her, he has the puppet say, "Would you like to be inside my skin? Think what I think, feel what I feel? It's good in here, Craig. It's better than your wildest dreams." Craig wants something more than Mertin wants: not just sexual satisfaction but the sense of being her, being inside her Cartesian theater, feeling and experiencing everything as she would. Sadly, this is the very thing the Cartesian view makes impossible: his project is bound to fail, for he and Maxine are irreducibly different minds.

Lotte has perhaps the most complicated set of desires. She wants to sleep with Maxine but as a man; before she hears of the portal, she tells Craig she's going to consult her dentist, Dr. Feldman, on the possibility of gender-reassignment. The Malkovich vessel provides the perfect solution: painless (if temporary) gender switching. But notice that she also gets the pleasure of 'penetrating' another person even more fully than physical sex would allow: on learning of the portal, she says, "it's as if Malkovich had a vagina."

For her part, Maxine enjoys her time with Lotte/Malkovich since it gives her a double dose of adoration. Craig alone has moral qualms with Maxine's relations with Lotte/Malkovich; he tells her simply, "you're evil." To justify herself, Maxine asks, "Have you ever had two people look at you with total lust and devotion through a single pair of eyes?"

There are essentially two varieties of erotic love in the movie. The first, Maxine's, is simple enough. Like Mertin, who fantasizes about being worshipped by Floris (Mary Kay Place) as "the Love God Eros," Maxine wants not just sexual pleasure but dominance over her partners. One senses that Maxine, at the end of the movie, couldn't be happier than where she is, at the center of a love rectangle: Lotte, Craig-inside-Emily, and presumably Emily herself, all in their different ways, love Maxine. Maxine doesn't want Craig but is pleased that he loves her: this is another soul she can dominate, and if she has no interest in the sexual pleasure he can afford, Craig offers a convenient object of ridicule ("The puppeteer declared his love for me today," we hear her telling a friend on her cell phone.) It's only when Craig learns to control the vessel and takes complete possession of it that Maxine marries 'him' (Malkovich/Craig). The essential emptiness of Maxine's psyche is impressed on us over and over again during the movie.

The second kind of love, Craig's, is at first sight more sophisticated. What he wants from Maxine is not just "lust and devotion"; he wants, so far as possible, to escape himself and the confines of his own mind. For him, "consciousness is a terrible curse. I think, I feel, I suffer, and all I ask in return is the opportunity to do my work and they won't allow it because I *raise issues*." Craig wants to use Malkovich not primarily to control others but to get as far as he can to his goal of dissolving himself in Maxine, escaping his Craig-ness in what he envisions as the warmth and love of Maxine. Sex is the closest he can come to this, but the scene with his Maxine puppet indicates that it is a second-best to the ideal state of affairs, in which he basks in the glow of Maxine's own consciousness, seeing and feeling the world from her point of view, experiencing what she experiences.

Unfortunately, as the movie suggests, this second kind of love cannot be had. There is no portal to Maxine. Knowing what we know about her, and what Craig *ought* to know about her, this is an act of kindness on Kaufman's part, for stepping into that beautiful skull the Craig-homunculus would discover anything but warmth. Moreover, such a portal, even if it existed, would only serve to illustrate the essential separateness of persons, on the Cartesian view: he can tour her subconscious and feel the same sensations as she, but they will remain distinct minds or souls. Maxine will go on despising him and would only despise him the more if he got inside her head.

The lesson seems to be this: only power over others and bare sexual pleasure are goals worth aiming at. Whatever the true content of Craig's higher form of love may be, it is impossible, a romantic illusion on which those of us who "see what they want and go after it," like Maxine, delight in pouring scorn. If we really are Cartesian minds, love can at best be an attachment to another such soul: what counts, what makes the person you now live with the same person you fell in love with, is just the persistence of one and the same mind. Such a mind can lose all of its qualities, change all of its likes and dislikes, and still remain the same. It as if there were an enduring essence of the person, permanently hidden within the prison-house of the body, that is the object of love. However attractive mystical hooey about 'soul-mates' can seem, the Cartesian view gets things radically wrong. Cases in which a person's changing qualities preclude the same attitude are all too common. We often say things like, 'she's not the same person I married,' and presumably we don't mean that a different mind inhabits the same body, but only that the qualities that made the person who she was have changed.

Death and the Meaning of Life

When Lester/Mertin explains the secret of his longevity—carrot juice—he adds, "I piss sitting down like a goddamned girlie-girl. But nobody wants to die." The claim is patently false: life is not a good thing in and of itself, and some of us, when life becomes too painful, too humiliating, or just too boring will look for and find a way to die. Mertin cannot see this because his desires are so powerful he cannot conceive of anyone wanting to die. The longing for immortality is parasitic on some other interest or set of interests around which one can construct a life. Absent these 'ground projects', as philosopher Bernard Williams calls them, it is an open question what reason one has to go on living at all, much less to live forever. So it makes no sense to want nothing other than to live forever: we must want this, if at all, because we think it will allow us to satisfy some of our desires and carry out our ground projects.

Should we want to live forever? The 'should' here is rational, not moral: our question is not whether it is morally right to want this, but whether it's rational to want to live forever. What gives us a reason to do anything? Our desires are part of this, but so is the fact that our time as living beings is limited. This familiar fact is brought home by our behavior. Suppose you have an entire weekend in which to write a take-home exam. Chances are good that you will not write it Friday night, for you have Saturday and Sunday in which to do it. Now suppose that you have an infinite amount of time in which to do it: what reason do you have to do it *now* as opposed to tomorrow, or ten years from now, or a million? Our reasons for doing things are conditioned on our nature as temporally limited beings. Obviously, we always have reasons to seek our own pleasure. But larger projects only make sense if we will, someday, die. Captain Mertin is a fine example of this: what else can he aim at, besides shtupping Floris?

At the end of the film, we find Craig imprisoned in the body of Emily, a girl who turns out to be Maxine's and Malkovich's daughter. The tragedy of his position is offset by the apparently happier ending for Maxine and Lotte, who are now raising this Oedipal monstrosity. They, at least, get to be together. But we cannot help but wonder whether Maxine and Lotte will, in the end, be any happier or more fulfilled than Craig.

Many of our goals are no more laudable or more likely to be satisfied than Craig's or Mertin's. Even if they were ultimately satisfied, as in the case of Maxine and Lotte, what would we do then? We would either be forced to pick out a new desire to try to satisfy or, perhaps even worse, we would find ourselves without any desire to propel us forward. It's hardly surprising that this predicament should inspire Craig's "dance of despair and disillusionment."

Immortality cannot be the goal of a rational person. Our lives make sense to us only on the assumption that they will end. We can be interesting to ourselves only to the extent that the narrative of our lives is limited. Imagine embarking on an infinitely long book: there is no reason to continue reading, since, although you don't know the ending, you know that *there is* no ending. Each event in the book would to that extent become meaningless. It is hard enough to motivate ourselves to read *Ulysses* or *Moby-Dick*.

For any project we can think of, we can step back and ask, in what way would achieving this goal make my life meaningful? Whether we choose sexual conquest or helping the poor of Calcutta, achieving the goal only presents us with the problem of meaninglessness all over again. Trapped in such an endless succession of more or less ephemeral desires and goals, we might well wish, with Craig-in-Emily, to "look away."

Liberation

Happily, the movie's presuppositions are incoherent. The events it depicts are conceivable or imaginable but not possible, just as an M.C. Escher drawing can present us with a scene that is, by the laws of geometry, impossible.

What view of the self, then, is open to us? Here's one worth considering. On this view, each person, Malkovich, Maxine, Lotte, is not a distinct being but a convenient grouping of more or less continuous successions of projects, desires, and memories. Whether Craig-in-Malkovich is numerically the same as Craig-prior-to-entering-Malkovich is an empty question. There are similarities in their desires, goals, and memories; but these similarities do not ground, and are not grounded by, a single, persistent self. Descartes wasn't entitled to infer I am (*sum*) from I think (*cogito*); what follows is something like, there's thinking going on here now. There's no mystical self which performs these acts of thinking: there is only a heap of thoughts. If we eliminate the Cartesian homunculus, what we are left with is a complex set of interrelated experiences.

On this view, the Cartesian self is what we might call a 'deep illusion'. Some illusions, like the Müller-Lyer illusion,[6] are easily

---

[6] In this illusion, subjects are asked to compare the lengths of two line segments, one of which is bounded by greater-than signs, the other, by less-than signs. Although the segments are in fact of equal length, subjects routinely say that the former is longer than the latter.

corrected. But some persist in the light of better knowledge. Although we all know that physical objects have nothing corresponding to our phenomenal perception of color and are only disposed to bounce different wavelengths of light at our eyes, the intuition that objects really are red, blue, or what have you, dies hard. It is similarly hard to conceive of ourselves as nothing more than a haphazard collection of desires, thoughts, sensations, and projects; but that is what we are.

To some, this will seem even more depressing than the Cartesian view. And so it is, if we cling to the desire for immortality. But that desire is irrational. There are practical advantages to my view as well. The separateness of persons, transformed into a metaphysical divide between Cartesian minds that can communicate only indirectly, disappears. We are no longer compelled to view love as either the desire to dominate the other or to achieve a kind of union with another soul, a union that is ruled out by the Cartesian view.

There is a further moral consequence. Consider pain. On the Cartesian view, I have a special reason to prevent my own future pain simply because it will be mine; I have only derivative reasons to prevent the pain of others. But if my continued existence is a matter of degree, and the future 'self' I shall become is only more or less related to the current set of beliefs and desires that constitute me, the picture changes. I still have a reason to avoid causing this future self pain simply because pain is bad and I am in the best position to do something about it. But the ineliminable divide between me and others is gone. I now have reasons to be less selfish, less caught up in Lotte's project of 'self-actualization.' The pain of others matters to me in much the same way as my own future pain. Where there is and should be a difference, it is a difference of degree, not kind.

Coming to hold a view like the one I have sketched can be consoling and liberating. Derek Parfit reports that when he believed that his own continued existence was an all-or-nothing matter, as the Cartesian view has it,

> My life seemed like a glass tunnel, through which I was moving faster every year, and at the end of which there was darkness. When I changed my view, the walls of my glass tunnel disappeared. I now live in the open air. There is still a difference between my life and the lives of others. But the difference is less.

Other people are closer. I am less concerned about my own life, and more concerned about the lives of others.[7]

The question, 'What is the meaning of *my* life?', presupposes that there is a genuine, unified self whose life can have or lack meaning. Giving up on the Cartesian ego can help reconcile us to the fact that no answer could ever satisfy us. And without the presupposition of an immaterial homunculus imprisoned in our skulls, we shall be less prone to ignore the suffering of others and less vulnerable to myths about romantic love. *Being John Malkovich* shows that belief in a Cartesian ego is not just a metaphysical blunder but a powerful source of human misery.

---

[7] *Reasons and Persons* (Oxford: Clarendon Press, 1984), p. 281. Parfit's own view is considerably more sophisticated than the one I have sketched here.

TO THINK ABOUT

1. If you had the chance to inhabit someone else for fifteen minutes, whom would you choose, and why? Would it be any different, morally speaking, from spying on the person through a window? Why, or why not?

2. The memory theory says that continuity of consciousness underwrites personal identity. Do you think this is right? What would this view have to say about someone who suffers from amnesia, or permanent short-term memory loss? Can you think of a way to reply to the criticisms offered in this essay?

3. Would you want to live forever? Is Captain Mertin irrational? Is he morally evil?

4. What role does Elijah the chimp play in the movie? What does the movie say about the inner lives of animals? How could we go about figuring out whether chimps have souls?

TO READ NEXT

René Descartes. *Meditations on First Philosophy*. Cambridge: Cambridge University Press, 1986. This is the classic statement of the Cartesian view of the self, presupposed in the movie, Being John Malkovich.

A.O. Rorty, ed. *The Identities of Persons*. Berkeley: University of California Press, 1976. A good collection of essays on personal identity.

Gilbert Ryle. *The Concept of Mind*. London: Hutchinson, 1949. Chapter 1 is the The classic critique of Descartes's theory.

Richard Taylor. *Good and Evil*. Amherst: Prometheus, 2000. The final chapter is a good place to start on the contemporary debate on the meaning of life.

David Wiggins. Truth, Invention, and the Meaning of Life. In Geoffrey Sayre-McCord, ed., *Essays on Moral Realism* (Ithaca: Cornell University Press, 1988). A reply to Taylor.

6

Popping It In: Gender Identity in *Boys Don't Cry*

REBECCA HANRAHAN

In the 1990s, a recurring sketch performed on *Saturday Night Live* centered around a character, Pat, whose gender was unclear to all those who met him or her. No one could tell whether Pat was a man or a woman. The other characters in this sketch were either obsessed with discovering Pat's gender or they were immobilized in their interactions with Pat because they didn't know his or her gender.

Imagine that you are Pat and imagine that the reason other people don't know your gender is because you, yourself, don't know whether you are a man or a woman. Think about what your life would be like. Where would you go to the bathroom or shop for clothes? Which kind of deodorant would you use? When you danced with another, would you lead or would you let yourself be led? To whom would you direct your affections? If you directed them towards a woman, would you be a lesbian or would you be a heterosexual? The confusion other people experience while interacting with you would pale in comparison with the turmoil you would experience as you negotiated your way through life.

From this thought experiment we can see that in a very real way our ability to make sense of our lives depends on our having a gender identity. To understand why this is so, consider that there is a connection between the meaningfulness of life and personal identity. Imagine a Jewish doctor living in Germany during the 1940s. Imagine that he survives the War by burying his great love for his religion and by making himself indispensable to the

Nazi Regime. Specifically, he helps beautiful but seemingly infertile Aryan couples produce the next generation of the master race. This man surely helped the couples under his care. We can even imagine that he had moments of happiness while tending these people. But, nevertheless, this man's life has to be considered meaningless for under different circumstances he clearly would have rejected the actions and beliefs that shaped his days.

Thus, the meaningfulness of life depends on our living in accord with a sense of self that we can affirm as our own. In *this* way, the meaningfulness of life depends on our personal identity. Moreover, as we just learned from the example of Pat, our personal identity depends on our gender identity. What each of us do, believe, and feel is a function of our gender. Thus, having a gender identity is seemingly necessary for our lives to be meaningful. But what makes some of us women and some of us men? What, in other words, is the source of our gender identity?

This question is explored in Kimberly Peirce's *Boys Don't Cry* (1992), a film inspired by the actual events that surrounded the death of Teena Brandon/Brandon Teena. Teena Brandon (Hilary Swank) cuts her hair short, stuffs socks down her pants, and tapes her breasts down, all for the purpose of transforming herself into a boy—Brandon Teena. Brandon then moves to a town, Falls City, Nebraska, where no one knows anything about him. There he meets Lana (Chloe Sevigny), and they fall in love. But Lana's friends, Tom and John (Peter Sarsgaard and Brendan Sexton III), discover Brandon's secret. They both feel betrayed, for they believe themselves to have been lied to. In their anger they beat, rape, and eventually kill Brandon.

But did Teena/Brandon lie to these people? Did Teena/Brandon trick people into thinking that she was a man when she was really a woman? Or did Teena become a man, Brandon, by behaving in such a way that others accepted him as a man? In what follows I will answer these questions. Specifically, I will argue that from the perspective of the film Brandon did more than merely pass as a man. Brandon was a man during his time in Falls City, and Tom and John punished Brandon for his successful transformation by forcing him to become a woman again (or) a woman once more.

Three Theories of Gender

As background to this argument, let's consider the three most prominent theories on the nature of gender. Each of these three theories agree that a person's *sex* is biologically determined. That is, it is agreed that whether or not you are a male or a female is determined by the constitution of your body. Where there is disagreement is with regard to whether or not your *gender* is determined by your *sex*. Are all men males? Are all women females?

To most people, these questions seem silly. Of course, all men are males and all women are females. Thus, for most people, the question I'm looking at in this chapter isn't much of a question. Is Brandon a man or a woman? Most would say that Brandon is a woman, for Brandon has and always has had a vagina. Those who offer this answer are working with *a realist theory of gender.*

To be a realist about something is to take the position that facts about that thing hold independently of human beliefs, attitudes, and opinions. Instead these facts are determined, usually, by some physical, biological, or chemical state of the world. You can be a realist about all sorts of things. So, for example, to be a realist about electrons is to believe that whether or not electrons exist does not depend on your believing in their existence. Rather, their existence depends only on whether or not there are actually elemental particles in the world that are negatively charged.

Similarly, to be a realist about gender is to believe that a person's gender isn't determined by what s/he or others believe his-her gender to be. Instead, a person's gender is determined by certain physical, biological, or chemical facts about the body. Does the person in question have a penis and XX chromosomes? Well, then he is a man. Does this person, instead, have a vagina and XY chromosomes? Well, then she is a woman. As far as the realist is concerned, the body can answer all the questions we could ever ask about a person's gender. Thus, for realists, a person's gender is determined by their sex.

In opposition to this theory, many feminist have noted that we can determine each other's gender without running blood tests and without pulling each other's pants down.[1] If this is

---

[1] Marilyn Frye, "Sexism," in *The Politics of Reality: Essays in Feminist Theory*, (Freedom: The Crossing Press, 1983), p. 27.

possible, then gender must not rest solely in the body and hence it must in some sense be separate from our sex. Instead, gender must either be *socially constructed* or it must be *subjectively* determined.

Social constructivists hold that each society constructs a set of criteria for determining certain aspects of an individual's identity. Thus, whether or not a person possesses a particular identity will be determined by society's estimation of how well that person has fulfilled the criteria it has set forth. Gang affiliation is a prime example of social constructivism. Tony (from *West Side Story*) is a Jet because from the perspective of other members of his community—most notably the police, the Sharks, and the Jets, themselves—he has successfully met all the requirements associated with being a Jet. Specifically, he lives in a particular community, a section of Brooklyn. He associates only with a certain kind of person, people of European descent, and he engages in illegal activities, such as rumbling with the Sharks.

If you're a social constructivist about gender, you believe that gender is a lot like gang membership. That is, you hold that within a particular society a person is, for example, a man, if that person possesses those characteristic that society associates with men. Within western societies a man is expected to be strong. He is not expected to wear skirts. He should like sports and cars. He should want kids, but he shouldn't want to spend all of his time raising those kids. Rather he is expected to work outside of the home on important matters having to do with business or government.

Unlike realists, constructivists draw a distinction between sex and gender. Your sex is still determined by your anatomy. But your gender is determined by your ability to meet those criteria society associates with one gender as opposed to the other. But even though constructivists distinguish between sex and gender, they also acknowledge that a person's sex will often play some role in determining his or her gender. So, most societies see having a penis as a characteristic associated with being a man. But, more importantly, this characteristic is merely associated with this gender. It is not a characteristic that you must have in order to be a man. Thus, for a constructivist, you can be a man and lack a penis or you can be a woman and lack a vagina. In fact, according to social constructivism, there is no one characteristic that you must have, or fail to have, to be considered either a man or a woman.

The final theory we need to consider is the subjectivist theory of gender. Subjectivists, in general, hold that the nature and existence of certain objects, properties, or identities depend solely on our individual beliefs. Consider a person's political leanings. To determine whether a person is a conservative or a liberal, you need not consider that person's biology. You don't even need to consider his/her position within society. You only need to consider that person's beliefs. For whether a person is a conservative or a liberal depends solely on that person's beliefs about the role a society's government should have within its citizen's lives.

So, to be a subjectivist about gender is to hold that whether a person is a man or a woman is similarly determined by his or her beliefs. That is, what makes a person a man is that he believes himself to be a man. Importantly, he can be a man without having a penis and without engaging in any particular activity. His manhood rests solely in his belief that he is a man.[2]

Which of these three theories does the film *Boys Don't Cry* endorse? Is this film promoting the realist position on gender? If it is, then from the film's perspective Brandon was merely passing as a man when in fact she was a woman. She was in effect lying to others when she made them believe that she was a man. Or is the film promoting the constructivist position? In which case Brandon became a man during those times he successfully fulfilled those criteria his society associated with being a man. Hence, he shouldn't be charged with lying. Or finally, is the film promoting gender subjectivism? If it is, then, again, Brandon shouldn't be charged with lying if he believed himself to be a man. For this belief that he was a man was, in fact, what made him a man.

Rejection of Gender Realism

One might think the film is promoting a realist perspective because of the attitudes of many of its characters. In one scene,

---

[2] For a fuller discussion of realism, constructivism, and subjectivism see Judith Butler, *Gender Trouble: Feminism and the Subversion of Identity* (New York:

Tom and John claim that "there is a real easy way" to determine Brandon's gender. Brandon need only take down his pants. Later in this same scene, the two violently pull Brandon's pants off of him and Tom upon seeing that Brandon has no penis declares that it, "Don't look like no gender identity crisis to me." In Tom's mind, a person's gender can be in doubt only if it is unclear what kind of genitalia s/he has. Since it is clear that Brandon does not have a penis and does have a vagina, Brandon can't be suffering from a gender identity crisis; he must be a woman.

But, even though many of the characters in this film take the realist perspective, the film rejects this perspective. This rejection of gender realism can be seen most clearly within the unfolding of the scene described above. To fully appreciate this scene we need to briefly consider Lana's relationship with Brandon.

From a realist perspective, Lana had good reason to question Brandon's gender identity. During their first sexual encounter she saw that Brandon had cleavage. She also noted how smooth his face was. Later, Lana goes to visit Brandon in jail (he is being kept for passing bad checks); and she discovers him imprisoned in the women's wing. There he tells her that he is a hermaphrodite and that he has both male and female genitalia.

But, despite these two incidents, Lana never gives any explicit voice to doubts she might have about Brandon's gender identity. In fact, in the scene when Tom and John forcibly remove Brandon's pants, Lana initially tries to stave off any direct confrontation between these men by taking Brandon into her bedroom. There Brandon offers to show Lana his genitalia. But, she tells him to button up his pants. "Think about it," she says, "I know you are a guy." For Lana, Brandon's anatomy is irrelevant when it comes to determining his gender.

Next Lana lies to her friends by telling them that she has seen Brandon in the "full flesh." But Tom and John don't believe her declaration that Brandon is a man, and it is then that they strip Brandon. Afterwards, they force Lana to look at Brandon by prying her hands away from her eyes. Upon fully

---

Routledge, 1990); Ruth Hubbard, *The Politics of Women's Bodies,* (Rutgers: The State University, 1990); and Charles Mills, *Invisible Blackness: Essays on Philosophy and Race* (Cornell: Cornell University Press, 1997).

viewing Brandon, Lana looks up at John and screams "Leave *him* alone."

For the most part *Boys Don't Cry* was conventionally filmed with most of the action shot from a third- person perspective. But after Lana screams at John, a four- shot sequence follows unlike any other sequence in the film. In each of these four shots the characters pictured are virtually still and there is no sound. Brandon is illuminated as he looks directly into the camera while the other characters are for the most part in shadow, averting their eyes from the camera. Each of these shots concern the same scene, depicted from different perspectives.

The first shot is a close-up of the faces of John, Brandon, and Tom. In this shot, John and Tom are still, while Brandon tilts his head up so that he is looking directly into the camera. The second shot is of Brandon, Lana's mother (Jeanetta Arnette), and two of Lana's friends, Candace and Katie (Alicia Goranson and Alison Folland). They are all standing in the doorway of the room in which Brandon is being assaulted, looking into that room. Brandon is the only character in this shot positioned outside of the narrative of the film. The other characters occupy the physical position they were occupying and will again occupy when the action continues. Brandon, though, is surrounded by these women and he is dressed differently than in the scenes that precede and follow this shot. Again, he is the only character who moves. He tilts his head up, seemingly to meet his own gaze from the first of these four shots.

The third shot illustrates what these four characters are seeing in this room. It is a wide-angle shot (instead of a close-up) of the first shot. In this third shot, Tom and John hold Brandon up, while Lana is on her knees in front of Brandon. The arrangement of the various characters evokes the classical form of a deposition. That is, Brandon is positioned as if he were Jesus being taken down from the cross; Lana is positioned as if she were Mary kneeling at Jesus's feet. The fourth and final shot is a repeat of the second shot. Except in this shot, Brandon is still and the three women in this scene start to move as they will when the action resumes. The sound, light, and action then return and the first utterance we hear is a repetition of Lana's last line, "Leave him alone."

Because these four scenes are stylistically so different from every other scene in this movie, it is safe to assume that the filmmaker is trying to emphasize a point. Whatever is communicated through these scenes must be of great importance. But what is it?

Obviously, these four shots foreshadow Brandon's execution. But, more than that, these shots can be read as the filmmaker's rejection of gender realism. First off, these shots are sandwiched between Lana's demand to "Leave him alone." This demand is made after Lana has been forced to confront the fact that Brandon doesn't have a penis. Thus, through Lana, we have here a clear rejection of gender realism. This rejection is emphasized by its repetition and by these four shots, that seem to be prompted by this demand.

Secondly, the main action in these four shots is Brandon meeting his own gaze. And, again, this is happening right after Lana has reaffirmed Brandon's identity as a man. To meet your own gaze, as you do when you look into your own eyes in the mirror, is an act of self-recognition. You are in those instances seeing yourself for who you are. Thus, by meeting his own gaze in response to Lana's declaration, Brandon seems to be acknowledging his identity as a man despite his anatomy.

Third, within at least two of these four shots, Brandon is positioned as a Christ-like figure. Jesus is not of his body. He, instead, transcends his body. Thus, by positioning Brandon in this way, the film communicates to us that Brandon, like Christ, is not of his body. Symbolically, the body is eliminated here. Consider also that Brandon's legs are positioned within this third shot as Jesus's legs are often positioned on the cross. They are bent to hide his genitalia. Prior to these four shots the question that was the main focus of concern was, What is between Brandon's legs? But, by positioning Brandon as Christ, this film implies that neither this question nor its answer are important. Contrary to the realist position, Brandon, like Christ, isn't defined by his body.

From all this, it should be clear that *Boys Don't Cry* rejects the realist position. The next question we need to consider is whether it goes further to endorse either the constructivist or the subjectivist position. Here is where things get a little tricky.

Gender Constructivism

On the one hand, as I will argue, the film operates from a constructivist perspective. But, on the other hand, this film also critiques constructivism. Through this critique, it seemingly moves towards a kind of gender subjectivism. Consider the first of these two points.

As far as most constructivists are concerned, for any particular society, there is no definitive list of properties or characteristics that one must possess to be considered a man as opposed to a woman, or a woman as opposed to a man. But, even so, for most constructivists, there is usually one property (or set of properties) that is especially important when it comes to the way a society constructs gender. That is, within a particular society it might not be the case that, for example, every man will possess this certain property, but most people who do will be considered men by that society. Moreover, this property will loom large within that society's understanding of what it is to be a man.

I contend that from the film's perspective the property that is central to determining a person's gender is that person's position with respect to the act of penetration. Specifically, if a person is seen as someone who is to be penetrated, then that individual is, most likely, a woman. If instead that person is seen as someone who penetrates others, then that individual is, most likely, a man. In support of this thesis, consider the following exchange from the scene in which the police chief of Falls City, Sheriff Laux (Lou Perryman), interrogates Brandon about his confrontation with Tom and John.

> **SHERIFF LAUX:** After they pulled your pants down, seen you as a girl, what did he do? Did he fondle you any?
> **BRANDON:** No.
> **SHERIFF LAUX:** Didn't that kind of get your attention somehow? That he wouldn't put his hand in your pants and play with you a little bit?
> **BRANDON:** I don't know what he did.
> **SHERIFF LAUX:** I can't believe that he pulled your pants down and *if you are a female* that he didn't stick his hand in you or his finger.
> **BRANDON:** Well, he didn't.[3]

---

[3] It is worth noting that this dialogue comes virtually word for word from

Here a connection is drawn between gender and penetration. In the sheriff's mind, a man's failure to penetrate Brandon can only be explained by Brandon's failure to be a woman. For women by definition are those who are to be penetrated.

In response to this, a realist might argue that this scene reveals nothing about the nature of gender; rather, it reveals something about our attitudes towards women. Women, we learn in this scene, are to be penetrated, though being penetrated isn't what makes a person a woman. Rather, it is the mere presence of a vagina that makes a person a woman, just as it is the mere presence of a penis that makes a person a man.

But one of the characters in this film has a penis and he isn't considered a man. Recall one of the first scenes of the movie. Teena with the help of her gay cousin Lonny (Mark McGrath) has just finished transforming herself into Brandon.

> **LONNY:** If you was a guy, I might even want to fuck you.
> **BRANDON:** You mean, if *you* was a guy, you might even want to fuck me.

Lonny has a penis but Teena doesn't classify him as a man. Why not? As a gay man, he is seen as someone who is to be penetrated. Because he is seen as someone who is to be penetrated, he isn't really a man. Thus, we see here that from the film's perspective a person's position with respect to the act of penetration takes precedence over anatomy when determining his/her gender.[4]

The kind of penetration involved here need not be sexual. Midway through the movie Tom reveals to Brandon that he cuts himself. He then gives his knife to Brandon and encourages him to cut himself. Brandon refuses and proclaims "I guess I am a pussy compared to you." Tom then explains that while he and John were in jail, they often cut themselves, though he, Tom, could always go deeper. In this scene, Brandon implicitly con-

---

Teena Brandon's actual interview with the Falls City Police. See the documentary, *The Brandon Teena Story* (DVD, New Video Group, 2000).

[4] This theory that a person's gender identity is connected to his or her position with regard to penetration echoes Monique Wittig's work. See Monique Wittig, *The Straight Mind and Other Essays*, (Boston: Beacon Press, 1992); and for a concise commentary on Wittig's work see Jacob Hale, "Are Lesbians Women?" *Hypatia*, 11:2 (Spring 1996), pp. 94–122.

cedes that he isn't a man. He is a woman because he refuses to cut himself. Tom, though, is a man. In fact he is the manliest of men. For not only does he embrace this act of penetration, but when he penetrates, he goes deepest of all.

To see how this conception of gender is constructivist, note that it makes gender an activity. According to both the realist and the subjectivist, no one has to do anything to make him/herself a man or a woman. Rather, a person's gender is a passive state of either the body or the mind. But, for constructivists, gender is a kind of performance, an activity one must engage in.[5] For to be a man as opposed to a woman or to be a woman as opposed to a man, a person needs to satisfy certain criteria, and the satisfaction of these criteria will often involve that person doing something. So, for example, a person might need to dress him/herself in skirts as opposed to suits to be a woman or s/he might need to play football as opposed to field hockey to be a man.

To conceive of gender in terms of penetration is clearly in line with this constructivist notion that gender is an activity. For in order to be a man, a person needs to position himself as someone who is to penetrate others, and the best way to do this is to penetrate others. To be a woman, a person needs to position herself as someone who is to be penetrated, and the best way to do this is to "let" others penetrate her.

Next, consider how this conception of gender is employed to reinforce the gender hierarchy among the characters in this film. For a constructivist, society decides what it is to be a man and what it is to be a woman in so far as it establishes the criteria associated with these two genders. Society also decides who is to be a man and who is to be a woman in so far as it decides whether or not a person has satisfied the criteria at issue. More importantly, the way in which a society makes these decisions is shaped by the desires of those in power to preserve their position within society.

John and Tom (through his alliance with John) are in control of their community, but the person who is most valued in this community as a mate and as a friend is Lana. John is portrayed as having a special relationship with Lana. He considers Lana's family and home to be *his* family and *his* home. Thus, Brandon

---

[5] See Butler, *Gender Trouble* (1990).

becomes a threat to John's power because of his relationship with Lana. In response to this threat John tries to reassert his power over Lana. He does this by trying to control Brandon's gender identity.

After learning about Brandon and Lana's relationship, John speaks to Lana in her bedroom: "What do you see in him?" John asks, "I mean I know he is nice and everything but he is kind of a wuss." After this exchange in which it becomes clear to John that Lana and Brandon have slept together, John makes a point of giving Lana to Brandon as a birthday gift. Not only is John trying to assert his power over Lana and Brandon, he is also trying to reassert his power to define what it is to be a man and who is a man by acknowledging that Brandon is in a position to penetrate Lana. John, in other words, is implicitly claiming here that though Lana and Brandon might have forgotten, Lana is his and he gets to decide who is man enough to penetrate her.

The most obvious demonstration of these powers is found in Tom and John's rape of Brandon. John's desire to uncover Brandon's "true" gender identity stemmed from his desire to control or, as he would say, "protect" Lana. But merely forcing Lana to confront the fact of Brandon's anatomy wasn't enough to break Lana's alliance with Brandon. To John's amazement, she still saw him as a man. Thus, to break this alliance, Brandon needed to be made over into a woman. Brandon, as far as John and Tom were concerned, had to be raped. Consider here the actual transcripts of Teena Brandon's interview with the police.[6]

> TEENA: Tom told me are you going to make this easy or you going to make this hard? And then he goes, in fact he said that, he said that either you can have the shit beat out of you and then have it happen anyway.
> SHERIFF LAUX: Have what happen?
> TEENA: When he raped me.[7]

---

[6] To distinguish between the movie character and the actual person, I will refer to the actual person as Teena, and I will continue to refer to Hilary Swank's character as Brandon.

[7] *The Brandon Teena Story.*

Teena here explains that Tom and John saw the rape as inevitable, as something that had to happen. Echoes of this exchange can be heard in the dialogue from the film's rape scene. Prior to raping Brandon, Tom explains that, "You [Brandon] can make this easy or you can get the shit knocked out of you." Here Tom is explaining that there was nothing Brandon could do to avoid being raped, but if he was good, he might avoid being beaten. Similarly, John claims that Brandon "brought" this rape on himself, and Brandon concedes that "it is all my fault." John's assertion and Brandon's concession again present the rape as inevitable. To regain control over Lana, Tom had to rape Brandon; Brandon had to be made over into a woman.

Both of these incidents illustrate the constructivist notion that within a society those in power desire to maintain that power. As as a consequence this desire affects how that society constructs gender. The constructivist perspective on gender is clearly present within the film, but that doesn't necessarily mean the film endorses gender constructivism. It doesn't, in other words, mean that the filmmaker thinks gender should be socially constructed. Actually, I think the film critiques the perspective of constructivism.

Gender Subjectivism

Tom's and John's attempt to make over Brandon into a woman doesn't succeed. After the rape Brandon doesn't suddenly become a woman. Instead, his gender becomes indeterminate. While some of the characters refer to him as a "she," many more of the characters refer to him as an "it" or a "he." Even Tom and John refer to Brandon right after the rape as "little man" or "little buddy." Given John and Tom's position within this society and given the constructivist perspective at play here, through the rape they should have been able to reconstruct Brandon as a woman. But, they don't. So, something must be wrong with this constructivist perspective.

One thing morally wrong is that this particular brand of gender constructivism licenses rape. Those in power within society are ultimately in control of its member's gender identity, and this identity is determined by one's position with respect to the act of penetration. Clearly, this conception of gender eases the way for those in power to rape those who lack power. For it is the clearest expression of their power to define gender.

But the rape of Brandon is strongly condemned within the film. All the women in this film come to Brandon's aid in response to the sexual assaults he suffers. Katie calls the cops. Candace gives him sanctuary in her house. Lana brings him to the police. Even Brandon's mother who ultimately betrays Brandon tells Brandon that, "no one has a right to do this to you." Consider again the four shots that occur right after Lana is forced to look at Brandon's genitalia. In two of these shots, Candace, Katie, and Lana's Mom are looking into the room where Brandon is being assaulted. But, though these women are looking at Brandon, Brandon is pictured as being surrounded by them. Thus, these women are both bearing witness to his assault and at the same time they are symbolically standing with him. This repeated shot can be read as the filmmaker calling women to stand together against rape. The rape is being condemned.

Through this condemnation, the film is saying that each of us should be able to control for ourselves this act of penetration. But, of course, if we do control this act, given the conception of gender at work here, we will also be constituting our own gender identity. This points us towards a gender subjectivism.

Other hints towards gender subjectivism can be found within the film's presentation of Brandon's transformation. Brandon is very much the author of his own gender transformation.

> **LANA:** What were you like before all this? Were you like me, a girl-girl?
>
> **BRANDON:** Yeah, a long time ago. And then I guess I was just like a boy-girl. Then I was just a jerk. It's weird. Finally, everything felt right.

These transformations can't be explained by referencing a change in Brandon's society for these transformations all occur within a year or so and they all occur within a seventy-mile radius of each other. Brandon's gender changed because he changed it. Moreover, the impetus for these changes were his feelings. Brandon stopped his transformations in Falls City because everything "felt right"; it was finally "working."

Admittedly, the fact that Brandon basically chooses his own gender is compatible with social constructivism. For sometimes the criteria associated with a particular identity are such that it is up to the individual whether they want to satisfy those criteria. And if they choose to satisfy those criteria, they are choosing in effect to have that identity.

For example, an individual chooses whether or not to be a gang member. But, not only does Brandon choose his gender, he also defines for himself what it is to be a man. He initially tries to be a "he-man" but later he becomes a man unlike any of the other men who surround him. To the dismay of the women and the disdain of the men, he cleans up and cooks for others. He encourages Lana to develop her talents and cares for her when she is sick. Thus, while from a constructivist perspective a person might at times be able to choose his/her gender, they certainly don't get to decide what it is to be a man or a woman. But this is a decision an individual gets to make from a subjectivist perspective.

Thus, the film's condemnation of rape and its presentation of Brandon's gender transformation is evidence that this filmmaker thinks that each of us should be able to choose our own gender. Still, we can't forget that Brandon made this choice and he was punished for it. So, while we *should* be able to choose our own gender, the film, by portraying Brandon's brutal rape and murder, acknowledges that this decision isn't *yet* ours. So, where does this leave Brandon? Was Brandon a man or a woman? Was he or wasn't he a liar?

Brandon or Teena?

Brandon didn't have a penis. But, given this film's rejection of gender realism, this wasn't as important as many would have thought. Brandon clearly believed himself to be a man and hence chose to live as a man. But, as the film acknowledges, this choice wasn't yet his to make. Gender subjectivism is false. Thus, from the film's perspective, gender must be socially constructed. This by itself, though, doesn't make Brandon a man. For Brandon to be a man, he must have fulfilled to society's satisfaction the criteria associated with manhood. Did he fulfill these criteria? Yes, he did. He was accepted by others as a man and this can be seen through his relationship with Lana. So, for a time, he was a man and he was no liar.

Brandon had an identity, a sense of himself, which he could affirm. Contrary to his anatomy, he identified himself as a man. As Brandon said, when he was a man, "Everything felt right.". Moreover, in so far as could affirm his identity as a man, his life was meaningful. Unlike when he was a "girl-girl," his life as a man made sense; it worked. The rape ended this. Because of the rape, Brandon could no longer identify himself as either a man or a woman. Everything then was just "screwed up." His life was rendered senseless. Brandon's only possible response to this destruction was to start over again, and that is what he intended to do when John and Tom killed him.

To have a meaningful life, you need to be able to live in accord with your own sense of self. But your sense of self, your identity, is determined in large part by your gender. Thus, if you are forced to live a life as a gender you can't affirm it as your own: you (like Brandon) will be hindered, if not crippled, in your ability to live a meaningful life. But if gender is socially constructed, then not only can society change how it constructs gender, it can also abandon gender as a constructed category. It can instead let its individual members determine both their own genders and what it is to be gendered. It can even let its members reject gender all together. Thus, the endorsement of gender subjectivism or, alternatively, the rejection of gender as a category increases the possibilities that every one will be allowed to live meaningful lives. And this can only be considered a good thing.[8]

---

[8] Angela Curran commented extensively on an earlier draft of this paper. Her help is greatly appreciated.

TO THINK ABOUT

1. How would your life be different if you were a woman as opposed to a man, or a man as opposed to a woman? In what ways would you act, speak, or think differently?

2. Why is it significant that Tom and John raped Brandon (as opposed to just beating and/or killing him)?

3. Brandon at times concedes that he has brought the wrath of Tom and John down upon himself. In these moments, he seems to be admitting that he has done something wrong during his time in Falls City. Has he? What?

4. When Teena makes herslf over into Brandon, does she have a set of expectations about what it should be like to be a male? Does Teena simply adopt social stereotypes about male behavior? Do you believe she ultimately succeeds in this transformation?

TO READ NEXT

Judith Butler. *Gender Trouble: Feminism and the Subversion of Identity.* New York: Routledge, 1990.

Marilyn Frye. *The Politics of Reality: Essays in Feminist Theory.* Freedom: The Crossing Press, 1983.

Carol C. Gould, ed. *Gender.* Amherst: Prometheus, 1997.

Ruth Hubbard. *The Politics of Women's Bodies.* Rutgers: The State University Press, 1990.

Monique Wittig. *The Straight Mind and Other Essays.* Boston: Beacon Press, 1992.

7

We All Need Mirrors to Remind Us Who We Are: Inherited Meaning and Inherited Selves in *Memento*

MICHAEL BAUR

The movie *Memento* (2000) broaches several interrelated philosophical questions concerning human knowledge, personal identity, and the human search for meaning. For example, is our knowledge based mainly on conclusions reached through our own reason, or is it based instead on habituation and conditioning brought about by forces outside of us? What is the role that memory plays in our knowledge? Furthermore, what is the relationship between memory and personal identity? And what is the relationship between memory, personal identity, and the human search for meaning? Can one meaningfully pursue projects in life that one has not chosen for oneself? While *Memento* does not resolve all of these issues, it does suggest some provocative answers that are bound to make us think differently about human knowledge, personal identity, and the meaning of life.

Many of *Memento*'s segments are presented in reverse chronological order, and for good narrative, cinematic, and even philosophical reasons. First, on a narrative level, the reverse ordering allows the film-maker (Christopher Nolan) to withhold from the viewer the very same information that Leonard (Guy Pearce) is also withholding (until the end of the film) from us and even from himself; the information being withheld is the fact that it is Leonard himself who has deliberately set himself up to kill Teddy (Joe Pantoliano). Secondly, on a cinematic level, the reverse ordering draws us viewers into the movie more fully. Like Leonard, we viewers are forced to make inferences and decisions about the trustworthiness of various characters in the movie, for example, Teddy, Natalie (Carrie-Anne Moss), and Leonard himself. And also like Leonard, we must draw our conclusions on the basis of radically incomplete information. Finally, on a philosophical level, the reverse ordering forces us—like Leonard—to struggle with our memory of events in the movie, and thus forces us to realize that Leonard's condition is not just his condition alone, but is in fact—though in a less severe form—our very own condition as well.[1]

What If Each of Us Is Really Made Up of Several, Consecutively-Existing Selves?

Leonard explains throughout the movie that he has a "condition" which prevents him from forming new long-term memories. He tells us that he retains his long-term memory of events prior to and leading up to the assault and killing of his wife ("the incident"), but that he has been unable to form new long-term memories of events since then. As a result, he is now unable to experience the passage of time beyond the usual ten-minute segments available to him through his impaired memory. Thus the center of experience that constitutes Leonard's personal identity lasts only for about ten minutes, and when this brief time period is over, Leonard forgets what he has just experienced, and begins having new experiences afresh, as if his immediately preceding experience did not happen at all. Leonard really does not experience himself as a single, unified self that endures unbroken over time, but rather as a series of different selves. Each of his separate, consecutively-existing selves comes into being and passes away in segments of about ten minutes.

---

[1] Only the movie's color segments are presented in reverse order, while all of the movie's black-and-white segments are presented in correct chronological order. More specifically, the movie alternates between color segments and black-and-white segments, with all the black-and-white segments being presented in correct chronological order, and all the color segments being presented in reverse chronological order. Thus, if one wanted to see all of the segments in correct chronological order, one would first have to see all of the black-and-white segments (skipping the color ones) in the order in which they are presented, and then see all of the color segments (skipping the black-and-white ones) in reverse of the order in which they are presented.

What Leonard's broken experience suggests is that his personal identity over time—or for that matter, anyone's personal identity—is not based simply on physical or material continuity over time, but depends rather on the "continuity of consciousness" that unites the various sensations, thoughts, memories, and ideas that make up one's experience. In other words, the conditions of an individual's personal identity over time seem to be different from the conditions of the identity of an inanimate object, or the conditions of the identity of a living thing that is not a person. An inanimate object such as a table maintains its identity over time simply so long as it maintains a continuity of material parts over time. Similarly, a living being that is not a person, such as a plant, maintains its identity over time simply so long as it maintains a continuity of life-processes over time. Unlike inanimate things and unlike living things that are not persons, persons seem to depend on altogether different conditions of identity over time. One's identity as the same person over time seems to depend on the contents of one's conscious experience. Thus if a person's living, physical body were to remain the same, but if he or she were to be given an entirely separate set of conscious experiences, then it would apparently be wrong to say that he or she was still the very same person. There would be no change in his or her identity as a physical being or as a living being; but there would be a change in his or her identity as a person, since that which seems to constitute his or her personhood (the contents of consciousness) would be altogether different and discontinuous with the preceding segments of consciousness.

This consciousness-centered notion of personal identity was expounded by the English philosopher John Locke (1632–1704), in his *Essay Concerning Human Understanding*.[2] *Memento* makes use of this notion in order to raise several philosophical questions, and eventually to question this very notion of personal identity altogether. According to Locke, one's identity as the same person over time is determined by the continuity of one's conscious experiences; because of this, one and the same physical, living human being could actually be connected with

---

[2] See John Locke, *An Essay Concerning Human Understanding*, edited by Peter H. Nidditch (Oxford: Oxford University Press, 1990), Book II, section xxvii, "Of Identity and Diversity."

multiple persons or selves. And so according to the Lockean notion, two unconnected, discontinuous segments of consciousness are not part of the same person, but belong instead to two different persons. *Memento* employs this consciousness-centered notion of personal identity in order to suggest that we should perhaps not think of Leonard as a single person, but rather as a set of several different, consecutively-existing persons. After all, Leonard's experience is not a single, continuous unified experience, but rather the experience of many disconnected segments of consciousness—or many selves—that come into being and pass away every ten minutes.

Along these lines, Leonard explains to the motel clerk, Burt, that his experience "is like waking; it's like you just woke up." This is significant for two reasons. First of all, the experience of "just waking up" is an experience that we all have. In other words, it's not just Leonard, but we ourselves, whose experience seems to be the experience of several, disconnected persons or selves. This point is reinforced in the short story, "Memento Mori," on which the film *Memento* is based. In the short story, we read:

> Every man is broken into twenty-four-hour fractions, and then again within those twenty-four hours. It's a daily pantomime, one man yielding control to the next: a backstage crowded with old hacks clamoring for their turn in the spotlight. Every week, every day. The angry man hands the baton over to the sulking man, and in turn to the sex addict, the introvert, the conversationalist. Every man is a mob, a chain gang of idiots.[3]

The lesson here is that Leonard's condition is not different in kind from our own condition; it is only different in degree. Leonard's condition is simply an exaggerated version of our own condition. Whereas Leonard "wakes up" and comes into being as a new self every ten minutes, we do the same thing, but usually just once and not several times each day.

Secondly, Leonard's comparison of his experience to the experience of "just waking up" is significant because it makes clear that we need to distinguish between two types of memories. First

---

[3] The short story, "Memento Mori," by Jonathan Nolan, was first published in the March 2001 issue of *Esquire* magazine. The short story is available online at: www.esquire.com/features/articles/2001/001323_mfr_memento_1.html

of all, there are relatively short-term memories that I form from within the present segment of consciousness that is my present self. Secondly, there are relatively long-term memories that I have not formed within my present experience, but that my present self *inherits* from a previous segment of conscious experience (from a previous self). My present self is dependent on another self (a previous self) for its long-term memories, and as a result, the inferences and decisions made by my present self depend on the reliability of the memories that it inherits from the other (previous) self.

In accordance with the image of "just waking up," the short-term memories that the present self forms within its own experience can be called "post-waking memories," since these short-term memories are formed by the present self after it has "woken up." By contrast, the long-term memories that the present self inherits from a previous self can be called "pre-waking memories" or "inherited memories." Leonard tells us that ever since the time of "the incident," he has been unable to form any new long-term memories, and that all of his long-term memories are inherited from a previous self. Even though this description of Leonard's experience seems to make him unique, it is clear—upon further reflection—that this characterization is also meant to describe our own experience. Within our own experience, we always seem to find ourselves with "inherited" memories that have simply been given to us by a previous self, but also with the ability to form our own short-term, post-waking memories.

Two Types of Memory, Two Types of Knowledge, and Two Sources of Meaning

In addition to suggesting that each person might really be made up of multiple selves, Leonard's story also suggests that there is an important difference between two types of knowledge, which are based on two different types of memory. For example, when I rely on long-term, inherited memories, I must rely on a source (a previous self) that is external to my present self. My pre-waking, inherited memories give me knowledge that has been formed in me outside the scope of my (or my present self's) own conscious awareness; as a result, such knowledge is knowledge that is "implanted" in my present self. It is knowledge that I simply must "wake up" with, and about which I apparently have no choice but to accept. The problem with inherited knowledge is that it is knowledge that the present self did not arrive at on its own. When the present self relies on inherited knowledge, it is always in danger of being misinformed, misled, or manipulated by some other, previous self. By contrast, when I rely on short-term, post-waking memories, I am evidently not relying on any source that is external to my present self. Knowledge based on my short-term, post-waking memories is knowledge that I myself have arrived at through my own experiences and inferences. Of course, the problem with such post-waking, short-term memory is that the time period within which I am able to have my own experiences and form my own short-term memories is usually very brief. It's about sixteen hours in the case of ordinary human beings, who are unconscious (asleep) for about eight hours of every twenty-four-hour cycle; and it's about ten minutes in the case of Leonard, who loses all of his short-term memories roughly every ten minutes. As a result, any knowledge that is based only on post-waking, short-term memories is radically incomplete, fragmentary, and thus of limited use. It follows that Leonard's condition, which is meant to represent our own condition, seems to present us with a fundamental dilemma: If I rely only on the memories and inferences formed by my present self, then I will be very limited in the knowledge I can gain and the decisions I can make; on the other hand, if I want to expand my knowledge and my capacity for decision-making, then I must rely on inherited memories and knowledge, in which case I run the risk of being misled or manipulated by an unreliable, external source.

Let us recall that the new, short-term, post-waking memories that Leonard is able to form on his own (within his present experience) last only about ten minutes. Once the ten minute period is over, the short-term memories and knowledge that Leonard himself has formed (along with his present self) are extinguished. Once Leonard's previous self is extinguished, a new Leonard "wakes up" and begins at the same "starting point" from which all of his previous, short-lived selves had to wake up and begin their conscious experience. That is, he wakes up with the memory and knowledge that "I am Leonard Shelby of San Francisco, former insurance investigator, whose wife has been raped and killed, and whose death I must now avenge."

In one respect, this inherited memory and knowledge is what gives each of Leonard's present selves a meaning: each time a new Leonard "wakes up" with his inherited memories and knowledge, he immediately knows that his purpose and goal in life is to avenge the death of his wife. Every waking moment of Leonard's present self is consumed by, and dedicated to, the project of avenging his wife's death. His present self can have no meaning apart from this goal.

Now it would seem that the very thing that gives Leonard his purpose in life (namely, his pre-given set of inherited memories and knowledge) might also undermine his quest for genuine meaning. For Leonard's problem is not just that he must pursue his purpose in life (avenging his wife's death) in periods of only ten minutes each; as Leonard himself realizes, this logistical problem can be addressed through a system of tattoos and notes.[4] The more serious problem for Leonard is that his meaning in life is not based on a goal *that he has chosen for himself*, but is rather derived from a purpose or goal that he has *inherited*, or that has been *implanted* in him, from a previous self. Leonard's problem—and by implication, our own problem—is not just that a person has a limited time within which to pursue the projects that give meaning to one's life. The deeper problem is that the projects that give meaning to one's life never really seem to be chosen by that person's own (present) self, but are always inherited from another (previous) self. But how can a person's own life really be meaningful, if such meaning is supposed to be derived from goals that have been dictated by some other (previous) self? Don't my most cherished goals in life have to be chosen by me (my present self) if they are to have meaning for me (my present self)?

In the movie's final segment, Teddy touches upon this issue of meaning when he tries to convince Leonard not to worry over the fact that he may have just killed the wrong person (Jimmy Grantz). In effect, Teddy argues that the meaning that Leonard's present self derives from the killing of Jimmy Grantz should not be based on any external events involving Leonard's past life or

---

[4] Leonard writes copious notes and tattoos information on his skin, in order to record the clues that he has gathered and thereby preserve them for a future self. Leonard must do this, since his present self cannot be trusted to remember anything beyond a brief, ten-minute period.

past self. More generally, Teddy is claiming that the goals that give meaning to one's life should not be goals that are imposed on one's present self by some other (previous) self; rather, the only goals that are truly meaningful are simply those that one's own present self chooses. What matters, Teddy says, is only that Leonard's *present* self enjoys the experience of having avenged the death of his wife. According to Teddy, then, the fact that Leonard may have just killed the wrong person is irrelevant, since Leonard will soon enough forget about what he has done. But Leonard will have none of this. He insists that the finding and killing of the right person is crucial to the very goal that his present self aims to achieve. After all, his present self would not even try to kill another human being, if it never were the case that some other human being had at some previous time destroyed his memory and murdered his wife. In other words, Leonard insists that the meaning experienced by his present self is inescapably dependent on a goal that his present self did not directly choose on its own, but rather inherited from a previous self. As Leonard had tried to explain to Natalie earlier in the movie, the meaning of one's present actions must refer to something beyond the scope of one's present consciousness: "Just because there are things I don't remember, it doesn't make my actions meaningless. The world just doesn't disappear when you close your eyes, does it?"

So is Teddy right to say that the meaning experienced by one's present self should not depend on goals inherited from a past self? Or is Leonard right to insist that the meaning experienced by his present self is inescapably connected to the goals that he has inherited from a previous self or a previous state of affairs? In one respect, Teddy seems to have a good point, since it is clear that Leonard's present self is always free to interpret the meaning of the evidence presented to it from a previous self or selves. As an example of this, Leonard's present self remains unconvinced by the Polaroid photograph which apparently depicts him celebrating after having successfully avenged his wife's death. It seems that Teddy is therefore right to claim that it is Leonard's present self alone that can decide what is meaningful or not within the scope of its present experience. On the other hand, Leonard also seems to have a good point. For it appears that Leonard's present self has no choice but to derive its meaning and purpose from the memories and knowledge that it inherits from a past self. Precisely because he cannot form any new long-term memories, Leonard cannot move beyond the pain of his wife's death. As Leonard explains it, the last long-term memory that his present self retains is always the memory of his wife being killed. As a result, Leonard cannot learn to "forgive and forget," and thus cannot avoid the purpose that is freshly imposed on him every ten minutes. Along these lines, he asks (while sitting in bed with Natalie): "How am I supposed to heal, if I can't feel time?" Because he cannot experience sufficiently long passages of time, it seems that Leonard is perpetually condemned to "wake up" every ten minutes with the same goal or meaning that he inherits from another (previous) self.[5]

The Role of the Future Self and the Possibility of Self-Conditioning

Now even if both Teddy and Leonard seem to make valid points, the lesson of *Memento* is that both of them are wrong: Teddy focuses too much on the present self's ability to make its own decisions about what is meaningful, while Leonard focuses too much on the present self's dependence on goals and meaning inherited from a previous self or previous state of affairs. In their exchange, both Teddy and Leonard focus on the past self, the present self, and the possible relations between them, but they both overlook the crucial role of the *future self*. Contrary to Teddy's claim, the present self that I am at any given moment does not acquire meaning by entirely ignoring or denying its dependence on a past self or on past events. And contrary to Lenny's claim, my present self does not gain meaning by just uncritically accepting the goals that have been dictated to it by a past self. Rather, the truth of the matter is that my present self achieves meaning by *looking forward* and by making decisions in the midst of its present experience with an eye towards creating a *new past* for the *future* self that it is yet to become.

---

[5] In the short story, "Memento Mori," the difficulty is expressed in this way: "And as for the passage of time, well, that really does not apply to you anymore, does it? Just the same ten minutes, over and over again. So how can you forgive if you can't remember to forget?" The text can be found online at: www.esquire.com/features/articles/2001/001323_mfr_memento_1.html

Even though Leonard is not quite clear about it, he is vaguely aware of this solution when he discusses his ability to "condition" himself. The key to such self-conditioning does not have to do with the past self or with the present self alone, but rather with the future self that Leonard is to become. Through self-conditioning, Leonard's present self neither denies its own past, nor simply ignores it, but rather forms new memories that will be forgotten by the *present* self that it is, but nevertheless retained as the seemingly unchosen past that its *future* self will inherit. Through such self-conditioning, the present self chooses or "sets up" the past that will have to be inherited by a future self. The fundamental philosophical lesson implied by the possibility of self-conditioning is this: *The past that you seemingly have no choice but to inherit is the past that you yourself have set up for yourself, but through the actions of your now-deceased previous self.* Memento deliberately provides evidence that such self-conditioning (the setting up of one's own past) is possible. For example, it is through his post-incident self-conditioning that Leonard learns that Polaroid photographs have to be burned in order to be destroyed; and it's also through his post-incident self-conditioning that Leonard learns how to "fake it" when he does not recognize the people he encounters.

As the short story, "Memento Mori," makes clear, the possibility of self-conditioning can be a good thing or a bad thing. After all, each of us is deemed to be a chain of multiple selves. And the present self that sets up the past for a future self can be a genius or a dolt. The tragedy of life is that our better and more insightful selves must frequently give way to lesser selves. The key to finding meaning in life is to ensure that my present self—in its fleeting moments of clarity—takes steps to bequeath to its future selves a better past than it has inherited.

That's the miserable truth. For a few moments, the secrets of the universe are opened to us. Life is a cheap parlor trick. But then the genius, the savant, has to hand over the controls to the next guy down the pike, most likely the guy who just wants to eat potato chips, and insight and brilliance and salvation are all entrusted to a moron or a hedonist or a narcoleptic. The only way out of this mess, of course, is to take steps to control the idiots that you become. To take your chain gang, hand in hand, and lead them.

> The best way to do this is with a list. It's like a letter you write to
> yourself. A master plan, drafted by the guy who can see the light,
> made with steps simple enough for the rest of the idiots to under-
> stand. . . .[6]

If one's present self does not act with wisdom and foresight,
then one risks condemning one's future selves to a limited,
meaningless existence—an existence in which one is increasingly conditioned to crave only potato chips. In other words,
one is conditioning oneself to forget about the future and to
live only in the present moment, as a dumb animal lives. And
by now it should also be clear that the boundaries that properly define a "present self" don't depend on some pre-
ordained segment of time (such as ten minutes for Leonard or
sixteen hours for us). The boundaries that distinguish one self
from another depend on the insights that each self has (no
matter how long these last), and not on some fixed measure
of time.

   The possibility of self-conditioning also reveals that the
Lockean, consciousness-centered notion of personal identity is
ultimately wrong, or at least very misleading. For the possibility of self-conditioning implies that the future self's own self-
understanding will depend on the previous choices made by
the present self. And since any present self is really just a
"future self" in relation to a "past self," it follows that the present self's own self-understanding will also depend on the previous choices made by the past self. Because of this, the
present self doesn't come to know itself simply by looking
inward, but rather must depend—even for its own self-understanding—on sources external to itself. These external sources
may include not only the past selves that are "external" to the
present self, but also other selves altogether (such as Teddy
and Natalie, on whom Leonard depends for crucial information
and insight into his own situation). As Leonard poignantly
observes at the end of the movie, we need to look outside of
ourselves in order to have our very own purposes and goals
reflected back to us: "We all need mirrors to remind ourselves
who we are."

---

[6] "Memento Mori."

What If Long-term Memories Could Be
Altered by Short-term Memories?

The present self depends on past selves and other external sources for its own self-knowledge and for its sense of purpose in life. But this does not mean that the present self is not responsible, or cannot be held accountable, for its self-understanding or for its sense of purpose in life. This is because the boundaries that allegedly separate a present self from a past self are not airtight or impermeable. And so just as *Memento* leads us to question Locke's consciousness-centered notion of personal identity, it also leads us to question the seemingly obvious and clear-cut distinction between past selves and present selves, and between long-term memories and short-term memories. By the end of *Memento*, we're led to see that—contrary to initial appearances—the pre-waking, long-term memories that a present self inherits from the past are not immune from the influence of the short-term, post-waking memories that the present self forms from within its own experience. So what appear to be unchanging, long-term, inherited memories can actually be modified or altered by the decisions and inferences that a present self makes within its experience. Accordingly, we come to realize that some of the seemingly fixed, long-term memories that Leonard's present self has apparently inherited may have in fact been altered—or perhaps even created—because of the memories formed and decisions made by the present selves that Leonard has become. For example, in the prostitute scene, Leonard wakes up after hearing the bathroom door being slammed, and upon waking he believes that is wife is still alive (we know this, because he wakes up saying, "Honey, it's late—is everything okay?"). But how can he have forgotten that his wife is dead—and how could he believe that his wife is still alive—if the last truly reliable, long-term memory that he has (the last memory that he acquired before suffering his head-injury) is that of his wife dying?

Leonard directly tells Natalie that the last fixed, long-term memory he has is that of his wife dying. And throughout most of the movie, we viewers are led to believe that Leonard is correct about this. But the prostitute scene shows that Leonard's post-waking, present self is actually able to forget that his wife is dead. This implies that Leonard's memory of his wife's death is actually *not* a fixed, unchanging, long-term memory that each of his present selves must passively inherit from his earlier, pre-injury self, but might be a memory that was formed in him *after* the time of his memory-impairing injury. Now if this is the case, then it is possible that Leonard's wife did not die at the time of the assault but rather survived the assault and was killed some time later. And if this is the case, then Teddy might be telling the truth when he suggests that the story that Leonard tells of Sammy Jankis (Stephen Tobolowsky) is really Leonard's own story. In other words, it is possible that Leonard's wife survived the assault, became frustrated with Leonard's memory-loss, "tested" Leonard (as Sammy's wife allegedly tested him), and died when Leonard unwittingly injected her with a lethal dose of insulin.

Before addressing the question of whether Sammy's story is really the story of Leonard himself, it will help to make a further observation about the idea of self-conditioning. As we've just observed, the seemingly fixed and unchanging long-term memories that one inherits from a past self are not hermetically sealed off from the influence of the short-term memories that one forms within one's present experience. A present self can have experiences and form new memories that will change one's seemingly fixed memories of a long-gone past. Thus the meaning of the past and the grip that it is has on a person can be altered by the decisions one makes within one's present experience. Stated differently, the meaning of the past that one must inherit is actually not fixed for all time, but can be transformed indirectly through one's present decisions. As a result, one is inescapably responsible not only for the decisions one makes as a "present self," but also—indirectly—for the meanings one inherits from "past selves.[7] "In his disagreement with Teddy, Leonard was right to say that we must always inherit or "wake up" with a past that gives meaning to our life. However, Leonard was wrong to suggest that our present selves must simply accept and live out the projects that have been given to them by an entirely external (past) self. Though he was not quite aware of it, Leonard's own activity in self-conditioning was gradually and retrospectively transforming the meaning of his own past.

---

[7] Conversely, one is also responsible for the purposes and goals that one bequeaths to "future selves."

Interestingly, our own viewing of the movie shows just how such retrospective transformation can take place. Throughout most of *Memento*, we are led to believe that Leonard is speaking truly when he says that, just prior to his injury, he formed a fixed and reliable long-term memory of his wife dying. By the end of the movie, however, we have doubts about this, and our doubts cause us to recollect the movie's earlier scenes in a very different light. In this respect, we are again like Leonard: our subsequent insights transform the meaning of our past experience. Of course, we are inescapably dependent on the meanings and purposes that the past bequeaths to us. But we are never just purely passive victims of what the past has given to us. Rather, we always have the freedom to transform the meaning of the past—and transform the hold that it has on us— through the decisions we make in the present. The twentieth century German philosopher, Martin Heidegger (1889–1976), refers to this kind of freedom as "thrown projection." For Heidegger, even though we are always *thrown* into the world with a past that defines who we are and what is meaningful for us, we are nevertheless also free to transform the meaning of the past by *projecting* ourselves into the future.[8]

Is the Story of Sammy Jankis Really the Story of Leonard Himself?

We can now return to our final question. Is the story of Sammy really an altered and transmuted story of Leonard's own past self? There are good cinematic reasons for believing so. For example, early in *Memento* Leonard explains that Sammy's poor memory prevented him from watching anything but commercials on TV. But when Leonard himself is alone at Natalie's house, we see him changing the TV channel to watch a commercial for Cal Worthington Ford. Furthermore, the film-maker presents us with a consistent and revealing system of flashbacks.

---

[8] Martin Heidegger, *Being and Time*, translated by John Macquarrie and Edward Robinson (New York: Harper and Row Publishers, 1962), pp. 182–88. Richard Polt explains Heidegger's point very nicely when he says: "Our lives are always a process of taking over who we have been in the service of who we will be." See Richard Polt, *Heidegger: An Introduction* (Ithaca: Cornell University Press, 1999), p. 96.

All of the flashbacks about Sammy are in black-and-white, while all of the flashbacks about Leonard's wife are in color. In one color flashback, we see an insulin needle being pre- pared, obviously implying that it was actually Leonard's wife who had diabetes. Finally, in a flashback depicting Sammy's institutionalization, we see—just for a split second—Leonard sitting in the chair where Sammy had been sitting.

Now in addition to these cinematic suggestions, there is also a good *logical* reason for believing that Leonard may not be giv- ing an "objectively true" account of Sammy and his wife. The logical reason is this: the only two witnesses to the "insulin test" that Leonard describes were Sammy and Sammy's wife. But how could Leonard have known about this test? The only two wit- nesses to the test would have been unable to tell Leonard about the test. One witness (Sammy's wife) was killed as a result of the test, and the other witness (Sammy) did not know that he was being tested. And besides, even if Sammy did know about the test, he now remembers nothing about it. Does this suggest that the "insulin test" was actually a test that Leonard knew about through his *own* experience, and not from Sammy or Sammy's wife? Should we conclude that it was *Leonard's* wife who became frustrated with Leonard after "the incident," and that it was Leonard himself who killed his wife through an "insulin test"? It is tempting to draw these conclusions, but there is an important question that should give us pause: How could Leonard know about the insulin test, if it were *he himself* who was tested and who killed his wife? If Leonard himself really were tested in this way, and if he really did kill his wife because of his faulty memory, then Leonard could not have learned about the test from his own experience. In other words, the idea that Leonard was tested by his wife is just as questionable as the idea that Sammy was tested by his wife. In either case, there are simply no remaining witnesses who would be in a position to inform Leonard about the test.

So now we come upon a final philosophical lesson to be drawn from *Memento*. Because there are no remaining, reliable, "expert" witnesses to the "insulin test," we must learn to live without a final and definitive answer to the question of whether Sammy's story is really Leonard's story. That question simply cannot be answered once and for all. But what we have just said about the insulin test can also be said about the meaning of the past in general. That is, *Memento* shows us that the meaning of the past and thus also the meaning of our future goals in life are not externally imposed on us once and for all. Because of this, we must learn to be unlike Sammy's wife, who—according to Leonard's story—turned to Leonard in order to know definitively whether Sammy was "faking it" or not. Sammy's wife did not care which answer she received: she simply wanted an answer—any answer—because she sought certainty and direction in her future relationship with Sammy. She simply wanted the testimony of an "expert" (she wanted the testimony of Leonard, the "expert" insurance investigator) so that she could escape the responsibility of making her own difficult decisions in life. But *Memento* teaches us that Mrs. Jankis's quest is misguided. While our quest for meaning in life always depends initially on the memories and testimony that we have received from past selves and from other external sources, we should not pretend that this dependence can eliminate our responsibility for making difficult decisions and seeking our own meaning in life. While we always need mirrors to know who we are and to know what we seek in life, we are nevertheless inescapably responsible for what we have made of ourselves, and thus responsible even for what we behold when we look into the mirror.

TO THINK ABOUT

1. Is it possible to have a personal identity without having a past that one can consciously remember? Conversely, is it possible to have a personal identity without having a future that one can consciously anticipate? Finally, is it possible to have a personal identity if one's conscious awareness is restricted to the present moment alone?

2. Is it possible to find meaning in life without having a past that one can consciously remember? Conversely, is it possible to find meaning in life without having a future that one can consciously anticipate? Finally, is it possible to find meaning in life if one's conscious awareness is restricted to the present moment alone?

3. Some philosophers have observed that there is an important connection between memory and personal liability. More specifically, they have argued that one cannot be held liable for that which is entirely absent from one's memory. Is this theory of personal liability a good one? Why or why not?

TO READ NEXT

Daniel C. Dennett. *Brainstorms: Philosophical Essays on Mind and Psychology*. Cambridge, Massachusetts: MIT Press, 1981.

Martin Heidegger. *Being and Time*. Translated by John Macquarrie and Edward Robinson. New York: Harper and Row, 1962. Especially Section 31 ("Being-there as Understanding").

John Locke. *An Essay concerning Human Understanding*. Edited by Peter H. Nidditch. Oxford: Oxford University Press, 1990. Especially Book II, Section xxvii, "Of Identity and Diversity."

Frederick A. Olafson. *What Is a Human Being? A Heideggerian View*. Cambridge: Cambridge University Press, 1995.

Richard Polt. *Heidegger: An Introduction*. Ithaca: Cornell University Press, 1999.

John Perry, ed. *Personal Identity*. Berkeley: University of California Press, 1975.

Take Three

Am I Alone?

8

The Indifferent Universe: Woody Allen's *Crimes and Misdemeanors*

MARK T. CONARD

In his earlier, funnier works (*Love and Death*, *Sleeper*, *Bananas*), Woody Allen raised certain philosophical issues, but typically only in passing, and he treated them in a humorous fashion. Then, in his more mature period, and prior to *Crimes and Misdemeanors*, Allen made three completely dramatic (and Bergman-esque) films, *Interiors*, *September*, and *Another Woman*, which dealt with the personal crises of the characters, as well as profound and universal human themes, and in which he (Allen) did not appear.

In his best and most mature works, however, Allen combines the serious (and philosophical) with the humorous.[1] *Crimes and Misdemeanors* (1989) stands among these best works; but it also stands out, insofar as it deals with some of the most important and serious questions about the meaning of life and the existence of God, and at the same time amuses and entertains with Allen's characteristically New York, Jewish, neurotic humor. Allen is able to achieve this by brilliantly interweaving two stories, one largely comedic and the other dramatic, into a unified whole.

---

[1] These works include *Manhattan*, *Stardust Memories*, and *Hannah and Her Sisters*.

The Misdemeanors

In the (largely) comedic story, Clifford Stern (Woody Allen) is an unemployed filmmaker who is hired to make a PBS biography about his wife's brother, the rich and successful TV producer, Lester (Alan Alda). While shooting the film, Cliff meets Halley Reed (Mia Farrow), the producer of the project, and the two of them hit it off. Cliff has been working on a film about philosophy professor Louis Levy (Martin Bergmann), who is a sensitive, life-affirming holocaust survivor. Halley appreciates Cliff's work and believes that together the two of them can produce the film about Levy for the PBS series, which would assure Cliff a wider audience and some measure of success. Cliff and Halley also share a contempt for Lester, who is vain, pompous, and crass towards women. Cliff's marriage is in its last stages, and as they work together, he becomes more and more interested in and attracted to Halley.

In the end, the life-affirming Levy commits suicide (thus wrecking Cliff's film project); Cliff exposes Lester's faults in the PBS documentary, comparing him to Mussolini and a talking mule, and is subsequently fired from the project; and, last, after having been separated from Cliff for several months while she was in England, Halley returns to New York as Lester's fiancée. Cliff's life is in ruins, and his worst fears have been realized (and, yes, this *is* the funny part of the movie).

The Crimes

In the (more) dramatic story, Judah Rosenthal (Martin Landau) is a wealthy and successful ophthalmologist, who has been having an affair with the neurotic Dolores (Anjelica Huston). Judah wants to break off the affair, but Dolores threatens to reveal their relationship (along with some questionable financial moves on Judah's part) to his wife and the community if he does. Judah was raised very religiously, and although he has abandoned his faith for science, he confides in his lifelong friend and patient, Rabbi Ben (Sam Waterston), who is also Cliff's brother-in-law, and who is progressively going blind. Ben advises Judah to come clean to his wife about the adultery, but Judah rejects the advice and instead seeks help from his brother, Jack (Jerry Orbach), who has ties to the underworld. Jack arranges for Dolores's murder, and at first, after the deed is done, Judah is guilt-ridden, and his religious background re-emerges to weigh on his conscience. The final scene of the film is the wedding of Ben's daughter, where Judah and Cliff meet at the reception, after Cliff has learned that Halley is going to marry Lester. Judah relates to Cliff the story of the murder as if it were the plot of a movie. As it turns out, after a few months the protagonist of the story—Judah himself (as we know)—is more or less guilt-free and has gone back to his former, happy life in which he has even prospered.

The Existence of God and the Meaning of Life

In *Crimes*, the issues about morality which drive the film are deeply connected to questions about the existence of God and the value and meaning of life. In one telling scene in which Judah confides in Ben about his affair, Ben remarks that the two of them have had the same discussion their whole adult lives, in which they express contrasting views about the universe. Judah sees the world as "harsh and empty of values and pitiless," says Ben. That is, Judah believes that we live in a godless universe, which contains no inherent and absolute meaning or value. Whereas, speaking for himself, Ben says:

> I couldn't go on living if I didn't feel with all my heart a moral structure, with real meaning, and . . . forgiveness. And some kind of higher power. Otherwise there's no basis to know how to live.[2]

This dispute between Judah and Ben is the central theme of *Crimes*. Life is meaningful, and there is a moral structure, *only if* God exists. If God doesn't exist, then there's no "real meaning," and "no basis to know how to live." As Judah himself expresses it, initially reeling under the weight of the guilt of Dolores' murder: without God, "the world is a cesspool."

It's clear that if the Judeo-Christian monotheistic God (loving father-figure, creator of all) exists, then meaning and value are built into the universe. We're God's children, made in his image. Good and evil exist in the world; and we know what we have to do to achieve salvation, and what to do to avoid damnation.

---

[2] All movie quotes in this chapter are from *Crimes and Misdemeanors*, directed by Woody Allen, 1989.

But if God doesn't exist, why can't our lives still be meaningful? The answer to this in Allen's films is that both meaning and value require permanence. That is, any real meaning and value in life would have to be something that doesn't change, that is inherent in the universe, that is absolute. For Allen, nothing that is fleeting, that is corruptible, that doesn't last can be truly meaningful or valuable. So, without God, given that everything in the universe is continually changing and breaking down, there can be no permanent, absolute meaning or value.[3] Again, *only if* God exists can there be meaning and value.

God Doesn't Exist

The title of Allen's film, *Crimes and Misdemeanors*, is clearly intended to be an allusion to Dostoyevsky's *Crime and Punishment*. In the latter story, the main character, Raskolnikov, murders an old woman and initially gets away with it. However, he comes to be haunted by the action, and plagued with guilt; and so he experiences remorse, confesses to the murder, goes to prison, and eventually finds redemption. But note the significant change in the title of Allen's film. For Dostoyevsky, there was crime *and punishment*. For Allen, there are crimes and lesser offenses, misdemeanors, but there's no punishment in sight.[4] I'll mention in passing, too, that in Dostoyevsky's *The Brothers Karamazov*, the intellectual, atheist brother, Ivan, says that (to paraphrase) "if nothing is true, everything is permitted." This seems to be one of the central themes of *Crimes and Misdemeanors*: Without God, and thus without eternal and absolute truth, there are no values, no moral guidelines, no reward or punishment.

The change in the title of the movie hints at Allen's second premise: that in fact God doesn't exist, and so there is no one to punish us. This is neatly symbolized by Rabbi Ben's progressive blindness. One of the primary, and almost overwhelming,

---

[3] For further discussion of this issue, see my "God, Suicide, and the Meaning of Life in Woody Allen's Films," in Mark T. Conard and Aeon J. Skoble, eds., *Woody Allen and Philosophy* (Chicago: Open Court, 2004).

[4] See Mary Nichols's discussion of the alteration of the title in her *Reconstructing Woody: Art, Love, and Life in the Films of Woody Allen* (Lanham: Rowman and Littlefield, 1998), pp. 149–151.

symbols of the movie is sight. Recall that Judah is an ophthalmologist; he's told as a boy that God sees all; and there are
numerous other references to vision.[5] Since the time of Ancient
philosophy, sight has been a metaphor for truth and understanding. Plato, for example, in his "Allegory of The Cave, found
in his *Republic*, likens grasping and understanding truth to sight
and the things seen in the visible world around us.[6] And when
we talk about reason or the intellect discovering truth and gaining wisdom, we refer to "enlightenment"; finally, when we
understand something we say, "I see!" So, the literal blindness
of Rabbi Ben symbolizes his metaphorical blindness to the truth
about God and the nature of the universe. As Judah contemplates the murder of Dolores, Ben appears in his thoughts as the
voice of conscience:

> **JUDAH:** What choice do I have, Ben? Tell me . . . I will not
> be destroyed by this neurotic woman.
> **BEN:** It's a human life. You don't think God sees?
> **JUDAH:** God is a luxury I can't afford.
> **BEN:** Now you're talking like your brother Jack.
> **JUDAH:** Jack lives in the real world. You live in the Kingdom
> of heaven.

In believing in a God who provides a moral structure to the universe, Ben blinds himself to reality; he doesn't live in the real
world. In an interview, Allen confirms that this is indeed the
message: "Yes, my own feeling about Ben is that, on the one
hand, he's blind even before he goes blind. He's blind because
he doesn't see the real world." Allen goes on to say:

> Ben is the only one that gets through it, even if he doesn't really
> understand the reality of life. One can argue that he understands it

---

[5] A few examples: Dolores says that the eyes are the windows to the soul.
Joking with his niece, Cliff tells her that she shouldn't listen to her school
teachers; she should just *see* what they look like, and that's how she'll know
what life is really like. Through most of the film, Halley wears glasses, as do
most of the principal characters, but when she appears at the end as Lester's
fiancée, she's not wearing them. Notice that the camera pans down to the
headlight on Judah's car, and we see it go dark, when he pulls up to Dolores's
apartment, immediately after she's been murdered.
[6] See his sun metaphor, 507a–509d.

more deeply than the others. I don't think he does myself. I think
he understands it less, and that's why I wanted to make him blind.
I feel that his faith is blind. It will work, but it requires closing your
eyes to reality.[7]

Interestingly, Allen seems to consider these coping mechanisms
to be useful, if not necessary, fictions. He refers to Ben as lucky
and blessed "because he has naïvety."[8] I'll discuss this more
below.

Further, in one powerful scene, Judah visits his childhood
home and imagines looking in on one of his childhood Seders.
His very religious father, Sol (David S. Howard), is attempting to
pray in Hebrew, when he's interrupted by his sister, Judah's
Aunt May (Anna Berger), who is an atheist. A discussion ensues
about the nature of truth and morality:

> **AN UNCLE:** And if all your faith is wrong, Sol? I mean, just
> what if? If?
> **SOL:** Then I'll still have a better life than all of those that
> doubt.
> **AUNT MAY:** Wait a minute. Are you telling me you prefer God
> over the truth?
> **SOL:** If necessary, I'll always choose God over the truth.

Judah's father juxtaposes God and truth, so that the lesson here
is that God is opposed to truth; God is tantamount to falsity. In
other words, Allen is telling us, God doesn't exist.

So Everything *Is* Permitted?

So if morality and a meaningful existence are only possible if
God exists, and God doesn't exist, then the conclusion would
have to be that there is no moral structure to the universe, and
life is inherently without meaning (it's a "cesspool"). Everything
is in fact permitted. At the imagined Seder, Aunt May remarks
that six million Jews were killed in the Holocaust, and yet the
Nazis "got off with nothing," and this is because "might makes

---

[7] From Stig Björkman, *Woody Allen on Woody Allen* (New York: Grove Press
1993), pp. 223–25.
[8] *Ibid.*, p. 223.

right." The conversation goes on thus (and Judah steps into his own imagined scene to interact with the others):

> **SOMEONE:** What are you saying, May? There's no morality anywhere in the whole world?
>
> **AUNT MAY:** For those who want morality, there's morality. Nothing's handed down in stone.
>
> **WOMAN:** Sol's kind of faith is a gift. It's like an ear for music, or the talent to draw. He believes and you can use logic on him all day long, and he still believes.
>
> **SOL:** Must everything be logical?
>
> **JUDAH:** And if a man commits a crime . . . if he kills?
>
> **SOL:** Then one way or another he will be punished.
>
> **AN UNCLE:** If he's caught, Sol.
>
> **SOL:** If he's not, that which originates in a black deed will blossom in a foul manner . . . Whether it's the Old Testament or Shakespeare, murder will out.
>
> **AUNT MAY:** And I say if he can do it, and get away with it and he chooses not to be bothered by the ethics, then he's home free. Remember, history's written by the winners. And if the Nazis had won, future generations would understand the story of World War Two quite differently.

Again, the faith of Rabbi Ben and of Judah's father blinds them to reality, and leads to a belief in fictions. And so it's Aunt May who seems to express the lesson of *Crimes and Misdemeanors*: In a world without God, there is no moral structure to the universe, and thus "no way to know how to live," as Ben says, and consequently—as we've seen—there is no inherent meaning to life.

This lesson is also vividly manifested in the fact that Judah reports having gotten away with the murder: he escaped punishment, was able to leave behind or overcome the guilt, and has even prospered and become more happy in his life. In the documentary, *Woody Allen: A Life in Film*, Allen tells us that one of the essential messages of *Crimes and Misdemeanors* is that:

> there's no God, and that we're alone in the universe, and that . . . um, there is nobody out there to punish you, that your morality is

strictly up to you. If . . . if you're willing to murder and you can get away with it, and you can live with it, that's fine.[9]

In addition, Professor Levy seems in the end to grasp the truth about the universe that Allen is expressing.[10] Despite his overall positive outlook on life, he claims that "the universe is a pretty cold place," and that under certain circumstances, we figure out that life "just isn't worth it." As I mentioned above, Professor Levy, having gained this understanding, subsequently commits suicide.

The Indifferent Universe

Admittedly, the end of *Crimes and Misdemeanors* seems to suggest a different position or outlook than the one I outlined above. In a very touching scene, the now-completely-blind Rabbi Ben dances with his daughter at her wedding, while we hear Professor Levy's voiceover.

> We are all faced throughout our lives with agonizing decisions, moral choices. Some are on a grand scale. Most of these choices are on a lesser scale. But we define ourselves by the choices we have made. We are in fact the sum total of our choices. Events unfold so unpredictably, so unfairly. Human happiness does not seem to have been included in the design of creation. It is only we with our capacity to love that give meaning to the indifferent universe. And yet most human beings seem to have the ability to keep trying, and even to find joy from simple things, like their family, their work, and from the hope that future generations might understand more.

Levy seems to be suggesting here that even if God doesn't exist, and the universe is "indifferent," we can still invest our lives and the world with meaning and value. And this has led a number of commentators and critics to conclude that *Crimes and Misdemeanors* is ultimately a hopeful, optimistic film. In her *Art, Love, and Life in the Films of Woody Allen*, for example, Mary Nichols says that Levy articulates a middle ground between

---

[9] *Woody Allen: A Life in Film* (Turner Classic Movies, 2002. Directed by Richard Schickel).

[10] We only ever see Professor Levy in film clips that Cliff has shot.

Ben's pious blindness to reality and Aunt May's nihilism, since "while he acknowledges that human happiness is not included 'in the design of creation,' he does not claim that it is precluded by it. An 'indifferent universe' is not a hostile one."[11] Sander Lee likewise takes *Crimes and Misdemeanors* to be optimistic in its outlook, and even goes so far as to argue that Judah is not guilt-free at the end, that he's deluding himself or lying when he claims to have gotten over the moral crisis (even over the objections of Woody Allen himself!)[12]

This optimism, however, is not warranted. 1) Accepting Allen's position over Lee's, consider first that Judah has gotten away with murder, scot-free. He feels no guilt, no remorse, and is happily back with his family, his position in the community secure. 2) Remember that Cliff, the good guy, attempted to do exactly what Levy suggests: to invest his life with meaning and value through love, family, work, and so forth; yet all his efforts were in vain. As his soon-to-be-ex-wife remarks, Cliff makes these little films and in the end "they come to nothing."[13] He has aspirations, but they don't pay off, and his attempts to reveal the truth about Lester resulted in his getting fired and losing the one opportunity that might have given him a real career.

Further, and shockingly, Halley—his beloved—shits on him. In a very funny but disgusting scene, Cliff's sister, Barbara (Caroline Aaron), relates to him a misadventure that she had while on a date with a man from the personals. The man tied her to the bed and defecated on her. The suggested metaphor

---

[11] Mary Nichols, *Reconstructing Woody*, p. 159. Her optimism includes arguing that Judah is in the end punished "by having to face an empty universe that does not punish" (p. 158), and thus Judah doesn't get away scot-free. Yacowar says: "Allen wields Levy's words against the moral darkness." Maurice Yacowar, *Loser Take All: The Comic Art of Woody Allen* (New York: Continuum, 1991), p. 279.

[12] In an interview contained in Lee's book, Allen says: "You are wrong about Judah; he feels no guilt and the extremely rare time the events occur to him, his mild uneasiness (which sometimes doesn't come at all) is negligible." Lee says: "While the reader is free to accept Allen's response as the final word on this point, I would argue that the film's text gives stronger support to my interpretation." Sander Lee, *Eighteen Woody Allen Films Analyzed* (Jefferson: McFarland, 2002), pp. 162–63.

[13] This could be understood as self-referential on Allen's part, reflecting his true feelings about his own work.

couldn't be clearer: this is what we do to one another in relationships—we shit on each other. This undercuts Levy's suggestion that love can provide meaning and value to an
indifferent universe. 3) Last, consider that the suggested optimism comes from the voice of a man who killed himself
because of the emptiness and coldness of the universe; and that
we hear that voice while watching the blind rabbi, the one who
has closed his eyes to reality.

So why does Allen present us with this false optimism? One
reason might be that the movie would just be too dark, too
bleak, if it concluded with the good man's life in ruins, and the
murderer happy; and so Allen had to give us viewers *something*
to make us feel better. This is certainly possible, but I want to
suggest too that the ending is meant to be ironic. Ironic certainly
because of the elements I listed above—Cliff's ruin, Judah's happiness, Levy's suicide. But also ironic because of something that
Judah tells Cliff in their conversation at the wedding. As I mentioned, Judah tells the story of the murder to Cliff as if he's relating a movie plot. In his story, of course, the murderer gets away
with the crime. Thinking that Judah is really talking about a
movie, Cliff suggests a different ending:

> **CLIFF:** Here's what I would do. I would have him turn him-
> self in. Because then, you see, your story assumes tragic
> proportions, because in the absence of God or something,
> he is forced to assume that responsibility himself. Then
> you have tragedy.
>
> **JUDAH:** But that's fiction. That's movies. You've seen too
> many movies. I'm talking about reality. If you want a
> happy ending you should see a Hollywood movie.

Cliff is suggesting the kind of ending that Dostoyevsky provides
in *Crime and Punishment*, but, as I noted, here there is no punishment. As Aunt May says, if you can commit the crime and
choose not to be bothered by the ethics, then you're home free.
Note too the interesting shift in the way Judah describes the
story. It's no longer fiction; his story is about *reality*, it's about
the real world. And this real world is *so* harsh and *so* bleak that
tragedy would in fact be a happy Hollywood ending (that's how
bad things are).

So Levy's voiceover at the end is exactly the kind of happy Hollywoodish ending that Judah scoffs at and rejects.[14] And therein lies the irony: the ending is falsely and naively optimistic and is at odds with our understanding of the real world, which is expressed throughout the rest of the film. To accept the Hollywood ending, we have to close our eyes to reality, as Ben does.

Thus, *Crimes and Misdemeanors* is deeply pessimistic. Allen is telling us that we live in a godless universe which is devoid of meaning and value; and that the best that we can hope for is to blind ourselves to, or deceive ourselves about, this ugly truth. Regarding Levy's claim that we invest the universe with value and our own feelings, Allen says:

> Right, so we create a fake world for ourselves, and we exist within that fake world . . . In the same way we create for ourselves a world that, in fact, means nothing at all, when you step back. It's meaningless. But it's important that we create some sense of meaning, because no perceptible meaning exists for anybody.[15]

The world of love, meaning, and value that Levy describes is a fake world, a self-deception, if a necessary one.

---

[14] See Sam Girgus, *The Films of Woody Allen* (New York: Cambridge University Press, 1993), p. 127, for example, on the Hollywoodish nature of the ending. Like others, Girgus argues that Allen is presenting us with a picture of "moral ambiguity." He also claims that Cliff misunderstands the nature of tragedy, so that he's offering Judah a "neat ending," which is why Judah dubs it a Hollywood ending and rejects it. This misses the point, I think, insofar as Allen is presenting us not with moral ambiguity, but rather with a picture of the world as amoral. And, as I said, the point of the discussion about tragedy is that Judah's picture of the world (which is also Allen's) is so bleak that even tragedy would seem like a happy ending.

[15] Björkman, *Woody Allen on Woody Allen*, p. 225.

To Think About

1. How are the issues about morality in *Crimes and Misdemeanors* connected to questions about the existence of God and the value and meaning of life?

2. Would life lack meaning if some evil actions were never punished or some good actions were left unrewarded?

3. Do you think that the only thing that keeps most of us from acting like Judah is the belief that God is watching us?

4. Is there any good reason to believe that being overly intellectual, like the professor, or too idealistic, like Cliff, will only cause us to be unhappy?

To Read Next

Stig Björkman, *Woody Allen on Woody Allen*. New York: Grove Press, 1993.

Mark T. Conard. God, Suicide, and the Meaning of Life in the Films of Woody Allen. In Mark T. Conard and Aeon J. Skoble, eds., *Woody Allen and Philosophy* (Chicago: Open Court, 2004).

Sam B. Girgus. *The Films of Woody Allen*. New York: Cambridge University Press, 1983.

Sander H. Lee. *Eighteen Woody Allen Films Analyzed*. Jefferson: McFarland, 2002.

Mary Nichols. *Reconstructing Woody: Art, Love, and Life in the Films of Woody Allen*. Lanham: Rowman and Littlefield, 1998.

9

Rats in God's Laboratory: *Shadowlands* and the Problem of Evil

DAVID BAGGETT

Love is something more than an accident that bubbled to the surface of the human condition, a fortuitous experience or fuzzy feeling deriving from a particular collocation of atoms. It's the wild truth, the essence of what is ultimately real and what we as human beings were designed for. Love is the end towards which we rightly strive. Without love, life is an emaciated caricature of its true potential. Love on such a view goes all the way down to the core of reality. It's truly what life's meaning is all about.

Loving relationships—both earthly and divine—do however require a willingness to suffer. Grasping this truth may help us to cope with various aspects of suffering caused by these relationships. Richard Attenborough's beautiful 1994 film *Shadowlands* (based on a stage play written by William Nicholson) powerfully depicts such a hard lesson, learned in the context of an unlikely and moving love story between an Oxford don, C.S. ("Jack") Lewis (played by acclaimed actor Anthony Hopkins, who won a British academy award for his performance), and an American poet, Joy Gresham (played by Debra Winger).

Jack at Oxford

The opening scenes of *Shadowlands* showcase the complexity of C.S. Lewis (1898–1963). His colleague and fellow Inkling J.R.R. Tolkien once said of Lewis that we'll never get to the bottom of him. In the classrooms of the hauntingly beautiful

Magdalen College at Oxford, Lewis exemplifies the erudite professor of English literature. In an early scene from the movie, we see Professor Lewis closing the window to his classroom, and reading to his students about a garden and a fountain. In the midst of this garden grows one perfect rosebud, which he says is an image. But an image of what? The ensuing discussion makes clear that the rosebud is an image of courtly love, which prompts Lewis to ask his students, "What is love's one essential quality?" One student tentatively begins, "Un . . ." The professor interrupts his student, "Unattainability. The most intense joy lies not in the having, but in the desiring. The light that never fades, the bliss that is eternal, is only yours when what you most desire is just out of reach."

In the classroom, Lewis projects a persona that is polished, aloof, and dispassionate. At high table with his colleagues, or in the local pub, he can be found discussing his popular children's novels, which show him to be an expert storyteller with a rich and deep imagination. Beyond a teacher, scholar, and author of popular children's novels, Lewis is also a popular religious speaker and writer. *Shadowlands* includes excerpts from some of his more famous talks given to Christian lay people, most of which are addressed to what philosophers call the Problem of Evil. Perhaps the most succinct articulation of the Problem of Evil is to be found in the writings of the Scottish philosopher and skeptic, David Hume (1711–1776): "Is he [God] willing to prevent evil, but not able? Then is he impotent. Is he able, but not willing? Then is he malevolent. Is he both able and willing? Whence then is evil?"

Lewis himself had suffered in his own life. As a young boy, he lost his mother to cancer. Despite his prayers for her healing, she died. This unanswered prayer was likely one of the contributors to his atheism, which persisted for several years before he eventually reclaimed his faith later in his life. The movie takes some liberties to characterize Lewis's aloofness to be the result of this early traumatic loss. Having gone through the painful childhood ordeal of losing his mother, the movie suggests, he constructed a wall around his heart to prevent further hurt. Whether or not this is true of the real-life Lewis, such barriers likely serve to block intimacy and rob us of the best that life has to offer. For the meaning of life is bound up in loving relationships, which require an accessible heart and a willingness to be vulnerable, and this inevitably will involve pain and suffering.

A Megaphone to Rouse a Deaf World

The Problem of Evil is a very hard problem to resolve. For believers, or *theists*, it presents what is probably the biggest obstacle in the way of religious faith. A scene from *Shadowlands* includes the following snippet from Lewis's popular talks on religious questions, in which we can catch a glimpse of the sort of answer he provides. Referring to a tragic loss of life that had taken place not long before the talk was delivered, Lewis asks where God was on the night that it happened? "Why didn't he stop it? Doesn't he love us?" He continues, "I'm not particularly sure God wants us to be happy. He wants us to be able to love and be loved. He wants us to grow up." It's "because God loves us that he makes us the gift of suffering. To put it another way, pain is God's megaphone to rouse a deaf world."

Lewis then likens us to blocks of stone, and God to the sculptor who carves the forms of men. "The blows of his chisel which hurt us so much are what make us perfect." In a later talk containing similar reflections, he continues, "We think our childish toys bring us all the happiness there is and our nursery is the whole wide world." Then, unwittingly anticipating events to come, he adds, "But something must drive us out of the nursery into the world of others. And that something is suffering."

A moment's reflection on Lewis's words reveals that such sentiments do little to really solve the Problem of Evil. In fairness to Lewis, this smattering of insights does little to exhaust his writings and reflections on this philosophical topic. In real life, Lewis wrote an entire book devoted to this topic, *The Problem of Pain*. Such memorable phrases as "megaphone to rouse a deaf world," and images of pain planting "the flag of truth within a rebel fortress" come from this famous book. In writing this book, Lewis avails himself of perhaps the two most important resources that are at the theist's disposal in contending with the Problem of Evil. The first is human freedom, which accounts for those evils that are inflicted at the hands of other persons (what philosophers call "moral evil"). The second resource has to do with what philosophers call "natural evil": in an imperfect world—one that is littered with cancer, earthquakes, and heartache—pain seems required for us to develop both morally and spiritually.

Shadowlands highlights just one aspect of Lewis's thoughts on these matters: Why bother to love at all when losing loved ones hurts so much? Instead of providing a comprehensive catalogue of Lewis's insights, the movie highlights the difference between Lewis's theoretical reflections on the Problem of Evil, or what we might think of as "book knowledge" on the one hand, and his personal contentions with it, or "experiential knowledge," on the other hand. Philosophers sometimes make a similar sort of distinction between knowledge *about* something or someone on the one hand, versus actually *knowing* that thing or person on the other. Someone may know all *about* you—your gender, profession, marital status, hobbies, and interests—without knowing *you*. Likewise, thinking *about* pain and suffering is not the same as experiencing it in one's own life.

Shadowlands depicts Lewis, having lost his mother, as carefully guarding his heart to prevent further hurt, while at the same time engaging in academic reflections about pain and suffering. In Lewis's preface to *The Problem of Pain*, he admits that his treatment of the subject matter is more about the intellectual, or theoretical, aspect of the Problem of Evil than it is about the personal or experiential variant. Philosophers carefully distinguish between the theoretical, and personal (or pastoral), Problem of Evil. Most philosophers confine their attention primarily to the former. But the difficulty with this sort of approach towards this particular problem is that it threatens to ignore the fact that evil is typically *felt* in sometimes brutal experiences of an intensely personal nature. Merely reflecting on the fact that thousands of children die each year of cancer will typically not tug at our heart strings, but watching our *own* child die of the same disease is unbearable. Joy Gresham will provide that personal struggle with suffering that would bring Lewis out of his self-imposed shell and invest his life with new meaning.

Joy

Shadowlands portrays Lewis's tranquil and settled life being interrupted by the outspoken, and occasionally brusque, Joy Gresham. When we meet Joy, she has just come out of a stormy marriage, and has been corresponding with Lewis after having read several of his books. In real life, Joy had two sons, but the movie casts her as having only one son who is around the age of Lewis when he had lost his own mother. After cultivating a friendship with her, Lewis agrees to marry Joy in order to extend his British citizenship to her so she can remain in England. The marriage is strictly a formal affair, and both go on living separate lives just as they had before they ever met.

Lewis's willingness to marry Joy covertly, concealing it from even his best friends, suggests some sense in which Lewis is emotionally inaccessible. But Joy had already begun chipping away at Lewis's heart, preparing him to see an element of authenticity in her emotional life that was lacking in his. Joy touches an emotional and experiential chord in Lewis that had been silent for too long.

Early in their relationship, Joy claims that personal experience is everything. Lewis replies by asking if reading is thus a waste of time. "No, it's not a waste of time," she answers, "but it's safe, isn't it? Books aren't about to hurt you." To this, Lewis responds that just because something hurts doesn't make it truer or more significant. This interesting exchange between Jack and Joy demonstrates something important about the nature of their relationship. Although she is attracted to Jack's intellect, Joy is equally captivated by his emotional struggles.

This brief dialogue also shows that Lewis has retreated into the world of books and ideas, closing himself off to emotions and personal experience. In a pivotal scene that shortly follows this exchange, Joy sees this troubling aspect of the life that Lewis had arranged for himself. She accuses him of surrounding himself with those who are weaker, younger, or under his control. Neither the brother with whom he lives, nor his gang of friends with whom he associates, challenge him. They point him in the direction of doubt and fear, not hope or love. Nobody can touch him. Nobody can penetrate the walls he had constructed around his heart, not even Joy. Her willingness to confront him on this issue does eventually have some impact, and offers a refreshing challenge to his settled and studious life.

Rats in God's Laboratory

What happens next is summed up by Lewis in another of his religious talks.

Yesterday, a friend of mine—a very brave, good woman—collapsed in terrible pain. One minute she was fit and well, the next minute she was in agony. She's now in hospital and this morning I was told she's suffering from cancer. Why? See, if you love someone you don't want them to suffer. You can't bear it. You want to take their suffering onto yourself. If even *I* feel like that, why doesn't *God?*

The Problem of Evil comes home once again to Jack, now an adult, in an intensely personal way. Joy's prognosis looks bleak. At the very same time, Lewis is developing feelings for his wife. In a truly touching scene, Lewis apprehends the extent of his affections, "How could Joy be my wife? I would have to love her more than anyone else in this world. I would have to be suffering the torments of the damned at the prospect of losing her." As tears roll down his cheeks, Lewis finally recognizes the depth of his love for Joy, and the height of the barriers that he had erected around his heart. Lewis decides to marry Joy, but this time before God and the world. As a boy he had reacted to pain by guarding himself from further hurt. As a man, he opens his heart to Joy and allows himself to become vulnerable.

Treatments follow. Prayers are offered. And signs of hope appear. Joy's cancer goes into remission, and she's allowed to return home, where she and Jack enjoy a season of blissful married life. But in time the cancer returns, and the end draws near. At her deathbed Lewis movingly confides to his wife that she is the truest person he has ever known, and that he never knew he could be so happy as she had made him.

When Joy dies, Lewis plunges into despair, and his faith in God is shaken to its very foundations. Realizing that he will never see her again, unable to remember her face, terrified that suffering is just suffering after all, Lewis seethes in anger and resentment. Finding the consolations of faith empty, he becomes convinced that it is all a bloody awful mess, nothing more.

"I've just come up against a bit of experience, Warnie," he confides to his brother (played by Edward Hardwicke). "Experience is a brutal teacher, but you learn. My God, you learn!" A friend tries to comfort Lewis by reminding him that we see so little here, and only God knows why these things happen. Lewis replies, "God knows, but does God care? . . . No, we're the creatures, aren't we? We're the rats in the cosmic laboratory. I have no doubt that the experiment is for our own good, but it still makes God the vivisectionist, doesn't it?"

Notice that Lewis does not lose his faith. Instead he offers a poignant example of a person of faith who is wrestling with the anguish of unanswered prayer. And when we think about it, we realize that it is only the religious believers who really *have* to struggle with this problem. Atheists can and do struggle with pain and suffering, but to whom can they complain? For why should it be any different? The believer, though, faces the full brunt of the challenge. The believer can either renounce her faith altogether, or try to come to terms with the existential struggle and inevitable cognitive dissonance that comes from trying to make sense of such seemingly needless suffering in a world that was created by a loving God. For her the question of why God allows such evil to persist is almost insuperable. The very possibility that there is an ultimate answer to the Problem of Evil of which we are currently ignorant makes it all the harder to swallow.

For Lewis, rejecting belief in God is simply not an option. Both his intellect and his imagination point to theism. Another option would be to reject the traditional understanding of God's nature. If God is not wholly powerful (omnipotent) or wholly good (omni-benevolent), then there is no Problem of Evil, for he just might not have the power or will to do other than create an imperfect world with imperfect creatures. Harold Kushner, in his book *Why Bad Things Happen to Good People,* questions God's omnipotence, claiming that there are simply some things that God can't do, like heal certain diseases. Kushner claims that he'd rather believe in a less-than-all-powerful God, than one who is so cruel as to allow children to suffer and die for some exalted purpose. Although Lewis doesn't go that route, he *is* tempted by the possibility that God is not, after all, good, or if God is good, his goodness is so beyond our comprehension as humans that we do not even recognize it as such. Lewis becomes haunted by images of God as divine vivisectionist or cosmic sadist.

Suffering Over Safety

In one of the last scenes of *Shadowlands*, Lewis finds Douglas, Joy's son (played by Joseph Mazzello), and talks with him about his mother's recent death. Not knowing what to say to the young boy, Lewis had avoided saying anything at all. "Jack," Douglas eventually asks, "Do you believe in heaven?" After only a moment's pause, Lewis answers, "Yes, I do."

"I don't believe in heaven," Douglas replies.

"That's okay," Jack assures him.

"I sure would like to see her again," Douglas utters.

Then, as he begins to weep, Jack answers brokenly, "Me too," and envelops the boy with his arms.

This event is pivotal, for in the next scene Lewis seems more at peace. We find Lewis meeting with a student. In contrast to the opening scene of the movie, Lewis now opens his window. Instead of offering clean pre-packaged answers to his own questions, he now listens to the student. The movie ends with Jack contrasting his response to pain as a boy to that of a man. Now he chooses suffering over safety in order to love. Of course, neither this scene nor the movie addresses the entire Problem of Evil, but they do offer some insights into one important aspect of it.

So, why *should* we love when losing love hurts so much? Because to miss out on the love of friends and family is to miss out on much of what makes life meaningful. On our deathbeds, we won't be embracing our checkbooks or stock portfolios, for this is not what makes life worth living. Love does involve pain, for no relationship between imperfect persons can be pain-free. And death will invariably bring all earthly relationships to an end. We can try to avoid the pain altogether, but at the cost of those very relationships that invest our lives with so much of its meaning, as well as its pleasure.

Of course it's a mistake to encourage people to remain in (verbally or physically) abusive relationships in the name of love, or submission to God's will. Mutually self-giving relationships are wonderful, but relationships in which one person is doing most or all of the giving are a recipe for disaster. Love does not entail a forfeiture of self-respect, but it does require— at least this side of heaven—a willingness to sacrifice and suffer.

A Grief Observed

After losing Joy, Lewis began to keep a very personal journal about his grief over losing his wife. Published later as *A Grief*

Observed, this book has been considered by some to be Lewis's most spiritual, honest, and forthright work. In this book, Lewis faced head on his fear that God is a cosmic sadist, and that we're mere rats in his laboratory.

Lewis eventually rejected the vivisectionist hypothesis, if for no other reason than that it's too anthropomorphic—depicting God as too much in our image. The sort of moral obtuseness on which such a theology is based seems inconsistent with the sort of Creator responsible for love or laughter or a frosty sunset.

Lewis didn't think that God wanted us unhappy. As an oversimplification for the sake of projecting a particular artistic vision, it's fine for *Shadowlands* to characterize Lewis as saying he didn't know if God wanted us to be happy. But the real-life Lewis never said such a thing. What he said instead is that God is interested in *more* than *merely* making us happy. Unlike a kindly old grandfather willing to indulge his grandchildren's every whim, God has other intentions. God's love for us as fallen creatures, just as our love for others, introduces the necessity of pain. God is more like the divine surgeon who will not stop cutting until thoroughly removing the malignancy of sin. He is less interested in satiating our palate than in making us healthy, and sometimes the cure can be painful. Ultimately, on his view, our true happiness is attainable all right, and not out of reach after all, but to be found in fellowship with God. Since God is perfectly holy, such fellowship requires a profound moral transformation. Heaven may make the sufferings of this world pale by comparison, but it demands that we first be completely transformed by God's grace, and perhaps perfected through our own suffering. As Lewis himself put it in *A Grief Observed*, there are not only tears to be dried, but stains to be scoured.

Choosing Love and Choosing Pain

Shadowlands reminds us: To choose love is to choose pain. And this point can be applied to both the earthly realm and to our relationships with the divine. The Christian tradition has almost without exception heralded the truth that genuine saving faith is more than a mere matter of intellectual assent to certain propositions. To be made fit for heaven, we must be changed and made holy. Sin is no option in heaven. After we are graciously forgiven, salvation requires transformation of character. But this process of liberation from sin is not easy. Biblically, it's often depicted in terms of being refined by fire as our whole inward orientation has to change from being, in Lewis's terms, "mercenary and self-seeking through and through." But this process of the self becoming de-throned in favor of our heart's rightful inhabitant can be a painful one. Lewis believed our egoistic selves constantly attempt to regain the throne. Only by relinquishing control, and by submitting ourselves to God's plan, he thought, can full fellowship with the ultimate source and paradigm of love be enjoyed, and the deepest self-giving fellowship with others be made possible.

The central malady afflicting us is our self-consumed tendency to put our own desires and agendas above all else. Lewis came to see how egoistic and selfish he himself had been, both in his love for Joy and, even more so, in his devotion to God, especially after his faith proved so precarious when he did not get his way. Lewis thought this required a divine iconoclast. Experience needed to shatter the house of cards that was Lewis's false image of God, so that a stronger faith and a clearer image could emerge. That Lewis may have thought God used Joy's death in his life does not mean that God orchestrated it, however, even if Lewis was right. God's *redeeming* a situation is not the same as his *authoring* it. Nor is God's bringing good out of a tragedy a denial of its badness.

As the scene with Joy's son Douglas illustrates, although Lewis never stopped believing in God or heaven, he did become less confident that he knew all the answers to the most difficult of questions. His faith convinced him that there *were* answers, but not necessarily that he had been privy to them all. He came to understand that sometimes grief simply has to be endured. His own sufferings sensitized him to, and made him more sympathetic with, the sufferings of others. When Douglas claimed not to believe in heaven, Lewis did not correct him, but held him in his arms and cried. More than philosophical debate or theological admonition, sometimes such open-hearted participation in grief is the best and most spiritual response to pain. We can wait for greater clarity once our eyes are not blurred with tears.

Although a certain element of mystery remains in any discussion of the Problem of Evil, maybe the best we can do is echo contemporary Christian philosopher Nicholas Wolterstorff's insight (after his own tragic loss of a loved one):

> God is love. That is why he suffers. To love our suffering sinful world is to suffer. God so suffered for the world that he gave up his only Son to suffering. The one who does not see God's suffering does not see his love. God is suffering love.
>
> So suffering is down at the center of things, deep down where the meaning is. Suffering is the meaning of our world. For Love is the meaning. And Love suffers. The tears of God are the meaning of history.[1]

Suffering love is, for a believer like Lewis, both the abstract meaning of history, and the very personal meaning of life.[2]

---

[1] Nicholas Wolterstorff, *Lament for a Son* (Grand Rapids: Eerdmans, 1990), p. 90.

[2] Many thanks to Rose Alaimo, Greg Bassham, Kimberly Blessing, Elton Higgs, Stuart Noell, and Jerry Walls.

TO THINK ABOUT

1. Is the Problem of Evil especially a problem for people who believe in the existence of God? Do you think theism is able to answer it?

2. Can appeals to free will and a need for moral growth satisfactorily explain all the evils in the world? Why or why not?

3. Do you think there's a relationship between love and suffering? What's the difference between suffering and pain?

4. Some people think the goal of life is happiness. For instance, we want to to be in loving relationships because this will contribute to our happiness. Does the movie suggest that this view is mistaken?

TO READ NEXT

Marilyn McCord Adams. *The Problem of Evil*. Oxford Readings in Philosophy. Oxford: Oxford University Press, 1990.

C.S. Lewis. *A Grief Observed*. San Francisco: Harper, 2001.

C.S. Lewis. *The Problem of Pain*. San Francisco: Harper, 2001.

Nicholas Wolterstorff. *Lament for a Son*. Grand Rapids: Eerdmans, 1987.

10

Flying Without a Map: *Chasing Amy* and the Quest for Satisfying Relationships

JERRY L. WALLS

When I heard Kevin Smith speak at the University of Kentucky, he was introduced as "the King of Postmodern film." Well, I am not interested in the politics of who should be recognized as King of this domain, but if it were decided by election, I'm sure Smith would get a lot of votes. He is an astute observer of contemporary culture and his films are as rich with insight as they are laced with racy humor. Moreover, he has a remarkable ability to probe issues of perennial and passionate concern, and to do so in a way that resonates with the postmodern pursuit of purpose.[1] In this essay we will look at one of his films that portrays the moral ambiguities of postmodernism, and explore some important connections between the nature of morality and meaning of life.

While Smith's best known work is probably *Dogma* (1999), his irreverent look at religion, his own favorite is *Chasing Amy* (1997), a warmly personal movie inspired by his real-life relationship with Joey Lauren Adams, the female star of the film. He makes no secret of the fact that their relationship was threatened by his temporary inability to deal with her past. In his previous

---

[1] Postmodernism is the widely discussed and analyzed mindset that has become pervasive as the ideals of the modern period have lost their hold in western thought and culture. Postmodernism is very skeptical about the moral convictions that were largely a matter of consensus in the modern and premodern periods.

relationships, he was used to being the one who had done it all, the ultra-liberal who could teach any girl some new tricks. Then he met Joey.[2]

Why It's Called "Chasing Amy"

But enough about Smith himself for now—let us turn to the story he tells on screen.

Chasing Amy begins with all the main characters attending a comic book convention in New York as celebrity guests. Holden (Ben Affleck) and Banky (Jason Lee) are authors of a hit comic series called *Bluntman & Chronic*, which features crude sexual humor. Their fellow comic writer and friend Hooper (Dwight Ewell), a black homosexual, introduces them to yet another comic artist, Alyssa Jones (Joey Lauren Adams). Holden is intrigued by her smart-talking personality, and the two hit it off immediately. The next day, Hooper invites Holden and Banky to a nightclub on Alyssa's behalf, and Holden smells romance. Alyssa is called up to the stage to sing and she performs a throaty rendition of a love song, apparently aimed at Holden. But things are not always what they seem. Pushing through the crowd and in front of Holden is a blonde. Yes, a female blonde. And when the song is through, she and Alyssa begin kissing. Indeed, lesbian couples all over the bar are moved by Alyssa's performance and begin making out. While Holden is stunned, not to mention deflated, Banky soon finds delight in the situation, and revels in the opportunity to watch such things live and up close for free.

The next day Alyssa shows up at their apartment, and they begin talking about his feelings about what happened the night before and about the whole matter of what defines appropriate sexual behavior. They also learn that they both grew up in neighboring towns in Jersey. Despite Holden's initial misgivings, they are soon hanging out together constantly. While Alyssa seems to be just enjoying the friendship of a guy who can accept her for who she is, Holden is developing feelings that seem destined for disappointment. He is falling helplessly in

---

[2] For Smith's own account of this, see "The How's and Why's of 'Chasing Amy'" at http://www.viewaskew.com/chasingamy/index.html

love with her, and one night he tells her so in a speech that would do any "chick flick" proud. But Alyssa is not your typical chick, and she reacts first with shock and then with anger because Holden has simply failed to understand and respect who she is. She is outraged at his selfishness and insensitivity in thinking she can just change who she is because he has a crush on her!

But the scene has a happy ending. After getting out of the car into the pouring rain and telling Holden where he can get off, to put it nicely, she runs back to him and falls into his arms. Heterosexual kissing follows, and Alyssa seems just as passionate as she was in the lesbian bar. The romantic highlight of the film occurs a few scenes later when Alyssa tells Holden why she fell for him, breaking her previous pattern of female lovers. Her speech is as emotionally appealing as Holden's earlier one to her. She explains that she found him on her own terms having already explored the other side of the field. Holden is feeling pretty good that he has gone where no man has gone before in finding his way into Alyssa's heart.

Banky, however, is not pleased. Not only does he harbor anti-homosexual feelings, but he is jealous of the time Alyssa is taking with Holden and he fears it will ruin the career they have built as comic collaborators. Immediately after this scene, he drops a bomb, in the form of a high school yearbook, in front of Holden and instructs him to check out page forty-eight. There, we see Alyssa's senior picture with her nickname "Fingercuffs" printed underneath. Banky has been doing a little detective work and he has learned that she earned that name because she participated several years ago in a threesome with two guys, one of whom Holden and Banky remembered from their high school. (If the meaning of the nickname is not obvious, it is explained in the movie!)

This is more stunning to Holden than his initial discovery that Alyssa was a lesbian and he denies it vehemently, insisting that she had never been with a guy. But the hard truth that he wants to deny cannot be avoided; Holden confronts Alyssa about Banky's allegations while they are at a hockey game, a scene that is very cleverly choreographed. The exchange that follows is intense with raw emotion, as Alyssa confesses the incident, plus more. Indeed, she identifies herself as the "queen of suburban legends" because of her previous sexual adventures.

Holden is crushed as well as indignant that Alyssa had misled him about her past. While apparently not bothered by her numerous lesbian encounters, he saw her colorful heterosexual past as cheap and degrading.

Enter Jay and Silent Bob. While Holden is still reeling and confused, he meets the odd couple of Smith's films in a diner. Dispensing advice as only he can, Jay counsels Holden to dump Alyssa and forget her. But then Bob breaks his characteristic silence with two momentous words: "Chasing Amy." That is his diagnosis of what is going on with Holden. Silent Bob goes on at some length explaining that he had had a similar relationship with a girl named Amy, and he had pushed her away because he didn't know how to handle her past. He has come to realize she was the one, but now she is gone. Ever since, he explains, he has been "Chasing Amy . . . so to speak."

All of this brings us to Holden's ingenious solution to his quandary. This scene is very important to my analysis of this film and we will come back to it shortly. Before we proceed, however, let me state my central thesis. I believe "Chasing Amy" is a vivid picture of what happens to us emotionally, morally and relationally when we try to revise morality in some fairly radical ways, while still holding onto selected parts of traditional morality.

Morality and the Meaning of Life

Broadly speaking morality has been understood, in modern and pre-modern times, as something to which all human beings are accountable. It makes certain demands on us and prescribes how we ought to live our lives. However, morality has not been understood as a list of rules or obligations that are imposed on us as a burden. Rather, the rules of morality are the formula for true human fulfillment and flourishing. It is in following the moral way that we fulfill our nature and achieve lasting satisfaction.

Much of morality obviously pertains to relationships. The essence of morality is a concern to relate to other beings, and even things (such as the environment), in the right way. Persons have intrinsic value, and should always be treated with love and respect. In one of the most famous passages in the New Testament, Jesus says that the Ten Commandments could be summarized as two: We should love God with our whole heart and we should love our neighbor as our self.[3] So morality at its best provides direction for treating others, as well as our selves, in a truly loving fashion.

Now it is not easy to summarize the meaning of life in a sentence or two, but let's hazard this much: The meaning of life is loving relationships. It is what Alyssa, Banky, Holden and all the rest of us are looking for. And morality is about governing relationships and treating people in a truly loving way. Satisfying relationships depend, then, on proper moral guidelines to keep them on track. So there are obvious and important connections between morality and the meaning of life.

The connection is even stronger when we press on to ask one of the most basic of all philosophical questions, namely, where do our moral standards come from? What is the source or ground of morality? As we will see in a moment, this issue is raised rather pointedly in the movie. This is hardly surprising, for not only is this a longstanding philosophical issue, it is also a hot topic at the forefront of the so-called culture wars that currently rage in our society. Indeed, E.O. Wilson, a prominent socio-biologist, has stated that the dispute between fundamentally different views of morality is the twenty-first century's "version of the struggle for men's souls."[4]

According to Wilson, centuries of debate have left us with basically two different options. Either moral principles exist outside of the human mind and are independent of human experience, or they are the inventions of human minds. Those who hold the first view believe that morality is grounded in the eternal nature or will of God, or at least in self-evident moral principles that any rational person should be able to see as clearly true.

By contrast, people who hold the second view believe moral principles are the products of biology and culture. Moral demands are really nothing more than the principles we have hammered out over the years as we have made agreements and contracts with each other to govern our life together. Over the centuries of social and cultural evolution, these principles have

---

[3] See Matthew 22:34–40.
[4] Edward O. Wilson, "The Biological Basis of Morality," *Atlantic Monthly* (April 1998), p. 54.

hardened into requirements and obligations. On this view, a statement about what we "ought" to do is just shorthand for what society first chose to do and then later hardened into a moral code.

At the foundation of morality then, according to this view, lies human choice and experience, including the choices and experiences of Holden, Alyssa, and their friends. Understood this way, morality is open to our revision if it no longer seems to us to meet our needs or fit with our experience.

As Wilson, a proponent of the latter view recognizes, this dispute has great implications for religion and also for the quest for human meaning. Human beings, he admits, are incurably religious. They seek immortality and eternal significance for their lives. They hunger for communion with God and even to be united with him in a relationship of perfect love. Without such hope, human beings tend to feel lost in a universe that is ultimately without meaning.

Unfortunately for us, Wilson believes our deepest longings and hopes are destined for disappointment. Religion, like morality, is a human invention and has no independent reality. It is our misfortune that we have evolved with desires and aspirations that do not fit reality. The ultimate Lover we seek is a product of our creative imagination.

But maybe our misfortune involves even more than this. Perhaps even our quest for human love is a misguided one that will inevitably be frustrated. Jay suggests as much in the encounter with Holden in the diner. When Holden explains that he can't just dump Alyssa because he is in love with her, Jay replies: "Ah, there ain't no such thing. You gotta boil it down to the essentials. It's like Cube says—life ain't nothing but bitches and money." If these really are the essentials of our world, Jay may be right that love is an illusion.

Standard Without Substance

One of the most interesting scenes in the movie for moral analysis is the conversation that occurs after Holden has first discovered that Alyssa is gay. She opens the door for him to ask questions about her sexual preferences and the following exchange occurs.

HOLDEN: Why girls?
ALYSSA: Why men?
HOLDEN: Because that is the standard.
ALYSSA: If that's the only reason you're attracted to women—
because it's the standard . . .

Holden goes on a bit later to add that, "Girls feel right." Alyssa
says the same is true for her. Holden then infers that she is a vir-
gin if she has only been with girls and has never had intercourse
with a member of the opposite sex, again appealing to the "standard definition." And again, Alyssa proceeds to punch holes in
his definition.

Now this is very telling. While Holden keeps appealing to the
"standard" account of things, it is rather clear that he has very
little sense of how to defend his convictions or any convincing
reasons why his standards should be accepted.

Consider now Alyssa's explanation of why she was attracted
to Holden, despite her previous history of lesbian relationships:

> I came to this on my own terms. You know, I didn't just heed what
> I was taught. Men and women should be together, it's the natural
> way—that kind of thing. I'm not with you because of what family,
> society, life tried to instill in me from day one. . . . So here we are,
> I was thorough when I looked for you, and I feel justified lying in
> your arms—'cause I got here on my own terms, and I have no
> question there was someplace I didn't look. And for me that makes
> all the difference.

This brings into sharper focus why Alyssa feels no obligation to
accept the standard account of things. The standard is based
only on what family, society, and the like tried to instill in her
as the natural way we should behave. In doing things on her
own terms, she is merely preferring her own way instead of
what she sees as the rather artificial demands of others,
demands that have no real authority over her.

Alyssa's moral outlook is also clarified in the scene outside
the hockey arena when Holden asks her how she could have
done some of the outrageous things she had just confessed. She
replied as follows: "Easily! Some I did out of stupidity, some I
did out of what I thought was love, but—good or bad—they are

my choices, and I'm not making apologies for them now—not to you or not to anyone!" Alyssa goes on to point out that Holden also had sex in high school, to which he replies that there is a world of difference between "typical high school sex" and having sex with two guys at once. A bit later, she describes herself as "an experimental girl" trying to figure things out on her own. Contrasting herself to Holden, she says she was not given a "map at birth, so I tried it all."

Now, in view of Wilson's two basic views of morality, cited above, Alyssa seems to hold a version of the second view. She sees the "standard" view of morality as resting on a very flimsy foundation that cannot really bear the weight placed upon it. It may make grand claims, but it really amounts to nothing more than what parents or society have told us about how we ought to behave. Alyssa feels perfectly free to reject this and figure out from her own experience how she ought to behave.

But what about Holden? What is his view? While he appeals to the "standard" he hardly has a well-thought-out or consistent view on the matter. He apparently sees nothing wrong with sex outside of marriage, as long as it's "typical" sort of stuff. He even comes to the point that he is untroubled by Alyssa's lesbian past. He only draws the line, so to speak, at more unusual practices like sex with multiple heterosexual partners at the same time. Alyssa challenges the inconsistency in Holden's views when she puts the following question to him: "Do you mean to tell me that—while you have zero problem with me sleeping with half the women in New York City—you have some sort of half-assed, mealy-mouthed objection to pubescent antics that took place almost ten years ago?"

In one sense then, Holden's problem is caused by his moral standards. He has revised the "standard" account of morality to a large extent, but he still holds to certain parts of traditional morality. He is caught in a dilemma because he loves Alyssa, on the one hand, but he also holds certain moral convictions that she finds silly and "mealy-mouthed." His dilemma is a variation on the conflict we feel anytime we find ourselves at odds with our moral standards. This produces a tension that we need to resolve if we are to have emotional peace and personal integrity. The question, which is one of the truly fundamental issues human beings have struggled with as long as there have been human beings, is how to do this.

Holden's Brilliant Solution

This brings us to Holden's solution, which he unveils in a meeting he has arranged with both Alyssa and Banky. He arrived at his solution, he says, after dissecting the whole situation and looking at it a thousand different ways. When the answer finally came to him, he says everything made sense and "a calm came over me." If they will agree with him, not only will the tension be relieved between him and Banky, and Banky and Alyssa, but most importantly, he and Alyssa will be able to get past the wall they have hit in their relationship and go on to be stronger than ever.

After this buildup, he announces "We've all got to have sex together." While at one level this sounds so preposterous that you want to laugh, Holden makes the case so earnestly that the scene is actually charged with vulnerability and poignant emotion.

> Don't you see? That would take care of everything. Alyssa, with you I wouldn't feel too inadequate or conservative anymore. Because I'll have experienced something on a par with all your experience. And it'll be with you, which'll make it that much more powerful. And Banky—you can take that leap that everyone else but you sees that you should take. . . . And when it's over, all that hostility and aggression you feel toward Alyssa will be gone. Because you'll have shared in something beautiful with the woman I love. It'll be cathartic. This will keep us together.

Now the irony here is truly remarkable. What Holden viewed before in another context as the insurmountable stumbling block to an otherwise wonderful relationship has been transformed in his mind into a virtual sacrament. What he saw before as cheap and degrading and scandalous, he now describes as simply another level of experience, a level that he suggests is higher and richer than his own experience. To engage in three-way sex is now seen as something beautiful, as emotionally cathartic and as the means to true communion.

In short, Holden's solution to his dilemma was to further revise his moral views, to erase the line he still wanted to draw as a limit on acceptable sexual behavior. Once this offending "standard" was eliminated, the tension between him and his moral convictions would be resolved, and he could experience peace again.

Not surprisingly, Banky is blindsided by Holden's proposal, but he reluctantly agrees to go along with it. Alyssa, however, rejects the proposition firmly, but with feeling (to which Banky breathes a sigh of relief, and says "Thank Christ"). Holden seems truly perplexed, given her previous willingness to engage in such activity, but she insists that his solution will not solve anything, but only create more problems. She elaborates:

> Maybe you'll see me differently from then on, you know? Or maybe you'll despise me for going along with it, once you're in the moment. . . . Or what if—and God I sincerely doubt it, but what if—I saw something in Banky that I've never seen before, you know, and fell in love with him and left you? I've been down roads like this before; many times. I know you feel doing this will broaden your horizons and give you experience. But I've had those experiences on my own. And I can't accompany you on yours. I'm past that now.

This exchange represents a sort of reverse in their roles, with Alyssa now drawing a line that rejects three-way sex. However, her reasons for declining this encounter are much the same as her explanation for why she earlier participated in such behavior. She is still taking an experimental approach to morality, and her reasons for declining Holden's proposal can be summed up in the fact that she personally has already had those experiences and is now past them. But it is unclear what she means by this. The fact that she keeps open the possibility that she could fall in love with Banky and leave Holden suggests she is still following her feelings and doing things on her own terms, wherever that may lead in the realm of romantic relationships. The conclusion of the movie is also interesting in this regard, although ambiguous. In the final scene Alyssa is again at a comic convention with one of her female friends. Has she returned to the lesbian lifestyle? All that seems clear is that Alyssa has been down many roads in her experimentation and is unwilling to accompany others who feel the need to go where she has already gone.

So we are left with the suggestion that Holden's solution for resolving the moral tension he was feeling is not a satisfactory one, that he would probably not find the peace he thought he would achieve by engaging in forms of sexual expression he previously viewed as wrong or inappropriate. But Alyssa's refusal is finally only a statement that she cannot accompany Holden. It is not really a statement that Holden should not go down the roads she had already explored. On Alyssa's own terms, she must leave open the possibility that Holden might indeed find satisfaction in a threesome, just as she might find it in Banky, at least temporarily.

Another Option for Chasers Everywhere

So much for the attempt to resolve the moral tension by making more changes in one's moral standards. There is, however, another profoundly different way of resolving the tension that is never explored in the movie. In short, instead of changing one's moral standards, one can change one's behavior to bring it in line with the standards. This approach would require one to own up to the fact that any behavior that violated those standards was indeed wrong and should be recognized as such.

But this approach raises a huge question: what would moral standards have to consist of in order for us to be able to take them that seriously? If moral standards have nothing more behind them than society's expectations, parental authority and the like, then it is hard to get too worked up about violating them. Alyssa's attitude is perfectly understandable if "standards" amount to nothing more than this.

Recall Wilson's claim that "the battle for men's souls" in this century is being fought over just this question. Recall also that one of the sides in this battle holds that morality does indeed have a much more substantial foundation than human authority and consensus. Indeed, according to the view that has been dominant in Western culture for the better part of two thousand years, morality has as strong a foundation as can be imagined, namely, God Himself. There are various ways of spelling this out this in detail, but the basic idea is that morality is not an arbitrary matter at all, nor is it merely the product of human thought and experience. Rather, it is a reflection of God's nature or an expression of his perfectly wise and loving will.

It is this belief about the nature of morality that gives solid content to the traditional idea that the rules of morality are the formula for fulfilling our nature and achieving the satisfaction we all crave. Since God is perfectly wise and loving, he not only knows what is best for us, but also desires it. He has not left us on our own to experiment and figure out for ourselves how we ought to live. Rather, he has given us direction and guidance to help us find the satisfaction and happiness all of us are looking for.

Now all of this can sound rather theoretical or even stuffy. In reality, however, these ideas can help us avoid negative and heavy-handed notions of morality, particularly, the notion that it is just a legalistic matter of following certain rules for the sake of the rules. For if morality is rooted in the will of a personal being who is truly loving and good, then when we do what is wrong, we are not just breaking some impersonal rule. Rather, we are disappointing God and damaging our relationship to Him.

So when we acknowledge we have done wrong, and aspire to do what is right, we are ultimately acknowledging God and expressing our trust that He truly loves us and knows what is best for us. In following his rules for human behavior, we not only enrich our relationship with God, we also pursue the most promising route to satisfying relationships on the human level.[5] All of this helps us maintain the personal touch and the concern for happiness that morality at its best is all about.

Now Smith, the writer and director, is a practicing Catholic, so it would not be unthinkable that he might explore this option. In fact, however, no one in the film ever brings God into the picture or gives any consideration to the possibility that He might be relevant to sexual morality. Some of the characters refer to their Catholic upbringing, and there are a few jokes with Catholic references, but Catholicism comes into play in a serious way only as the source of whatever conservative moral instincts remain with them. For instance, when Silent Bob is describing his relationship with Amy, and says that it blew his mind when she told him she had participated in a threesome, he explains that he reacted that way because he was raised Catholic. But none of the characters seem to take their Catholic upbringing seriously, so the guilt feelings and other moral reactions that remain are experienced as a sort of emotional hangover that serves no positive purpose.

Whether or not this is part of Smith's intention for this film, I believe he has portrayed for us in a powerful way the sort of

---

[5] I have defended in more detail the claim that God is the ultimate ground of morality in *Heaven: The Logic of Eternal Joy* (New York: Oxford University Press, 2002), pp. 161–197.

quandaries that inevitably result for people who live in a post-modern, post-Christian world and who still retain shreds of traditional morality, particularly sexual morality, but have no idea why those "standards" should be followed. Those remnants of traditional morality are relics from a worldview they no longer hold with real conviction, and those moral judgments often make little sense outside the worldview that originally gave them life. As such, those standards often leave the persons who must deal with them feeling deeply confused and bewildered.

To put it another way, *Chasing Amy* illustrates for us the inevitable difficulties for those without a map, who fly by the front of their pants, or who fly with only shreds of a map they have discarded long ago.

Making moral sense without God is not easy. It is hard enough *with* God, but harder still without him. If there is no God to whom we are accountable, morality certainly does not have the same sort of authority over us as it would with his existence. Alyssa's refusal to apologize to "anyone" for her past behavior makes a certain amount of sense if there is no God to whom we are accountable, and morality is a human creation. If we feel guilty or ashamed of our choices, but there is no God, then there is no one to forgive us and make us right again. Indeed, there is no need to be forgiven, at least on any grand scale, for our moral and relational failures.

If there is no ultimate relationship to give our lives meaning, if the hope for this relationship is an illusion, as Wilson believes, then we are on our own to do the best we can to find satisfaction in human relationships or wherever else we may. But if our lives do have ultimate meaning, we also have help and guidance for those relationships, as well as the prospect of forgiveness where we have gone wrong. Certainly this is not the only reason to believe in God, but the fact that belief in God helps us make sense of our deepest longings for morality and meaning is one powerful consideration in deciding this ultimate question.

Perhaps then *Chasing Amy* is an image of an even larger quest. If He is out there, maybe we will find her too.[6]

---

[6] Thanks to Dave Baggett, Yukie Hirose, Bill Irwin, Tom Morris, and Pat Wilson for helpful comments on an earlier version of this essay. Thanks to the students in my class on Postmodernism and Pop Culture, and to Jonathan Walls for insightful discussion of the movie.

To Think About

1. Does a meaningful life have to be a morally good life? Is it possible to separate out questions of meaning from moral issues?

2. Many thinkers have claimed that a morality grounded in God would make morality objective. In what sense does it make morality "objective"? Does this just present us with one more moral viewpoint?

3. What does the movie say about our ability to choose whom we fall in love with?

To Read Next

John E. Hare. *The Moral Gap: Kantian Ethics, Human Limits, and God's Assistance*. Oxford: Clarendon, 1996.

Alasdair MacIntyre. *Three Rival Versions of Moral Inquiry*. Notre Dame: University of Notre Dame Press, 1990.

Basil Mitchell. *Morality: Religious and Secular*. Oxford: Clarendon, 1980.

Jerry L. Walls. *Heaven: The Logic of Eternal Joy*. New York: Oxford University Press, 2002.

Take Four

What Do I Want Out of Life?

11

American Beauty: Look Closer

GEORGE T. HOLE

> . . . beauty's nothing but the start of that terror
> We can hardly bear; still we love
> The serene scorn it could kill us with.
>
> — RAINER MARIA RILKE, *Duino Elegies*

Good movies give us opportunities to imagine into the drama of other lives and, indirectly, allow us to fantasize about our own. As a result we might gain insights into how to live our own lives better. Lester Burnham, the main character of *American Beauty* played brilliantly by Oscar-winning actor Kevin Spacey, has a revelation—and he acts on it. "It's a great thing to realize you still have the ability to surprise yourself. Makes you wonder what else you can do that you've forgotten about." Can we appreciate this and his end-of-life insight, which involves a mysterious sense of beauty that freshens and redeems life more radically than surprise?

With comic and tragic overtones, *American Beauty* allows us to witness two seemingly normal families, the Burnhams (Lester, Carolyn, and Jane) and the Fittses (Frank, Barbara, and Ricky), caught in suburban angst, breaking apart at the seams. The movie does more than entertain us with yet another story of a man going through a mid-life crisis. It offers us a philosophical challenge, not simply to intellectualize about the meaning of the movie, but to examine our assumptions about the meaning of our own lives.

Life Post-Mortem

As the movie opens, a voice (we will learn is Lester's) introduces us to his daughter Jane (Thora Birch): "Janie is a pretty typical teenager. Angry, insecure, confused. I wish I could tell her all that's going to pass. But I don't want to lie to her." Janie is also highly critical of her father: "I need a father who's a role model, not some horny geek-boy who's gonna spray his shorts whenever I bring a girlfriend home from school. Like he'd ever have a chance with her. What a lame-o. Somebody should put him out of his misery." A voice off-screen asks "Want me to kill him for you?" Later, replaying this conversation, she tells her boyfriend Ricky that she would pay for his murder with the baby-sitting money that she has been saving to get "a boob job."

In the next scene, as the camera pans Robin Hood Trail, Any Town, U.S.A., a well-laid-out suburban neighborhood, we hear the same off-screen voice of Lester telling us prophetically, "In a year I will be dead. I am dead already." Lester's wife and daughter think he is a "great loser." Lester agrees: "And they are right. I've lost something very important. I'm not exactly sure what it is, but I know I didn't always feel this . . . sedated." When his wife Carolyn reintroduces him to Buddy Kane, the regional real estate "king" (with whom she will later have an affair), Lester replies self-mockingly, "I would not remember me either." The voice off-screen continues, "[I]t is never too late to get it [my life] back."

Ricky Fitts (Wes Bentley), the new kid next door who has the odd habit of constantly videotaping whatever he finds curious, will become Lester's personal hero after he witnesses Ricky telling his catering boss, "I quit. Leave me alone." Lester too, quits—he quits playing his customary, un-dramatic roles as father, husband, employee and neighbor. The event that triggers Lester's journey of self-discovery takes place when he is introduced to Angela Hayes (Mena Suvari), the beautiful blonde and sexually promiscuous cheerleader friend of his daughter, Jane. Middle-aged Lester is determined to impress and seduce her, much to the disgust of his daughter and oblivion of his wife.

Following Ricky's lead, Lester quits his job and rebels against his adult responsibilities. (His rebellion leads to complications, humorous for us, as it leads to the exposure of self-deceptions in other characters.) He buys a 1972 cherry red Pontiac GTO convertible and devotes his days to lifting weights, jogging with his homosexual neighbors Jim and Jim ("I want to look good naked"), smoking pot, and listening to Bob Dylan tunes in his well-appointed up-scale, two-car garage. Lester's sexual fantasy almost becomes real. On the evening of his murder, when he is about to have sex with Angela she tells him that she has been lying about her sexual experience; this is her first time. Instead of laughing at her or even himself, he responds with compassion: "You have nothing to be sorry about." And Lester realizes that he has nothing to be sorry about either. *American Beauty* ends with us hearing Lester's disembodied voice expressing his gratitude "for every single moment of my stupid little life." The voice continues: "You won't understand. Don't worry. You will someday."

A Life Behind Things

What is it that we do not understand? What we need to understand is another line from Lester's concluding soliloquy: "It is hard to stay mad when there is so much beauty in the world." In fact, beauty pervades the movie and seems most enigmatic in the scene in which Ricky, Lester's personal drug-dealing hero, shows a video he recorded. In it a plastic bag is held captive in a wind for fifteen minutes, gliding aimlessly in the air in front of a non-descript red-brick wall. Ricky, the son of a stern, homophobic, retired military officer father and a mother who never speaks except to apologize, explains:

> It was one of those days when it's a minute away from snowing and there's this electricity in the air, you can almost hear it, right? And this bag was like, dancing with me. Like a little kid begging me to play with it. For fifteen minutes. And that's the day I knew there was this entire life behind things, and . . . this incredibly benevolent force, that wanted me to know that there was no reason to be afraid. Ever.

Ricky sees "an entire life behind things." Anticipating Lester's end-of-life insight, which he announces in his post-mortem soliloquy, Ricky exclaims, "Sometimes there is so much beauty I can't take it. Like my heart is going to cave in."

The dominant theme of *American Beauty* is the exposure, sometimes humorously, sometimes tragically, of different versions of transcendence, getting to some supposedly better place or state beyond where we are now. Instead of transcendence as a strategy for meaning in life, the movie suggests a redemptive possibility in beauty, here, in this life as it is. What is this view of beauty, so pervasive and powerful, that it will redeem a stupid life?

The ancient Greek philosopher Plato (around 428–348 B.C.E.) and the German philosopher Immanuel Kant (1724–1804) offer theories about transcendence and beauty. For Plato, we might reach some stage of transcendence by climbing out of our cave and attaining beauty by climbing the ladder of love. For his modern counterpart Kant, the transcendent realm of god, freedom, and immortality, while it must be postulated, is beyond the reach of our knowledge and experience. His theory of beauty resting on the paradoxical idea of "purposiveness without purpose"[1] comes close to Ricky's sense of beauty in the aimless movements of the paper in the wind. The Eastern Sage Buddha (560–480 B.C.E.) will be an instructive guide to help us figure out what we do not understand and what is alive in the core of beauty. But first let's consider the first movie theater ever constructed, as found in Plato's famous "Allegory of the Cave."[2]

The Urge for Something Beyond

Plato in his famous Allegory of the Cave constructs the first movie theater, figuratively, in order to answer a speculative question about us, namely, to what degree can humans be enlightened? We are to imagine an underground cave in which people seated in darkness are watching images flicker on the cave wall in front of them, much like we are seated in the movie theater—with a crucial difference; they are chained from birth to their place. Plato imagines what it would be like for a person to be unchained, turned around and face the fire, the puppets, and puppeteers who are producing the shadow-show. After an initial experience of blindness and confusion, Plato suggests that

---

[1] "Beauty is the form of the purposiveness of an object, so far as this is perceived in it without any representation of a purpose"—the concluding statement of Third Movement of the Judgment of Taste, article 17, Immanuel Kant, *Critique of Judgment* (New York: Hafner, 1951).

[2] See Book VII of Plato's *Republic*.

the freed person would comprehend the nature and cause of the shadow-show. Plato has us follow the prisoner through two more stages, emerging from the cave into full sunlight and then returning back into the cave, returning to his original seat alongside his friends, still engaged in their pastime of naming the shadows. At each stage the freed person suffers blindness and confusion, before gaining sight and understanding.

The sun represents what Plato calls the "form of the Good." Forms are ideal models or prototypes for all particular things that exist in the world that we experience through our senses. Furthermore, forms are unchanging and have an existence more real for Plato than the sensory things in which the forms inhere. Take for example a few of the many striking appearances of the color red in *American Beauty*: rose petals, rose bouquets, the front door of the Burnham house, and Lester's blood on the white tile and white kitchen table. For Plato, all these examples are manifestations of the form of redness (and the form of beauty) which must exist independent of its examples if we are to have any stable knowledge of our world. So, when the prisoner finally sees the sun it is like being able to comprehend Goodness itself, independent of any specifically good things. Moreover, just as the sun is the source of light in our sensory world, Goodness is the source of intelligible light by which we can truly apprehend good things. Since the Good is the highest form, it is last and most essential to know on the journey toward enlightenment. And, the Good is like the sun; it is the source of the intelligible light by which we know particularly good things—But like the sun, we cannot look directly into the Good without being permanently blinded. Finally, just as the sun is the source of life and nourishment in the sensory, physical world, knowledge of the form of the Good is the source of vitality and meaning in what Plato characterizes as the intelligible world.

In Plato's allegory, we notice that only one person apprehends the Good and thus becomes enlightened. When he returns to the cave, the transformed prisoner is eager to tell of his remarkable journey and discoveries. In dismay, the other prisoners threaten to take his life if he persists in interrupting their entertainment.[3] For those who are ignorant of their chains,

---

[3] Likely Plato is alluding to the fate of his teacher and friend, Socrates, who was put to death by his fellow Athenians for the crime of practicing philosophy.

his talk about some strange place outside the cave, along with his wild idea about knowledge of the Good, has no practical value. They are deeply fascinated by the flickers of shadows and the voices of puppeteers, so they know perfectly well what is good for them; don't they? And, as Plato suggests by analogy, we know too; don't we? But recall what Lester advised at the outset of *American Beauty*: There is a truth—one that will redeem even a stupid life—we do not understand yet.

Plato's "Allegory of the Cave"—essential and exciting reading for any student of philosophy—captures a fundamental assumption that is central to most religions and, to a lesser degree, animates contemporary American culture. The assumption begins with a distinction between appearances and reality. The world of appearances—the common, everyday world that we accept based on tradition and unexamined experience—is represented by images that constitute the "reality" of the allegorical cave dwellers. Even their dreams of some better life outside the cave, are shaped by the puppeteers[4]. By contrast, the "real-reality" lies in the knowledge of the Good, which is to be learned last of all, and, at least for Plato, is realized only by a few individuals. Christianity embraces this dualism in its fundamental distinctions between the body—Caesar's world—and the soul—God's world. The notion of "transcendence," which is found in both Plato and Christianity, captures the idea of a higher reality, or other world, vastly superior to the lower, inferior existence we experience in our everyday lives.

For Plato and Christians it is this higher realm of existence that one should seek to obtain in order to have a meaningful life. Both endorse special means that one must practice in order to transcend this inferior life of ignorance or sin, to attain a truly worthwhile existence of knowledge of the Good or God's eternal salvation. *American Beauty* satirizes a materialistic version of transcendence and portrays a different possibility: Goodness

---

While Socrates did not claim to be enlightened, he dedicated his life to philosophy as the love of wisdom. Thus, Plato suggests that, in addition to a method of questioning, a person needs a deep love of wisdom to be free of the chains of popular belief and begin the journey toward enlightenment.

[4] Lester echoes this idea of appearance: "Our marriage is for show, a commercial." But, in contrast to Plato, he suggests at this point that there is no more substantial reality in marriage.

and redemption are possible through the realization of the everyday beauty pervading even the most mundane things and the most stupid and smallest lives. A prominent sign on Lester's desk issues the simple command: "Look closer." [5] This is a clue for understanding the nature of beauty, as well as Lester's final declaration—there is something we do not understand, something that presumably will make a decisive difference in the experience of the meaning of our lives.

When Is a Rose Not a Rose and Much More?

American Beauty pokes fun at many of the idealizations of beauty held dear by many Americans: the beautiful house, the beautiful yard, the beautiful $4,000 Italian silk couch, the beautiful wife, the beautiful body, and so forth. One of the initial scenes of the movie, in which we are introduced to Lester's wife, brilliantly parodies this aspect of the American dream. We find Carolyn Burnham (Annette Bening) in her rose garden in front of the house, cutting flowers and placing them in a basket, with a determined, humorless look on her face. She is perfectly put-together and has lots of useful, and apparently new, expensive gardening tools. Lester remarks sardonically: "That's my wife Carolyn. See the way the handle on those pruning shears matches her gardening clogs. That's not an accident." We then see two well-groomed, model-like men, Jim and Jim, who are leaving their home for work. One Jim gets into a Ford Taurus while the other Jim crosses the street to greet Carolyn:

> **JIM:** Morning Carolyn.
> **CAROLYN** (*overly friendly and dramatic*)**:** Good morning, Jim! I just love your tie!
> **JIM:** And I just love your roses. How do you get them to flourish like that?
> **CAROLYN:** Well, I'll tell you. Egg shells and Miracle Grow.

The camera returns to Lester dressed in his bathrobe, drying his hair as looks down on them.

---

[5] Sam Mendes, in his directional debut, likely is directing us to look closer into the movie we're watching.

LESTER: Man, I get exhausted just watching her. She wasn't always like this. She used to be happy. We used to be happy. . . . But she doesn't have much use for me anymore. About the only thing that gets her excited now is money.

What is Lester's response to their mutual unhappiness? He has accepted the coma-like state of his life: He mumbles complaints to himself and he stumbles over his efforts to get into his wife's car on schedule and to be a friend to his daughter. When he eventually rebels, he exposes the shallowness of his stultified American dream.

Flowers, in particular roses, conventional things of beauty, appear prominently throughout the movie. In fact, "American Beauty" is the name of a kind of rose. In one striking scene (used in the movie's trailer) Lester fantasizes that Angela is lying in a white porcelain bathtub filled with red rose petals: As he reaches into the tub to touch her, Angela slowly spreads open her thighs. In reality, Lester's sexual encounter with Angela will prove much less idyllic, and much more beautiful. Other character's confrontation with disillusionment will be more comic and far more shattering.

Rebellion and Exposure

The adult ladder Lester has been climbing to achieve the American dream has led only to the discovery that with success he is unhappy. He now deliberately descends, breaking rungs on the way down. He quits his job. In the process, he exposes the (cowardly) double talk of his boss, Brad, self-proclaimed as "one of the good guys," who requests a job profile as a prelude for firing Lester. Exposing Brad's mean business ethic, Lester extorts a severance package by threatening Brad with a homosexual harassment charge. Empowered by his freedom from the traditional American work ethic of transcendence, Lester proclaims at home, "I rule."

Lester's choice of a new life, responsibility-free and coma-free, contrasts with the upward grasping of other characters for some idealized state of transcendence—one that is vulnerable to failure and comic exposure. We watch Carolyn psyching herself by repeating a mantra "I will sell this house today." She strips to her undergarments to spic and span the empty house. The contrast between the deadpan responses of potential buyers to her inflated enthusiasm for the house is humorous.

One woman complains with a tinge of outrage: "The ad said this pool was 'lagoon-like.' But there's nothing 'lagoon-like' about it. Except for maybe the bugs [as she slaps her arm]. There are not even any plants out here." Carolyn, ever ready to please in order to sell, replies, "I have an excellent landscape architect." The woman states bluntly what she means: "I mean, I think 'lagoon,' and I think waterfall, I think tropical. This is just a cement hole." She seems righteously angry for being disillusioned by the ad—the danger in believing in something transcendent. We are amused. The scene ends with Carolyn clearly disappointed that she has not satisfied her ambition to sell the house today. Her disappointment, first expressed as a pout, turns suddenly violent: She slaps herself repeatedly in the face.

Another comic scene of exposure takes place in line at the fast-food drive-through. Carolyn and Buddy are groping each other in her Mercedes SUV, after their earlier sexual "explosion" in a motel. (Later, Carolyn will follow Buddy's suggestion for power-after-sex, to shoot a pistol.) They are unaware that Lester, now the food dispatcher, is watching them. Exposed, they try to compose themselves and utter an unconvincing story. Lester is amused, giving them their two "smiley" orders and giving himself several more degrees freedom from responsibility. However, because he has witnessed their sexual tryst, their exposed fantasy completely deflates.

The chronically disillusioned character in the film is Barbara, Ricky's mother. Whenever she appears, she seems catatonic. Her mantra is "I'm sorry." His father, Colonel Fitts, is the person most dramatically exposed. When his doorbell rings, it seems as if he hears an alarm and suspiciously questions his wife and son whether they expect anyone. It is comic to watch him open the door and be greeted by two neighbors, Jim and Jim, who introduce themselves as partners. They are offering the Fitts family a welcome-to-the-neighborhood basket. Colonel Fitts, hearing "partners," thinks that they must be trying to sell him something. Slowly it dawns on him that they are men living-together as partners and his disgust for homosexuality surfaces. Later, to avoid his father's hostility Ricky pretends to share his father's disgust. Much later, in an incidental comment to Lester, Ricky says with a laugh, "My dad thinks I paid for all this [expensive video equipment] with catering jobs." He adds a statement that may be true not only for his father: "Never underestimate the power of denial."

Like others in the movie, Colonel Fitts misinterprets something he sees, which leads to two cruel actions. When he thinks he sees his son commit a homosexual act with Lester, the Colonel beats his son mercilessly. Ironically, the Colonel's own homosexual desires surface when he kisses Lester, only to be gently rebuffed. Later, the Colonel kills Lester. Presumably when he discovered a shameful reality beneath his own shadow-show sense of identity, murder, not a struggle to enlightenment, is his only face-saving necessity. (We might ponder Socrates's famous assertion, "The unexamined life is not worth living" and add a caution: Never underestimate the suffering from exposure and more authentic self-knowledge.)

Angela is another character whose fantasy, in her case of self-importance, gets exposed. Nothing is worse for her than being ordinary. So, to prove otherwise, she tells stories about being the object of men's sexual attention and boy's masturbation fantasies. Ricky, who is escaping home after his father has beaten him, has asked Jane to join him. Angela protests. Ricky challenges her friendship with Jane, "She's not your friend. She's somebody you use to feel good about yourself." Angela calls him a freak and then asserts in her defense, "Oh, yeah? Well, at least I'm not ugly." Ricky challenges her deceptive sense of self, "You are totally ordinary. And you know it." Minutes later as Lester is slowly and sensually undressing Angela, finally acting out his sexual fantasy, she confesses, "This is my first time." His aroused illusion of her is shattered. Exposure no longer is comic; it is painful to watch. The only more painful exposure would be to watch some dimly recognized vulnerability of our own laid bare.

American Beauty

Beyond our conventional understanding, beauty itself might be what we cannot understand. We have standard conceptions of what is beautiful: a red rose, a blonde cheerleader with a voluptuous body, a well-manicured lawn. Correspondingly, we have standard representations of what is ugly: a dead bird, a useless plastic bag, a loveless marriage. Not unlike the cave-dwellers who name the different images of the shadow-show, we do not even have to look at these particular things to know that they are beautiful or ugly—we have been taught these judgments as cultural truths. But, can we look for ourselves, as if seeing for the first time? Can we have an insight similar to the one Edna St. Vincent Millay (1892–1950) expressed in her poem, "Euclid alone has looked on beauty bare" The poem is dense and suggests a sympathy for Plato's idea of form:

> Euclid alone has looked on Beauty bare.
> Let all who prate of Beauty hold their peace,
> And lay them prone upon the earth and cease
> To ponder on themselves, the while they stare
> At nothing, intricately drawn nowhere
> In shapes of shifting lineage; let geese
> Gabble and hiss, but heroes seek release
> From dusty bondage into luminous air.
>
> O blinding hour. O holy, terrible day,
> When first the shaft into his vision shone
> Of light anatomized! Euclid alone
> Has looked on Beauty bare. Fortunate they
> Who, though once only and then but far away
> Have heard her massive sandal set on stone.

The poem speaks of something blinding, holy and even terrible in the experience of looking on beauty bare. Beauty is bare when our minds are bare, free of pre-conceptions of beauty. At that moment, something profound happens. Ricky has experienced it: "Sometimes there's so much beauty in the world I feel like I can't take it, like my heart's going to cave in." Lester has a similar experience of beauty bare, "Sometimes I feel like I'm seeing it all at once and it's too much, my heart fills up like a balloon that's about to burst."

As Lester discovers, the experience of beauty has redemptive powers. Beauty can heal. It can heal the disappointment and anger at a life not lived as one would have hoped. Lester states what other characters and we might express, "I guess I could be pretty pissed off about what happened to me." But he adds this remarkable and rare realization, "But it's hard to stay mad, when there's so much beauty in the world." Ricky, too, could have been pissed off, when his parents sent him to a mental institution. Hearing this, Lester responds in an obvious way, "Yeah, but you lost two whole years of your life." Ricky has a different perspective, one that may be the eye-opener to beauty bare: "I didn't lose them. It taught me how to step back and just watch, and not take everything so personally. And that's something I needed to learn. That's something everybody needs to learn."

"Step back and just watch" might not seem like a hard lesson to learn. But it depends on how we understand its meaning. Philosophers attempt to "step back and watch;" in order to explain beauty; some of them focus attention on a particular kind of attitude that is necessary to experience it. Immanuel Kant, for one, emphasizes disinterestedness as an essential aspect of the aesthetic attitude.[6] Disinterestedness marks a boundary where we separate from our usual attitudes, practical, cognitive and moral, so that we are free to contemplate beauty bare, for its own sake.

Kant notes that our repertoire of concepts is not adequate to account for the beauty we behold. Matching concepts to objects—for example applying the concept of a freshly opening rose to our experience of this richly particular rose, in this unique setting—gives us, at best, conventional beauty and thin experience. Once free of our conventional matching of concepts to objects, we can enjoy the free play of imagination, an aspect of being creative with our experience that Kant describes paradoxically as "purposiveness without purpose." It seems as if the beautiful object has some purpose, some final objective, beyond simply being what it is. Yet, it is just what it is, a gift, a bag blowing in the wind, for our imagination and experience.

Ricky has a similar insight when he watches the bag blowing aimlessly in the wind: "And this bag was like, dancing with me. Like a little kid begging me to play with it. For fifteen minutes. And that's the day I knew there was this entire life behind things, and this incredibly benevolent force, that wanted me to know there was no reason to be afraid. Ever."

Lester, too, learns to be more fearless. Ricky had an earlier experience of a "life behind things": "When you see something like that [a dead bird] it's like God is looking right at you, just

---

[6] Kant, *ibid.*, article 2.

for a second. And if you're careful, you can look right back." Does he actually know there is a benevolent force or a God behind things? Ricky gives no evidence of belief in God (nor does any other character in the movie), or much else of traditional value. Ricky does seem to share Kant's intuition, that inherent in beauty there exists some greater purpose, which connects with transcendent ideas of God, freedom and immortality. For Lester, it was this intuition in beauty, which he optimistically believes we will understand someday for ourselves—an intuition that has the power to redeem "every single moment of [his] stupid little life."

In addition to "step back and watch," it is far harder to learn "not to take everything personally." Lester learns not to take everything personally, while all the other characters, except for Ricky, do take so much personally. Carolyn is not able to step back from her disappointing day: She takes it personally that she did not fulfill her self-imposed command to sell the house today. She continues to take it personally as she punishes herself, from a critic-like position, because she was not able to act and direct other characters and herself according to her script for the day. At this point she is a failed author, a failed actor, and a failed stage director. She can only satisfy her role as critic and punish herself.

The Ladder of Love

Plato describes for us a path to the greatest apprehension of beauty. In the *Symposium*, Socrates is given instructions on love. If he maintains a sense of honor and reverence for a beloved, not indulging in wanton desires, he will ascend, as if on a ladder, to higher forms of beauty, from the beauty of one person to many, from the beauty of persons to the beauty of laws. He will come "to understand that the beauty of them all is of one family, and that personal beauty is a trifle."[7] At the highest rung of this famous ladder of love Socrates will behold, in its awesome splendor, "the vast sea of beauty." As a result, "he will create many fair and noble thoughts and notions in boundless love of wisdom; until on that shore he grows and waxes strong, and

---

[7] Plato's *Symposium*, translated by Benjamin Jowett, found online at http://classics.mit.edu/Plato/symposium.1b.txt

at last the vision is revealed to him of a single science, which is the science of beauty everywhere."[8]

For Plato, this climb is as arduous a challenge as the prisoner's struggle to find the way outside the cave, to behold knowledge of the Good. Nothing short of beholding this final revelation is adequate for Plato: "He who has been instructed thus far in the things of love, and who has learned to see the beautiful in due order and succession, when he comes toward the end will suddenly perceive a nature of wondrous beauty (and this, Socrates, is the final cause of all our former toils)-a nature which in the first place is everlasting, not growing and decaying, or waxing and waning."[9]

Ricky and Lester have found a shortcut to the top of Plato's ladder: Look closer, without taking anything personally. They both realize that beauty is already here, waiting for one to let go of personal stuff, open "beginner's eyes"[10] and behold beauty bare wholeheartedly. Rather than being pissed off at not attaining the life he thought it was supposed to be, Lester appreciates his life as it is, with gratitude.

The Buddha on Beauty

Maybe we can understand Ricky's seeming obsession with videotaping as his attempt to capture and record beautiful images for later viewing. But, can he capture and replay his experience, much less beauty itself? Buddha offers a profound insight in regard to any experience, especially those great ones we try to hold onto and duplicate. About his long-sought and life-transforming enlightenment he states: "I obtained not the least thing from unexcelled, complete awakening; and for this very reason it is called 'unexcelled, complete awakening'."[11] He did not make his own enlightenment something personal, as if by holding onto it he would be special and entitled to claim for himself some privileged center of existence. In his concluding

---

[8] *Ibid.*

[9] *Ibid.*, 211b.

[10] The phrase is a variation on the title of a Zen Buddhist book: *Zen Mind; Beginner's Mind*, which teaches the importance of seeing as if for the first time.

[11] Alan Watts, *Zen Buddhism* (New York: Random House, 1957), p. 45.

revelation, Lester offers a similar bit of advice that is applicable when we are tempted to grasp or hold on to what we cherish in experience: "And then I remember to relax, and stop trying to hold on to it, and then it flows through me like rain."

Plato, in contrast with the Buddha, will not be satisfied until the enlightened one is free of all particulars and has a secure hold on the never changing, eternal form of beauty. Plato and Christianity share a similar vision of transcendence: By special practices—climbing the ladder of love or loving God, neighbor and self—a person can attain entry and status in a higher reality, the intelligible realm or after-life salvation. *American Beauty* shows a comic and tragic side to more mundane, competitive transcendence: To get somewhere and be somebody in America. While the movie exposes the life of grasping after "good" things, and pushing away or avoiding seeing "bad," it affirms and offers us the choice to transcend transcendence: Beauty is present even in a stupid life if a person takes a closer look and lets go of the personal stuff. What then is difficult to understand? We typically are seeking big meaning, a meaning that rests on an image of how our lives are supposed to be, if we do the right things. Consequently, we are like Plato's cave-dwellers in the sense that we have an image of how life would be if we broke free and could live outside our imprisoning cave. When life does not match our image and expectations we righteously get pissed off. *American Beauty* offers a glimpse of a more satisfying option: Meaning, like beauty, is always accessible in our lives, if we take a closer look, with beginner's eyes, and experience our lives with deep gratitude.

To Think About

1. Make a list of five things you find beautiful and five you find ugly. For one item from your beautiful list, do the following:

   Look at it again, this particular object, in this particular setting; look as closely as possible taking it in fully. This includes looking at it with sympathy for what it is, and without any cognitive, practical, or personal interest in it. Relax; take your time looking. Consider at some point that the object is looking back at you with gratitude. Note any difference from previous looking at it. Note any thoughts that make it difficult to contemplate the object simply for its own sake. Note (and better yet, write down) your experience.

2. Do you participate fully in your life as it is? In other words, is there some condition such that if it is not met you will not fully participate? For example, if you have been, or are likely to be "pissed off" by some person or activity, do you hold back from experiencing that person or activity fully? Or, if life is not fair, do you not try as hard to secure what you most want?

3. What does the movie say about our responsibility for our own happiness? Is our happiness completely with our control?

To Read Next

Edmund Burke. *A Philosophical Enquiry into the Origin of Our Ideas of the Sublime and Beautiful.* Edited with an introduction and notes by James T. Boulton. Notre Dame: University of Notre Dame Press, 1968.

Joseph H. Kupfer. *Experience as Art: Aesthetics in Everyday Life.* Albany: State University of New York Press, 1983.

Immanuel Kant. *Observations on the Feeling of the Beautiful and Sublime.* Translated by John T. Goldthwait. Berkeley: University of California Press, 1960.

Mary Mothersill. *Beauty Restored.* Oxford: Clarendon, 1984.

Plato. *Symposium.* Translated by Alexander Nehamas and Paul Woodruff. Indianapolis: Hackett, 1989.

Alan Watts. *The Way of Zen.* New York: Vintage, 1957.

12

Life Is Beautiful: The Lure of Evil and the Rebellion of Love

ANTHONY C. SCIGLITANO, JR.

The rose is without why; she blooms because she blooms; she pays herself no heed, asks not if one can see her.

— ANGELUS SILESIUS (Johann Scheffler)

Nothing is more necessary than the unnecessary.

— UNCLE ELISEO

Roberto Benigni was introduced to many Americans when he accepted the Best Foreign Film Oscar for *Life Is Beautiful* by straddling the tops of celebrity-filled seats to get to the aisle at the Academy Awards. While Benigni may be a bit loony, he is also brilliant—albeit in his own, bizarre way. Benigni finds room for both brilliance and lunacy in *Life Is Beautiful* to portray a father's love for his child in the midst of a terrible time, a time when the shadows of fascism threatened to swallow up all the light of goodness in Europe.

Life Is Beautiful is not primarily a movie about the Shoah.[1] It is first and foremost a love story through which Benigni offers a vision of life's meaning that he opposes to the vision held by Nazism. This may seem unnecessary. Nazism is clearly not an attractive vision of life. The first point I want to argue in this

---

[1] "Shoah" means destruction and seems much more appropriate than the more frequently used "Holocaust," which signifies a sacrificial offering to God for atonement.

chapter, however, is that a Nazi view of life's meaning can be more tempting, and more subtly tempting, than one might think. We might recall that Germans did not become Nazis because they wanted to think themselves evil, but because they found something seductive in Nazism, something that resonated with their own aspirations as human beings. The second argument of this chapter is that Nazism and what we might call "Benigni's vision" are so different because they spring from fundamentally different attitudes toward life: while an attitude of pride determines a Nazi vision of life, gratitude lies at the root of Benigni's vision. Each attitude serves to organize what one wills and how one reasons.

A Game of Life and Death

The action of *Life Is Beautiful* occurs in two places, Arezzo, Italy (birthplace of Petrarch), and an unnamed concentration camp. The film opens when Guido (Benigni) comes screaming downhill toward Arezzo while his friend, Ferrucio, attempts to control a suddenly brakeless vehicle. Flying ahead of the King and through a town parade, Guido wrongly receives the fascist salute as if he is the celebrated monarch himself. The car finishes its wild ride when it breaks down by a beautiful farm; soon, a beautiful woman drops from a hayloft into Guido's awaiting arms. He makes an eager hero, declares himself Principe Guido and Dora his Principesa.

Further "chance" meetings between the two in Arezzo are even more outrageous. Guido launches into her when his bicycle gets away from him; he later pretends to be a Fascist inspector sent from Rome so that he can visit Dora at her school; and on a horse named Robin Hood, he steals Dora (gold) from her own engagement to an upwardly mobile fascist. Dora later has a child by Guido, and they live near his Uncle Eliseo. Guido, Eliseo, and the child, Joshua, are Jewish; Dora is not. In other words, she chooses to marry a poor Jew who is a waiter—later a bookstore owner—rather than the upwardly mobile fascist. Her courage becomes more obvious later in the film.

The movie's tone gets progressively darker after Dora comes home to an empty, ransacked house. Her husband, father-in-law, and son have been taken for deportation to a camp.

Although she need not do so, Dora decides to join her family. The overseers of the camp separate women from children; somehow, Guido's son manages to stay with him and hide in the barracks as German soldiers snap orders to the prisoners. The rest of the film follows Guido as he struggles to maintain for his son's sake the illusion that the camp is an elaborately structured game at the end of which the last child left unfound by the enemy will win a real tank. With aid from others, Guido succeeds in maintaining the illusion, but at the cost of his own life. Guido's resourcefulness and imagination are credible throughout the concentration camp scenes because from the beginning Benigni has portrayed him as uncommonly adept both physically and intellectually. A German doctor at one point calls him a genius because of his uncanny ability to solve riddles. The story itself is related to us by the son as a way to honor his father's memory.

Benigni's Picture of the Nazi Mind

Nazism or Nazi ideology is often thought of as a mythology and exaltation of the will, of force and raw power. There can be no doubt that Nazism does extol the will. In addition, however, Nazism can be depicted as an abstract rationality, a system of calculations devoid of contact with the flesh and blood of human beings. Although these might seem like irreconcilable positions, Nazism reconciles them by subordinating the second to the first. Calculation serves power; reason is slave to irrational will. Even science gets taken up into this politics of power. Hitler commandeered a genetic theory to claim that by breeding certain human beings with other human beings he can achieve the superior race. This breeding policy involves the further conclusion that certain types of blood or certain ethnic groups constitute racial contaminants and must be eliminated.

Hitler makes claims; he does not make arguments or feel the need to persuade others rationally. Force does not debate. The story the Nazis tell themselves is that they are a superior race, and, therefore, that they have rights over against others, many of whom on this account have no right to exist. The meaning of life has to do, then, with cultural and racial domination, which some believe is theirs by right. There is a morality here, namely a kind of social Darwinism that would sacrifice the weak in view of the supposed creation of a superior humanity. Such an exalted end justifies every abominable means. In this light, Nazism may sound neither attractive nor alluring. But consider the following scenario.

One day, Upper Management Guy decides to approach one of the many corporate wage-slaves—let's call him "cubicle guy"—under his authority. Upper Management Guy tells cubicle guy that his talents are wasted in his current position, but that he can't promote him because of a nasty report filed by the much less talented, and obviously jealous Middle Management Guy. In fact, he says, he's seen this kind of thing happen a million times to just this kind of worker when middle-management types look to destroy the careers of the talented workers below them to ensure their job security. The unfortunate result is that the company remains mediocre, records low profits, and has to lay people off. "Hey," he says, "you want to get a drink after work? We can talk some more about this."

In this scenario, Upper Management Guy plays on cubicle guy's pride and feelings of discontent, identifies an enemy, and begins to present an alternative scenario where cubicle guy finally gets what he really deserves. Cubicle guy is also led to believe that not forming an alliance against Middle Management Guy hurts others, while forming this alliance is good for everyone. In other words, cubicle guy is able to think well of himself even while plotting to bring Middle Management Guy down. Of course, the truth is that Middle Management Guy never filed that report, and perhaps cubicle guy is not particularly talented. However, it serves upper management's interests to get rid of Middle Management Guy and to replace him with a loyal dupe. It also serves cubicle guy's interest not to grasp any of this—for that knowledge would give him an uneasy conscience. So he never investigates.

The point is not that cubicle guy then leaps upon unsuspecting Middle Management Guy, disemboweling him with his letter opener. It is the temptation we are after. It is tempting to think that our genius has gone unrecognized and that someone is to blame for our lowly position in life. Given the right conditions, the necessary spark, a combination of these elements can lead to violence. It is also tempting to think that in certain cases, with respect to particular people, we have special rights that they do not possess, rights that relieve us of the basic requirements for compassion and respect. We exalt ourselves to their detriment. There exist obvious cases: domestic abuse, office mistreatment, sexism, racism, and imperialism; and less obvious instances: verbal abuse, cutting wit, belittlement, intimidation, condemnation, or just forgetting someone's existence. In all of these cases, whether they articulate it or not, someone believes that they rightly dehumanize others, deify themselves, or both. Fascist, Nazi ideology makes doctrine out of these base human attitudes, summed up by pride.

Benigni proves expert at depicting the various Nazi doctrines or values in action and in conversation, even as they filter down in silly ways to the people. Of course he does so in a way that also shows their rank absurdity. We learn early on that Guido's traveling buddy, Ferrucio, is a fan of Schöpenhauer's philosophy of the will.

Schopenhauer was a nineteenth-century philosopher whose view of the will influenced Friedrich Nietzsche, a favorite philosopher of the Nazi regime.[2] Ferrucio believes that will power is the key to success. Ferrucio himself is a harmless character. More important is that some version of the philosophy of will has filtered into society and is taken seriously even by those who have little to gain from it. The irony here is that Guido's friend finds a job as an utter lackey to Oreste, the

---

[2] The debate regarding Nietzsche's influence on Nazi ideology still rages. It has been firmly established that he was neither an anti-Semite, a rabid nationalist, nor a believer in racial purity (quite the contrary—he seems to have thought that mixed races produced stronger cultures). Nevertheless, his genealogy of morals assigns to Christianity and Judaism the less than flattering label of "slave" morality and holds them responsible for Western cultural weakness. He sees the value of compassion, for instance, as a way for the weak to dilute the cultural strength borne by the "masters," those who are vital and alive. The masters then become self-conscious and encounter feelings of guilt regarding their strength. On the latter theme, see Friedrich Nietzsche, *On the Genealogy of Morality: A Polemic*, translated by Maudemarie Clark and Alan J. Swenson (Indianapolis: Hackett, 1998). See also Robert C. Solomon and Kathleen M. Higgins, *What Nietzsche Really Said* (New York: Schocken, 2000), especially pp. 103–124. Nietzsche's most avid defender is Walter Kaufmann. See Kaufmann, *Nietzsche: Philosopher, Psychologist, Antichrist* (Princeton: Princeton University Press, 1974). In his *Humanity: A Moral History of the Twentieth Century* (New Haven: Yale University Press, 1999), Jonathan Glover shows links between Nazism and a highly selective reading of Nietzsche's philosophy. See pp. 11–18, 40–47, and 355–364.

owner of a local furniture store. Apparently will power only gets you so far!

Benigni consistently ridicules Nazi racial ideology. Some of this ridicule is obvious and hilarious; at other times it is subtle. For Nazism it is the racism that justifies the right to power—because Nazis perceive themselves as belonging to a superior race, they judge that they have rights over other groups. Guido repeatedly encounters Oreste—the owner of the furniture store—who aspires to status in the fascist social-political world. The first encounter with Oreste yields the following:

GUIDO: What are your political views?
ORESTE (*distracted by his children*)**:** Adolfo, Benito, be good!

Guido quickly changes the subject and steals the merchant's hat. We then hear Oreste say, "He stole my hat." In Italian, however, we hear something else, namely, a nationalist who says "hat" in a local dialect. The nationalist fails to properly pronounce the national form of the Italian language. Guido accomplishes this theft several times, twice yielding the word "hat" from Oreste, as if to emphasize that this merchant's fascism runs contrary to who he really is. He must perpetuate a delusional existence to support a self-destructive ideology. And fascism, as an ideology of absolute loyalty to the state, is a *self*-destructive ideology. Only the will of the state matters. Of course, if the merchant is part of the superior race, we have to wonder why he is consistently fooled by this Jewish fellow.

Perhaps the most humorous scene in the film has Guido appear before young students at Dora's school dressed up as a fascist party official visiting from Rome. His job: to explain Italian racial superiority. Instead, he ends up in his underwear, the students left tittering wildly at the absurd picture before them. Argument being of little use against authoritarianism, Guido turns to mockery. He reduces racist ideology to its own absurdity. People must learn to see that beneath the shiny boots and goose-step procession lies a common, vulnerable humanity.

Within Nazi ideology, consequentialist reasoning comes to serve racial pride and a drive for power. Individual, irreplaceable lives bear little significance. Benigni is not subtle here. He has an Italian woman express her wonder at the mathematical acumen of German schoolchildren in relation to their more sluggish Italian counterparts. Her example is the following math problem that German youngsters reportedly dispose with ease:

> **WOMAN:** If the state spends 4 marks per lunatic a day, 4.5 marks per cripple, and 3.5 marks per epileptic, and there are 300,000 total, how much would the state save if it eliminated all of these individuals?

Dora responds that she "doesn't believe this," but the woman thinks that she is referring to the disparity of math skills. The example confirms for her German superiority! Of course, Dora is rejecting the appalling character of the example and how casually those around her, including her fiancé, speak of it.[3] She is also, however, rejecting the whole meaning of life represented by the Fascist worldview.

The Counter Story: An Ontology of Gift

The word "ontology" refers to that which is truly real, most real, as opposed to that which is only apparent, illusory, façade. We make this distinction all the time. If Coke is the real thing, the assertion is that Pepsi is somehow less authentic, the soda of falsehood. It's not "classic." Real grass versus Astroturf, real wood versus pulp board, outdoor stadiums versus domed, *Guinness* versus *Coors*.

The classic philosophical example of the real versus the illusory is Plato's allegory of the cave. In Plato's allegory, prisoners sit in a cave facing a wall and watch as movements occur on the wall which they believe are real, but which are actually the play of shadows from a fire which shines from behind them. They must be led out of the cave to perceive reality, and thus the difference between reality and mere appearance. That which is truly real is often said to be true, good, and beautiful as well. Guido, Dora, their son, and Guido's uncle Eliseo will present us with a vision of life's meaning more true, good, and beautiful than anything the Nazis put forth (admittedly not a

---

[3] This dialogue recalls the type of things that people like Adolf Eichmann would calculate in the dispassioned manner of a bureaucrat. See the classic study of Eichmann by Hannah Arendt, *Eichmann in Jerusalem: A Report on the Banality of Evil* (New York: Penguin, 1994).

high standard)—they offer a counter story or vision regarding life's meaning. Rather than pride, gratitude directs the use of will and intellect. We can start with Guido.

Guido is the classic comedic fool, the naïf who reveals what is highest in what appears lowest. He is like a child in the best sense: the beautiful world around him, whether the countryside, Dora, or Arezzo, captivates and energizes him. Guido's encounters with nature ("This is beautiful," he shouts), with Dora, with his uncle, and with his son come to him as gifts. Dora literally falls from above. He only meets Dora because his car breaks down and Ferrucio shoos him away from the vehicle to fix it. His Uncle gives him a job, a place to live, and much more.

Eliseo hires his nephew as a waiter, and trains him in one of the movie's great scenes. Rehearsing his servant's role, Guido practices bowing, but to a point where his forehead practically touches the floor. Learning to serve, he turns to groveling. Eliseo stops this buffoonery to teach Guido a lesson about service and dignity. "God serves men," he says, "but he's not a servant to men." Eliseo is the wise Uncle, a guide who helps Guido change from a clever, agile fool to a clever, agile Prince, willing to play the fool for a higher purpose. The meaning of Eliseo's other piece of wisdom—"Nothing is more necessary than the unnecessary"—provides what I take to be the interpretive key to this film.[4]

Two events in the film unpack the significance of this proverb most clearly. First, there is the surprising, spontaneous love that Dora gives to Guido and to her family. Not only does she descend from the hayloft, but by giving herself to Guido she also descends from a higher social class (and literally crawls under a table to kiss him). Guido is not only a Jew, he is a poor one. Her ultimate gift, however, comes when she boards the deportation train to share her family's destiny. This act was literally unnecessary; she is not Jewish. Love too is not necessary. It cannot be demanded by law, or arrived at by syllogism. In another sense, however, her expression of love at this point in the story is the most necessary act of all, for it manifests human solidarity in the face of Nazi belief in racial separation and sub-

---

[4] Eliseo's other memorable remark, "Silence is the loudest cry" and his need to have Guido understand that genuine evil is starting to arise are two other instances of his wisdom in the film.

jugation. We might say that love is both necessary and free in this case. Dora is not externally required to give her love, but she is internally compelled. If we could ask Dora about her choice to board the train, she might reply, "I had no choice," which is the right answer, even if we know that technically she did have a choice.

In another way, we often consider games unnecessary. "It's just fun and games," we say, indicating a lack of seriousness. Of course few who have ever played a game of Scrabble or Chess, basketball or golf, can believe that the competitors are not serious. A player who fails to take the game seriously lets everyone down. No one wants to win a game of Scrabble against someone who is too distracted by MTV to care. What we would seem to imply when we say that games are unnecessary is that they are not useful, or, if they are useful their usefulness is secondary to their real purpose which lies in pleasure. Along with games, we perhaps also place imagination in the "unnecessary" box. We can pull it out when we have time to spare, but otherwise better to keep it under wraps. We don't want to be dreamers. After all, calculation and hard work pay the bills, not imagination.

In *Life Is Beautiful*, however, games and imagination[5] play a central role. Dr. Lessing uses puzzles to cling to sanity; they fail him, perhaps because he is such an isolated figure. He always eats alone, and the only person to engage him is Guido. Guido's character loves games, pranks, and puzzles. He steals hats and hearts, he solves riddles, and he protects his child through an enormous effort of creativity. If games are normally considered unnecessary, it is nevertheless precisely a "game" that saves Joshua's life and manifests Guido's desperate love for his child. Guido's imagination becomes what is "most necessary" if his son's life is to be saved. Guido must strain every mental muscle to maintain the illusion that everything Joshua encounters in the camp exists as part of an elaborate game to win the real tank; certainly his will is at work to give his son a love worthy of Dora when she boarded that train. It is the only way to "pay forward" his wife's sacrifice. With Guido, however, love and gratitude direct will, reason, and imagination as they ought to be directed:

---

[5] Imagination can mean many different things. It involves the ability to create, to synthesize various impressions and ideas, to put oneself in another's shoes, to see a puzzle from more than one angle.

for the good of others. Of equal importance is the help that Guido receives at key points in his "game." Unlike Lessing, Guido is not a solitary figure.

Although the story is about Guido's sacrifice for his child (not just his death, but his whole existence in the concentration camp is a living sacrifice for the child), he is also kept alive because of the child. As Guido drags anvils up stairs to a furnace (essentially a picture of hell), he expresses his despair to a prisoner behind him. The prisoner explains that to stop would mean death. Guido's face reveals comprehension: if he dies, Joshua dies. Like Sisyphus rolling his rock up the mountain, Guido hauls the anvil to the furnace. Unlike Sisyphus, however, Guido has a purpose external to his climb and help outside himself. His child staves off Guido's despair by his very presence; in turn, Guido constructs stories to maintain the game illusion. When Guido is desperate, when exhaustion and anxiety cloud his imagination, Bartolomeo (a fellow prisoner) or the uncle pitch in, and the life-saving game, that which is "unnecessary," yet "most necessary," is saved.

Can we say that the meaning of life represented by Guido is more realistic than that of Nazism? It is tempting to view those who are successful or powerful as the ones who are realistic. They must hold a superior ontology, we tell ourselves (probably in simpler words). Success is surely helped by insight. But in the context of the film, it appears that the powerful fascists are simultaneously the most deluded of all. A clever contrarian might note that in fact, Guido dies at the end. If that's realism, then who wants it? But then, who doesn't die in the end? Neither power nor success purchase immortality. Such a view would represent an utterly false ontology, a forgetfulness of our finite nature. Like Guido and like the rest of us, each and every member of the Nazi party ceases to be. Death is the purest of democracies.

The hubris of Nazism is not merely dangerous to those against whom it arrays itself. A false view of the self also endangers the self. Pride on such a grand scale destroys those who hold it because their lives stand precariously perched over the abyss of self-delusion. Violence against others is necessary because their existence testifies to the lie at the fascist core. Pride makes of us fragile beings for whom truth is always a danger, something to be squelched lest it collapses our carefully constructed balsa wood identity. An ontology of racial superiority and power is ironically an ontology of fear.

The question that confronts Guido and the rest of us is what if anything is worth living and dying for, not whether or not we shall ever "go into that good night." A realistic conception of life might grasp existence, both ours and that of the world, as that which is given and that to which we are given to respond. This view suggests that our very existence—the community around us, the patterns of life that take shape before our eyes—we could not have procured for ourselves, but receive as a gift. We might say that existence is given and not grabbed; for Guido, life is not merely given, but also gift—it is good and beautiful. It's true, also, that nothing in this view precludes recognizing that we are capable of evil and ugly responses to the gift of being. We all know, for example, that people can receive a gift in the most gracious and in the most awful ways. The gracious extreme involves a spontaneous outburst, sometimes more fervent than expected by the gift giver; the opposite can also be the case: "What am I going to do with this?" The latter is wrong precisely because it forgets that the gift need not be given. "Awful gift receiver" guy seems to think that he ought to have received something better, when, in fact, he needn't get anything at all.[6]

Reception of a gift, then, carries with it certain appropriate and inappropriate responses. We recognize the giver as free (otherwise it is not a gift but an obligatory exchange) and therefore generous. We recognize ourselves as dependent upon the graciousness of another and in their debt. Primarily, then, our existence is receptive, humble, and rooted in generosity.[7] Our gratitude extends to a desire to return this generosity (not the gift!). Recognition that existence is a gift, given similarly to all, prohibits conceiving ourselves gods among men. Moreover, Guido's humility is not a lack of energy. Humility indicates a

---

[6] We are assuming here that the gift is appropriate. Utterly inappropriate gifts can of course be given (the proverbial baseball mitt that a child gives to his mother for Mothers' Day, for instance).

[7] Whether a god must be presumed here is an open question; it may be that Guido believes in God; he is Jewish, but we do not know from the film whether he is religious. Eliseo's comment about God points to this conclusion, but can also be construed as a useful observation drawn from the culture.

rightful estimation of one's place in the universe, not a low sense of self-esteem or an impoverished notion of one's responsibilities towards others. Indeed, reactions to gifts often include bursts of energy, renewed vigor and vitality. This is Guido's story. Gift begets gratitude begets generosity, vitality and creativity.

Life Is Beautiful?

Why beautiful? Why not true or good? An obvious answer is that Benigni is an artist. A second answer comes from Dostoyevsky, who tells us: "Only beauty can save us." We are back at our original question: Why focus on beauty? We said earlier that Guido must show the absurdity of Nazi ideology because there is no arguing with a fundamentally coercive ideology. The beautiful is that which can be grasped by the senses; beauty can move us sometimes despite ourselves. The difficulty that Guido confronts is that people around him have lost a taste for beauty and goodness, and with it a sense of humor about themselves (only the children and Dora laugh when Guido strips before them; Oreste is utterly humorless). Pride lacks beauty and humor precisely because it is so self-absorbed.

What do we mean by beauty? At the heart of beauty lies attractive form. It may be safe to say that life comes to us first as a series of forms and shapes. Prior to creed and duty, we encounter a world of edges and corners, colors and sounds, light and language. Our world takes shape as the smell of Grandma's perfume, the taste of milk, the light of the countryside. Form does not merely represent meaning that is somehow already present; without shape, our world has no meaning, like a language without grammar. Form is essential to meaning. Would anyone say, for instance, that the form a person's life takes over time is unrelated to the meaning of that life? Just as important, it is through form that meaning can happen as an event. An embrace not only expresses affection already present, but also impresses affection on a relationship—just as withholding an embrace does the opposite. Form and content work together; an embrace normally expresses and increases affection; a slug to the jaw does not.

Beauty is not simply "form," but form that compels, moves, attracts, fascinates. In Guido's world, beauty enchants, but does not coerce, an important distinction because enchantment can turn demonic, as in a charismatic figure like Jim Jones. The beautiful must also be good. It is the story of Guido and his family that fill out this vision of a beautiful life as a good life. Benigni's story specifies the beautiful life as ecstatic, a life formed through giving and receiving for others.

The word "ecstatic" means "to stand outside"; it is a form of self-forgetfulness that we experience[8] when we are "lost" in music or in a movie, when we are "in the zone" or when we "lose track of time." Beauty trains us to be less self-centered, like a rose: "The rose is without why; she blooms because she blooms; she pays herself no heed, asks not if one can see her." Like the rose, love does not calculate its own interest or pay itself vain heed. Love is, in a sense, whyless.

Guido is lost in the beauty around him. He exults in the countryside and gapes in wonder when Dora boards the train. Guido's ecstatic existence is true because he responds with gratitude and joy to the gifts he is given and good because he returns life's generosity in kind. Benigni knows that not everything attractive is beautiful, not every ecstasy good and true. We can be attracted to Nazi charisma, we can lose ourselves in an utterly evil cause, we can falsely assess our ontological status in relation to others, we can even fail to notice beauty when it appears. This family story shows us his vision of a truly beautiful and good life. Indeed, Benigni tells us at the beginning of the film that the movie is to be like a fable, a tale with a lesson. We might ask, then, what it all has to do with us, we who do not live among Nazis?

One of the great capacities of cinema is its ability to show us the drama that underlies our apparently prosaic lives. It does this by condensing all the drama of a life into two or three hours. Family love may appear mundane when it comes to bear the dust of the everyday. What Benigni shows, however, is something more familiar, so familiar in fact, that we often miss it. Guido's sacrifice, after all, is the sacrifice every loving parent makes for his or her children each day. To bear and love one's children is to live in their bones, to suffer their burdens, to fear for them when they are naively unafraid, to take joy in their life,

---

[8] Perhaps "we" don't actually experience, because the subject is gone in some sense and only comes back in a changed state.

sadness in their struggles, and to do anything to protect them against their enemies. In short, to give one's life. The goal of all this is sometimes survival alone; but a parent usually hopes for much more, for a child who can trust, who is strong and good, who has a richly textured life—happiness. Like Guido, all parents must battle their child's enemies: hunger, ignorance, pride, humorlessness, stupidity; glamour parading as beauty, falsehood dressed up as truth, evil costumed as goodness. If life, our life, is a beautiful gift, then we have something to lose. To Benigni, that constitutes a drama worth living and dying for.

TO THINK ABOUT

1. Explain the relevance of the two epigraphs at the beginning of this chapter.

2. Is the game Guido plays with his son morally justified? Would the act of deception be acceptable if instead of his son it involved his wife?

3. Does Guido's joy in life blind him to the impending atrocities? Is Guido naive?

TO READ NEXT

Hannah Arendt. *Eichmann in Jerusalem: A Report on the Banality of Evil*. New York: Penguin, 1994.

Augustine. *The Confessions*. Translated by Henry Chadwick. Oxford: Oxford University Press, 1998.

Jonathan Glover. *Humanity: A Moral History of the Twentieth Century*. New Haven: Yale Nota Bene, 2001.

C.S. Lewis. *The Four Loves*. New York: Harvest, 1971.

Plato. *The Republic*. Translated by G.M.A Grube and C.D.C. Reeve. Indianapolis: Hackett, 1992.

13

The Shawshank Redemption and the Hope for Escape

WILLIE YOUNG

> The soul is the effect and instrument of a political anatomy; the soul is the prison of the body.
>
> — MICHEL FOUCAULT, *Discipline and Punish: The Birth of the Prison*

Institutionalization and Despair

In *The Shawshank Redemption* (1994, directed and screen written by Frank Darabont), one of the most compelling scenes is when Andy Dufresne (Tim Robbins) walks into the prison library, and finds Brooks Hatlen (James Whitmore) with a knife to another prisoner's throat. Brooks, the long-time librarian, is hysterical, threatening to kill Haywood (William Sadler), the other prisoner, for no apparent reason. Everyone is quick to blame Haywood for setting Brooks off. Only afterwards do we learn that Brooks was threatening to kill Haywood because Brooks had been paroled, and would be let out of the prison where he'd spent the past fifty years. If he killed or injured Haywood, he would stay in Shawshank, the world he had come to know.

Shawshank follows Brooks into the outside world and we quickly learn why he had been so afraid of leaving the prison. Whereas he had been the head librarian in the prison, with a position of prestige and learning, on the outside he has no role or identity. He lives on the fringe of society, working as a bagger in a grocery store and staying in a boarding house. Utterly alone, bereft of friends, and without any hope for a future, he takes his own life in despair. His name carved above his hanging body seems to be the only lasting impression he made; suicide appears to be his only way out.

Brooks's despair resonates throughout the film. When Andy asks for a length of rope, the other inmates suspect he too might commit suicide. Red (Morgan Freeman) also appears to contemplate suicide when he is paroled years later and finds himself in Brooks's old room. Red's suicide looks likely because years of institutionalization strip the prisoners of all hope and all sense of who they are. Living in the prison leads one to depend on prison life; the routine, the walls, and one's place in the prison system give one a stable identity in a fixed place that provides security. As Red says, "At first you can't stand those four walls, then you get used to them, then you depend on them, and then you get to love them." The cost of such security is to give up any hope of another life, any memory of another way of being. All one can see beyond the walls is an abyss, where one's life fades into oblivion. Institutionalization produces despair, breaking one's spirit and destroying imagination; in Red's words the courts give you life, and that's what they take. Much as Foucault describes the modern penal system, in Shawshank one is disciplined by the institutional life, such that the soul's despair imprisons the body.

Unbeknownst to him, Brooks's name and identity live on; when Andy founds the prison library, he names it for Brooks. Brooks's library gives generations of inmates the opportunity to learn, acquire degrees, and find new ways of life. It provides them with a way out, and demonstrates that Brooks's life was not ultimately empty or hopeless. He received hope and an enduring legacy through Andy's memory of him. In the face of Shawshank's institutionalization and despair, the story of Andy Dufresne raises interesting questions about how one maintains hope. How does Andy keep his spirit so as to finally escape the prison? And, just as importantly, how do his actions and his story give hope and life to the other inmates, most notably Red?

The Shawshank Redemption, nominated for Best Picture but defeated by *Forrest Gump*, is a particularly striking film for reflecting on the meaning of life, because the institutionalization of the prison can be taken as a metaphor for everyday life. We too depend upon the security of a routine, role, or authority telling us who we are. In the process we may lose the hope for, or imagination of, another way of life. We may give up freedom for the sake of security. Our ways of thinking about the world may imprison us as well. Thus, Andy's story not only gives hope to Red, but also helps us imagine an escape from the institutionalization of modern life. In particular, *The Shawshank Redemption* suggests that hope is something one can have only by giving it to others, and that giving to others in friendship is the way that we can become free. Such freedom, while threatened by the brutality and violence of others, is also threatened by the desire for fantasy and escapism within us. Following the philosophy of Emmanuel Levinas, this essay will explore how, like Andy, we discover who we are, beyond despair and institutions, in responsibility for others.

Escapism and Freedom: Fantasy and Concrete Reality

In describing the effects of institutionalization, *Shawshank* starkly depicts the denigrating, destructive effects of prison life. Under such circumstances, Andy feels he must escape as a way to preserve some shred of humanity. All the same, he is the exception, as most prisoners don't try to escape; like Brooks, many come to depend on the prison environment. The movie's emphasis on institutionalization raises the important question of why prisoners don't escape, or even try, and how they cope with the violence of everyday prison life.

Red is a man who is able to get things; in Stephen King's novella, he says that liquor and cigarettes are the most common requests, along with sexual magazines and tools. Yet, close behind booze and cigarettes, posters, especially pinups, are one of the most common requests. Posters are so popular because they are a form of *escapism*—a fantasy that makes prison livable, by leading inmates to deny the concrete reality around them.

Posters function as a fantasy in several ways. First, they cover, and thus conceal, the concrete wall of the prison that confines an inmate. Second, an inmate sees an object of desire in the poster—in the movie, Rita Hayworth on the wall becomes the object of the inmate's desire. The inmate thereby reinforces, or restores, his desire and identity—which are deeply destabilized, given the frequency of rape and violence in Shawshank. His possession of her reassures him of his agency.

However, there is another side to fantasy. When one fantasizes, one does not want the fantasy to actually come true. As Slavoj Žižek has argued, for the fantasy to become real would bring the fantasy to an end—a possibility which horrifies the subject.[1] The fantasy serves to limit desire, as the desired object *appears* attainable within the fantasy, but is not. If one does not traverse the fantasy, passing through it, one remains confined within it. To fantasize about Rita Hayworth or other unattainable film stars is the safest way to desire, since one's fantasy will never become actual. In this light, it becomes clearer why prison officials don't object to posters in cells—they provide inmates with an escape, so that they *don't* escape. As Red says, "They live with it because they know that a prison is like a big pressure-cooker, and there have to be vents somewhere to let off steam . . . when it's something like posters, they wink. Live and let live."[2] As you dream of a Hollywood starlet, you don't see the hollowness of the prison walls, or the brittle, crumbling concrete that surrounds you. You forget the brutality of the prison, and that your life is reduced to a series of bed checks, labor, and miserable food. The poster and the fantasy effectively function as narcotics. As Red asks, "What harm could the posters cause?" Fantasy mentally imprisons the inmates, enabling their institutionalization to proceed all the more smoothly.

In King's novella, when Andy talks about the poster, its escapist connotations become clear. Red asks him what the poster meant. "Why, they mean the same thing to me as they do to most cons, I guess," says Andy. "Freedom. You look at those pretty women and you feel like you could almost . . . not quite but *almost* . . . step right through and be beside them. Be free."[3] The key, here, is the "almost": in looking at the picture, one can't step through. Fixing one's gaze also fixes one's position,

---

[1] Slavoj Žižek, *Organs Without Bodies: On Deleuze and Consequences* (New York: Routledge, 2004), p. 95.

[2] Stephen King, "Rita Hayworth and the Shawshank Redemption," in *Different Seasons* (New York: Signet, 1983), p. 38.

[3] King, "Rita Hayworth and Shawshank Redemption," pp. 55–56.

preventing freedom. The irony, of course, is that Andy does step right through—using the poster to cover his pick axing through the wall, on a journey that does lead to true freedom. By seeing through the illusion of escapism, Andy is able to really escape.

However, Andy's journey is not easy. To go beyond the fantasy, he must risk his life, crawl through excrement and sewage, and travel to an uncertain future—he doesn't know if the plans he has made will work. Where fantasy enables one to forget the "muck" of everyday life, Andy must immerse himself in it in order to find his way to Zihuatanejo, the city in Mexico he hopes to reach, thus symbolizing his freedom. In addition to traveling through the sewer pipe, he also must drop the concrete from his pants into the prison yard.[4] The plan costs him extensive time in solitary confinement, and he gets his hands dirty managing the warden's money-laundering for many years. He must become a crook to escape from prison. He even gives up his identity, becoming "Peter Stevens" instead of Andy. Freedom, then, is something fearful as well as something precious; the horror and disgust that one feels in watching his struggle for escape convey the fear that accompanies the pursuit of freedom.

Red's journey casts more light on the struggle for freedom. The world, in its bustle and speed, can take a person's identity and certainty from him. Having trained himself to go to the bathroom at a certain time, and only on the permission of his supervisor, Red now must face a world where his habits of action fall apart. The identity he assumed in prison dissolves. On the outside, one becomes invisible, on the margin of society—and Red, like Brooks, contemplates suicide. As Epictetus (55–135 C.E.) and the Stoics (the ancient school of philosophers, most influential from 300 B.C.E. to 200 C.E., who believed virtue was solely concerned with internal action) remind us, suicide is a way out that is always available, but *Shawshank* asks us if there is another path to escape.

The significance of Andy's escape grows when we consider that Rita Hayworth, and the subsequent starlets on his wall, are movie stars. Fantasy is not simply the product of a prisoner's imagination, but is itself created by the surrounding culture. In many ways, movies are *our* form of escapism, as we too have

---

[4] My thanks to Ethan Borg for highlighting this point.

celebrity images plastered on the walls in which we live. Thus, when Andy "steps through" the poster, it raises questions about how we relate to the fantasy posters on our walls. We often talk of going to movies to "get away from everything," or to forget about life for a while—in short, movies become a way to reconcile ourselves to the reality in which we live. Like the inmates, we forget ourselves through film.

Through film, we escape the sedentary routine of everyday life. As Alfred Hitchcock described it, "thriller" movies appeal to us because we desire excitement:

> Our nature is such that we must have these "shake-ups", or we grow sluggish and jellified; but, on the other hand, our civilization has so screened and sheltered us that it isn't practicable to experience sufficient thrills at first hand. So we have to experience them artificially, and the screen is the best medium for this.[5]

The "thrill" of the cinema is experienced at a distance, as we know that we are not really in danger, nor is the actor really in danger as well. What is interesting, here, is that Hitchcock connects thrills with speed. While the world around us is always accelerating, our lives lack thrills—they are devoid of excitement, fear, and passion. Yet, popcorn in hand, we can experience speed and passion, remaining secure in our stadium seating. Escapism helps us to bear our imprisonment, safely experiencing excitement while not really risking anything. One reason we hate the commercials at the beginning of a film is that they *remind* us of our daily imprisonment in a web of commercialization, when the point is to *forget* our imprisonment (how often do we say, "I don't want to see that at the movies— I can just turn the television on if I want to see commercials!" And oh, how we do!)

As horrifying as the solitary confinement, rape, and prisoner abuse are in *The Shawshank Redemption*, they may not be the most terrifying element of the film. Ultimately, we watch and fantasize Andy's journey to freedom. We experience the thrill of escape, while forgetting our lives, and thereby relieving our own

---

[5] Alfred Hitchcock, "Why 'Thrillers' Thrive," quoted in Peter Wollen, "Speed and the Cinema," in *Paris Hollywood: Writings on Film* (New York: Verso, 2002), p. 266.

need for escape. We live freedom vicariously through his action, but most often this escapism simply confirms our place in our social world. As we watch his journey, we remain fixed to our seats. What would it mean, for us to "step through the screen," as Andy steps through the poster? What would it look like, for us to take the journey to freedom that he takes? To answer this question, we need to explore how he embodies and gives hope inside the walls of Shawshank.

Outside the System: Having Hope or Giving Hope

You have to learn how to die—if you want to be alive
— WILCO

When one considers the brutality of *Shawshank*, its popularity is surprising. The film is scathing in its portrayal of the perverse violence of the institution on its inhabitants, stripping them of their humanity and dignity, and leading them to act out this violence on one another. When the guards beat one of the new inmates to death, the inmates don't even want to acknowledge that the inmate had a name, individuality, or personhood. The most horrifying scene is when the warden places Andy in solitary confinement and has Williams killed to keep Andy from having a new trial that would prove his innocence. The warden's actions show that his desire for power demands that he break the prisoners' spirits—as he says on Andy's entry into the prison, "Your ass is mine." Yet his intentional, malicious attempts to break Andy's spirit only concentrate the overall effect of prison life in the film—to unmake the world[6] of each and every prisoner. In the face of prison's brutality, Red tells Andy that hope is "a dangerous thing"—suggesting that forgetting hope is necessary for survival inside the walls. So, what message does the film give us about the nature of hope?

The appeal of *The Shawshank Redemption* lies largely in the hope, and the refusal of institutionalization that enter the prison in the character of Andy. To accept life within the walls, to depend upon them, is ultimately to give up the significance and

---

[6] I borrow this phrase from Elaine Scarry, *The Body in Pain: The Making and Unmaking of the World* (Princeton: Princeton University Press, 1994).

value of one's life. The prison imposes *nihilism*—the reduction of value and life to nothingness, the collapse of the world into an empty void—through its system of institutionalization, brutality, and discipline. In Brooks's suicide, and the constant awareness of this possibility, the film dramatizes how close we are to nothingness. By refusing to become institutionalized, Andy resists this loss of value and life. *Shawshank's* emphasis on escape and hope, as a refusal of this nothingness, takes on a poignant philosophical significance, suggesting a particularly radical way toward thinking about the meaning of life.

To help explicate this, we can turn to the work of Emmanuel Levinas (1906–1995), an influential twentieth-century French and Jewish philosopher. Levinas's work is best known for his emphasis on ethics as "first philosophy"—placing the emphasis of philosophy on ethics, as relation to others, rather than on knowledge or beauty. In a related way, his work deals with the idea of escape, as a form of transcendence that enables real freedom. In the process, however, he suggests a form of freedom very different from what most of us mean by that term.

In an early essay titled "On Escape," Levinas lays out some of the central problems he sees with the ontology (the philosophical investigation of how things exist) of Martin Heidegger, the German existential philosopher and author of *Being and Time* (1889–1976). Heidegger's thought focuses on what he calls the ontological difference—the way that particular beings come into being and pass away, as existence unfolds in the passage of time. In effect, Heidegger argues that we only truly grasp the significance of our being when we recognize that, in the passage of time, we come from and fade into nothingness. We grasp the significance of our being when we live toward our own death, recognizing the finite time that we each have. It is only in knowing our nothingness—the authentic recognition of our temporality—that Heidegger thinks that we can achieve any sort of real freedom.

For Levinas, Heidegger's thought remains fundamentally trapped—imprisoned within the bounds of Being, and thus a form of nihilism. Heidegger ultimately denies the possibility of any relation to God, or the good, or to anyone else that would transcend the nothingness of Being. By arguing that nothingness is the ultimate meaning of our lives, Heidegger questions the meaning of life for Levinas much as the nothingness of prison life problematizes the meaning of life for Andy and his friends in Shawshank. Like Andy, Levinas refuses to accept nihilism. Against Heidegger, he suggests that within ourselves, there is a need that remains unsatisfied—a need that carries us beyond being, breaking up the bounds of being that would confine us. The most basic need, for Levinas, is the need for escape—which is "the fundamental event of our being."[7]

The difficulty, however, is that we often seek to satisfy this need for escape in ways that are self-defeating. The most apparent of these is in our pursuit of pleasure. As Levinas describes it, in pleasure the self becomes ecstatic, losing itself or going outside itself in its pursuit of the object. In the phenomenon of pleasure "there opens something like abysses, ever deeper, into which our existence, no longer resisting, hurls itself."[8] However, while pleasure thus looks like something that carries us out of being, it is, as he says, a "deceptive" escape.

The false escape of pleasure in Levinas's work strongly resembles the escapism of prison life in *The Shawshank Redemption*—fantasy about movie stars, alcohol, drugs, and so on. If we confine ourselves to these forms of escapism, we unwittingly imprison ourselves. Another escape is required.

The question left unanswered in Levinas's essay, however, is what sort of escape from being one could achieve. In his later work, such as *Totality and Infinity*, he argues that it is only in relation to others that real escape, as transcendence, becomes possible. Beyond nihilism and the egocentrism it permits lies responsibility.[9] The central concept for Levinas is "the face" of the other; in seeing the face, I recognize the irreducible uniqueness of the other person. The face thus inspires, or commands, my responsibility for the other, moving me from working for my own enjoyment, to a concern for justice that leads to giving for the other. "Sociality will be a way of escaping being otherwise than through knowledge."[10] My response to the other, in face-to-face relation, gives each

---

[7] Emmanuel Levinas, *On Escape*, translated by Bettina Burgo (Stanford: Stanford University Press, 2003), p. 60.

[8] Levinas, *On Escape*, p. 61.

[9] My thanks to Keith Wilde for helping to highlight this point.

[10] Emmanuel Levinas, *Ethics and Infinity: Conversations with Philippe Nemo*, translated by R. Cohen (Pittsburgh: Duquesne University Press, 1985), p. 61.

of us a unique identity, free from the system, that cannot be taken away.

A similar theme emerges in *Shawshank*, as Andy "escapes" throughout the film precisely by *being for others*. In his responsibility to others, Andy demonstrates a freedom that cannot be destroyed by the prison walls, becoming free by giving hope to others.[11] He finds the purpose of his freedom in giving to and being for the other inmates. His acts of giving give him a sense of identity, discovering his inmost self in giving others their identities. As with Levinas, in a counterintuitive notion, his identity follows from his responsibility.

The most dramatic portrayal of this in the movie is the scene where Andy and his fellow inmates tar the roof. When the prison guard complains about being trapped by the IRS, Andy approaches him, risking a beating or even death (particularly with the provocative question, "Do you trust your wife?"). On telling the guard that if he gives his wife a gift, he can keep the money, Andy then requests beers for his coworkers; as he says, "I think a man working outdoors feels more like a man if he can have a bottle of suds." He gives his co-workers (and, incidentally, the guard) a sense of freedom, the vision of a world in which they are treated like men, rather than brutally reduced to slave labor with their spirits broken; he receives his humanity in giving them theirs (he doesn't partake of the beer that they get[12]). Likewise, when the library receives a gift of records, he puts Mozart on the public address system, and locks the door, giving the whole prison a memory they can carry in their hearts that can't be taken from them. The solitary confinement for this act was, he says, the "easiest time I ever did."

Andy's most important gift, however, is his gift of hope and friendship to Red. Red, over the years, has become a "man who knows how to get things." And, like Brooks, he sees himself as largely defined by this institutional role, forgetting his former harmonica-playing self and ability to get by in the outside world. Isolated and with no identity, in the shadow of Brooks's suicide,

---

[11] Levinas emphasizes that responsibility before the face is an infinite responsibility; we are, in a sense, responsible for others' responsibility. Andy reflects this idea when, though innocent, he takes responsibility for his wife's death.
[12] My thanks to Bill Irwin and Ethan Borg for highlighting this aspect of the scene.

the possibility of Red's taking his own life emerges. However, his friendship with Andy, Andy's dream of Zihuatanejo, and his letter telling Red how to get there, all show Red that the prison cannot capture him. Andy gives him not only a sense of freedom, but something and someone to live for. Andy becomes free precisely in giving others their freedom; through memory and hope, he gives Red the opportunity to respond in friendship and thereby escape the despair of institutionalization.

In light of Andy's story, the distinctiveness of Levinas's position emerges with increased clarity. Next to the escapism of pleasure, and the way out of suicide, another form of escape emerges in responsibility for others. In friendship and responsibility, one's life takes on a significance that does not collapse into nothingness at death. Our actions for others live on in them, much as Brooks's identity lives on in the library after he is gone. Friends, as "other selves," carry us beyond ourselves. There is no guarantee that our lives will have such significance, nor how long such significance can last, but in friendship we can *hope* that such significance endures.[13]

In this light, we can also see how Levinas challenges classical conceptions of freedom. On this view, one is only free in responsibility for others, much as Andy is only free in being for the other inmates. Levinas's understanding of identity is likewise counterintuitive: we only really discover who we are in being for others; there is no prior, stable identity that makes giving to others possible. For Levinas, and in *Shawshank*, one's identity and freedom are never certain, but rather only exist insofar as one relates to others. Andy only is himself, and has hope and freedom, insofar as he gives these to others. As Red says, "Hope is a good thing, maybe the best of things"—and perhaps that is because one only has hope by giving it.

Movies: Escapism, and the Meaning of Life

Since Plato, philosophers have viewed the arts with suspicion. In Plato's *Republic*, Socrates argues that the popular forms of poetry and drama central to Greek culture should be banned, as their emphasis on passion and grief lead away from a life of rea-

---

[13] My thanks to Erich Marks and Joanna Young for helping to develop this point.

son, and depict only an illusory virtue.[14] By contrast, Aristotle argues that tragic drama can play a central part in culture and politics, provided that it is written and performed so as to achieve the appropriate cathartic harmony of the soul, and thus supports the development of virtue.[15] However, overly passionate drama, by unseating reason, is still considered a danger. More recently, Levinas argues that there can be something "wicked and egoist" in artistic enjoyment—"There are times when one can be ashamed of it [art], as of feasting during a plague."[16]

Along with pop music, movies are one of the central artistic forms of our time, playing a role analogous to tragic drama in ancient Athens. Previously, I suggested that movies often serve as a form of escapism, and thus should be viewed with suspicion. Where art creates an illusion that separates us from others, rather than leading to being for others, it can undermine Levinas' idea of responsibility, and make hope impossible. However, does this mean that movies and pop culture should simply be viewed negatively, as destroying the meaning of life?

The Shawshank Redemption tells us otherwise. It does so, first, by giving us the hopeful story of Andy and Red's friendship. But it comments on the importance of movies in more subtle ways as well, most importantly in the scene where Andy asks Red for the Rita Hayworth poster. Red, along with the rest of the inmates, is watching Rita Hayworth in *Gilda* for the fifth time that week. The whole crowd hoots when Hayworth tosses her hair back. The inmates watch the film in what appears to be a chapel, suggesting that film may be a source of salvation. As Mark Kermode writes, "what we see is a picture of men at worship, entranced by the magical light which dances above their heads, momentarily removed from the grim meat-hook realities of Shawshank prison."[17] While the religious overtones are clear,

---

[14] Plato, *The Republic*, Book X, 595–608b, translated by T. Griffith (Cambridge: Cambridge University Press, 2000), pp. 313–330.

[15] Aristotle, *The Poetics*, translated by S. Bernadete and M. Davis (South Bend: St. Augustine's Press, 2002). For this interpretation of catharsis, I follow Jonathan Lear, "Catharsis," in *Essays on Aristotle's Poetics,* edited by A. Rorty (Princeton: Princeton University Press, 1992), pp. 315–340.

[16] Emmanuel Levinas, "Reality and Its Shadow," in *Collected Philosophical Papers*, translated by A. Lingis (Dordrecht: Nijhoff, 1987), p. 12.

[17] Mark Kermode, *The Shawshank Redemption* (London: British Film Institute, 2003), p. 38.

the scene also evokes a 1941 film, *Sullivan's Travels*, which raises deeper questions about the role of movies in our culture and our lives.

Sullivan's Travels is the story of a Hollywood director, John Sullivan (Joel McCrea), who is concerned with making socially responsible films. He wants to make a movie that will deal with issues of poverty, labor, and justice—but Hollywood executives tell him that the films must have romantic interest, and exciting chase scenes in order to have mass appeal (the threat of anti-Communist persecutions lurks in the background as well). While wrestling with this dilemma, Sullivan is mugged, convicted of murder and sentenced to prison. While on a work gang, he and other prisoners are invited to watch a movie in an African-American church. When he sees the audience laughing at the Disney cartoon *Playful Pluto* (1934)—like the Shawshank prisoners hooting at Hayworth in *Gilda*—he realizes that the escape that movies give "isn't much, but it's better than nothing in this cockeyed caravan."[18]

Sullivan's Travels highlights the equivocal nature of art as a form of escape. Hollywood movies help us to forget our troubles—but the troubles are still there. Suffering is only superficially relieved. Whatever deliverance is provided by cinema, it is qualified by the business of movie-making; as Christopher Ames writes, "That the viewers are prisoners [in *Sullivan's Travels*] comments on the ways in which audiences can be imprisoned by what they are shown, which is, in turn, a product of how they are conceived of in Hollywood."[19] When we recognize that *Shawshank* imitates this scene of escapism from *Sullivan's Travels*, we see that its message regarding movies is ambiguous: movies may provide salvation, or they may simply be escapist.[20]

Andy provides an answer to this dilemma: he pursues the arts for the sake of others, to give them the feeling of sublime freedom that the walls would crush. The arts—music, story,

---

[18] *Sullivan's Travels*, directed and written by Preston Sturges, produced by Paul Jones (Paramount 1941). Quoted in Christopher Ames, *Movies About Movies: Hollywood Reflected* (Lexington: University Press of Kentucky, 1997), p. 94.

[19] Ames, *Movies About Movies*, p. 93.

[20] My thanks to Noora Niskanen for the film reference, and several of the points of interpretation in the preceding paragraphs.

movies—can remind us of who we had been, in past times, and help us to imagine a different future so that we may act toward that goal. As *The Marriage of Figaro* plays on the phonograph, the camera sweeps over Shawshank, lifting the audience and the prisoners beyond its walls. When Andy gives Red the harmonica—which could be taken away—he is reminding Red that music touches something in our souls in a way that can never be taken away. Red's reluctance to play shows how deeply the institution has affected him, and that he has almost forgotten himself. And again, Andy tells Red the story of Zihuatanejo, to give him something to hope for—another life, and a place in which Red would be valued as Andy's friend beyond the confines of the prison. This story is crucial: it is the one thing that propels Andy through his final trials in prison and gives Red hope, so that he buys a compass in the pawnshop rather than a gun to end his life or send him back to Shawshank. Here, the movies, music, and stories by which we detach ourselves from the chains of reality become the bonds that cement the friendships between the inmates, tying Andy to others even after he has flown the coop.

So, as we face the institutionalization of daily life, which imprisons us in routines and established patterns of thought, what does it mean for us that Andy steps right through the poster to freedom? Movies, art, and music can give us hope, helping us to see beyond the illusory confines of our lives—but only if we see through *their* illusions. Such illusions are necessary, as they give us material for weaving friendships and histories that bind us together. Through them, we can find a freedom, identity, and escape in our relations to others. But we cannot depend on the arts to give us this escape. Ultimately, like Andy, we must recognize that "salvation lies within"—within ourselves and with one another.[21]

---

[21] My thanks to the following friends and family, without whose insights and suggestions I could not have written this essay: Kim Blessing, Bill Irwin, Noora Niskanen, Ethan Borg, Erich Marks, Joanna Young, Bill Young, Keith Wilde, Ajit Jagdale, Jonathan DeCarlo, and of course Melissa Sherman.

To Think About

1. *Shawshank* presents Andy as a character who gives hope to others. What are some ways that Andy receives hope from others, and that they contribute to his actions? How does this complicate the message of the film?

2. Are there ways of being for others that do not give hope or freedom? Can you come up with examples from the film of how characters are for others, in ways that deprive them of their identity, rather than restoring it? What, in your view, distinguishes hopeful ways of being for others from these more destructive ways of being for others? Use Andy as an example to explicate the difference. (My thanks to Keith Wilde for helping to develop this question.)

3. While *Shawshank* is about faith, hope, and love (or friendship), it is often critical of religion. What are some of the ways that the film is critical of religion? Given this, what do you take to be its message about where we can find faith and hope?

To Read Next

Stephen King. Rita Hayworth and Shawshank Redemption, in *Different Seasons* (New York: Signet, 1983).

Emmanuel Levinas. *On Escape*. Translated by Bettina Burgo. Stanford: Stanford University Press, 2004.

Emmanuel Levinas. *Ethics and Infinity: Conversations with Philippe Nemo*. Translated by Richard A. Cohen. Pittsburgh: Duquesne University Press, 1985.

14

The Roar and the Rampage: A Tale of Revenge in *Kill Bill, Volumes 1 and 2*

SHAI BIDERMAN

> Revenge is a kind of wild justice, which the more man's nature runs to, the more ought law to weed it out
>
> — FRANCIS BACON

> Revenge is in your soul: wherever you bite, there arises a black scab; with revenge, your poison makes the soul giddy.
>
> — FRIEDRICH NIETZSCHE

Socrates proclaimed that "the unexamined life is not worth living." Even if we agree with Socrates, we want more than merely to exist and reflect upon our existence. We also insist that our lives be meaningful. The quest for a meaningful life can start off as something vague and general. It becomes concrete once we come up with a plan for getting what we want out of life. Coming up with such a life plan involves defining a set of goals, which in turn involves determining the principles that will guide our conduct in our quest to obtain those goals.

The heroine of Quentin Tarantino's *Kill Bill, Volumes 1 and 2* (played by Uma Thurman) knows what she wants out of life. She's a contract killer, a mercenary, who finds meaning through her life's vocation, which consists of murdering at the behest of her operator and lover, Bill (played by David Carradine), the undisputed leader of the Deadly Viper Assassination Squad. Operating under the pseudonym "the Black Mamba," she goes about exterminating people in the skilful manner of a professional. That is, until she finds out that she is pregnant.

This discovery causes her to change her life. Now she wants to focus her energy on being a good mother. She leaves Bill and his band of mercenaries, moves to El Paso, Texas, and answers to the name of Arlene Machiavelli. Living in El Paso, her life's ambition is to create a nest for her future daughter. Her jilted lover Bill cannot forgive her for having deserted him, and sets out to find her. He finally tracks her down and shows up in the midst of the rehearsal for her wedding to Tommy, a local record-shop owner. After a short encounter between Arlene and Bill, Bill's "assassination squad" shows up. They embark upon what the local newspapers later refer to as "the massacre at Two Pines," or "the El Paso wedding massacre," in which Tommy, the priest and his wife, friends, family, and the organ player are all slaughtered.

Arlene, the former "Black Mamba," miraculously survives the massacre. She is brought to the hospital in a coma, still wearing her bridal dress, which leads the local sheriff to refer to her as "the Bride." After four years in a coma, the bride wakes up. Needless to say, she is no longer pregnant; instead she has a metal shield inside her head. Her old mercenary lifestyle takes on new meaning: to settle the score with her former allies in Bill's murderous squad, and kill them one by one. From this point forward, the movie follows her vengeful and bloody reckoning, which lasts for over four hours, separated into two movies, *Volume 1* and *Volume 2*. The saga ends with Bill's inevitable slaughter, and the Bride's emotional reunion with her long-lost daughter, whom she has believed, up to that point, to be dead. In the course of this lengthy ordeal, the Bride's real name is made known: Beatrix Kiddo.

As a rule, whenever a movie character has multiple names, it indicates an identity crisis. Beatrix Kiddo is no exception. She's torn between competing life goals and aspirations, each of which make different claims on her identity, which then supply her life with different meanings. Is Beatrix Kiddo really the devastating Black Mamba? Or is she Arlene Machiavelli, Tommy's cute wife from the local record-shop? Or is she the "bride," whose only concern is to be a good mother?

Tarantino offers us no clear answers. For him we aren't dealing with an evolving character who matures with the story's progression, but rather with a character torn between competing identities, and conflicting meanings. (It's for that reason that the plot doesn't unfold chronologically, and the "chapters" of the movies end up being muddled). Despite the character's obvious anguish, there is one endeavor that remains constant throughout her many incarnations. It is Beatrix Kiddo's violent and bloody search for revenge. So now "the unavenged life is not worth living." But is this enough? Can a life devoted to the search for revenge be meaningful?

That Woman Deserves Her Revenge: A Tale of Private Satisfaction

Before going any further, we should say a little more about what revenge is. Revenge, or vengeance, arises when one party inflicts pain or injury on another. This pain, often accompanied by humiliation, gives rise to wrath and hatred felt by the injured party who is in the position of victim. When the victim expresses his grievance, he will generally claim that he wants "to get back at" or "get even" with the perpetrator of the original violent act. The victim might act against the perpetrator in order to obtain relief or satisfaction, which would in some way redress the original harm.

Let's say, for example, that my friend James offended his friend Lisa when he stood her up on their first date, and that hurt her immensely. Wanting to rid herself of the hurt, or pain, and replace it with a sense of relief or satisfaction, Lisa finds James's BMW and rips off the antenna. For Lisa, the expression on James's face when he found his damaged Beamer was worth everything. Lisa has attained her goal—she has been avenged. Just as she was humiliated by James, so now James is likewise humiliated. This example suggests that revenge involves a relationship in which the victim extracts retribution from the perpetrator, which results in a sense of satisfaction and restoration of justice. But are vengeance and retribution the same thing?

Contemporary philosopher Robert Nozick (1938–2002) distinguishes between revenge and retribution as follows. First, retribution calls for a punishment that is normatively thought to complement the seriousness of the wrong; whereas in revenge the punishment is as great or as minimal as the perception of the wrong by the victim. Second, while the agent of retribution need not have special or personal ties to the victim of the wrongdoing for which he exacts retribution, revenge is personal. Third, retribution has no emotional component, while revenge involves a particular emotional tone, pleasure, and satisfaction in the suffering of another. Last, retribution is systematic. All similar acts would be met with the same punishment. In contrast, revenge need not be universal. Not only is the avenger not committed to avenging any similar act done to anyone; he is not committed to avenging all wrongs done to him.[1]

Unlike some writers, Nozick believes that revenge and retribution are mutually exclusive; he does not see revenge as a form of retribution. Revenge, according to Nozick, is natural, limitless, personal, and emotional. Kiddo can take her revenge on Bill by killing him. She can just as well avenge herself by humiliating him, or by inflicting on him whatever she'll find gratifying. She can kill hundreds of black-robed warriors in a Japanese dance club, and she can spare the life of the last one of them as a didactic statement. The extent of Kiddo's revenge depends wholly on Kiddo's understanding of the injustice done to her. The severity of the punishment reflects Kiddo's understanding of reasonable punishment for her attempted assassination, the murder of her soon-to-be-husband and unborn child, and for 'stealing' four years of her life.

Having seen the movie, we understand Kiddo's sense of just deserts, including the killing of Nurse Buck (who, we learn, repeatedly raped her when she was comatose in the hospital) and stealing his car; the killing of her ex-partner Vernita Green (A.K.A. Cobra-head, played by Vivica A. Fox) in front of her daughter; the massacre of O-Ren Ishii (played by Lucy Liu) and her army; tearing out Elle Driver's (A.K.A. California Mountain Snake, played by Daryl Hannah) eye; and finally the killing of Bill. In Kiddo's case, we may assume that satisfaction and a sense of restored justice are attained. But how can we understand the meaningfulness of these acts of revenge, acts private and specific to Kiddo?

---

[1] Robert Nozick. *Philosophical Explanations*. (Cambridge: Harvard University Press, 1982), pp. 366–68.

There's Nothing Sadistic in My Actions:
Freud and the Vindictive Drive

Sigmund Freud, the founder of psychoanalysis, assumed that human behavior could be mapped, categorized, and explained. Those behaviors that seem unique to one person in fact exist in all of us. It was his contention that these behavioral patterns, common to all human beings, are motivated by drives and needs, the most basic of which are hunger, sex, and the fear of death.

When we suppress these drives and needs, we inhibit them, and curtail their immediate gratification. Consistent suppression of these drives and needs, and their sublimation into moderated alternatives, is what allows the child to enter the functional life cycle of adulthood. Adulthood thus depends on the sublimation of such drives. A drive that has not been sublimated, in other words a drive that remains primordial, wild, unrestrained, and necessitating immediate gratification, is either the remnant of a childish behavioral imprint, or else symptomatic of neurotic behaviour, or in the worst case, of psychotic behaviour.[2]

Towards the end of *Volume 2*, there is a scene that depicts Kiddo's return to Mexico to meet Esteban (Michael Parks), who is referred to as Bill's "first father figure." The presentation of Esteban as a father figure echoes the Freudian theory of drives and needs, and provides an interpretation of how this theory shapes the concepts of justice and vengeance within different individuals. In Bill's case, we need to understand his violent childhood, his love for movies and icons, and his weakness for blonde women. If we can understand the circumstances of his upbringing, we can understand the way his drives were nourished and what motivates him. Most importantly, we can understand his response when he learns that Kiddo—his protégé, confidant, lover, and mother of his future daughter—is about to marry another man.

According to Freud, each person's early childhood holds the key to his current behavior. Can we assume that Kiddo's past also holds the key to understanding her present actions?

---

[2] See Joseph Reppen, ed., *Beyond Freud: A Study of Modern Psychoanalytic Theorists* (Hillsdale.: Analytic Press, 1985), pp. 212–300; see also Anthony Storr, *Freud* (Oxford and New York: Oxford University Press, 1989).

Moreover, can we say that Kiddo's past provides a context within which her acts of revenge are meaningful? According to Freud the answer to both these questions is "yes." Kiddo's actions cannot be understood in a void, but must be analysed in the context of her past experience, which inevitably reflects her internal drives and needs.

Freud's theory helps to understand why most people, when feeling they were unjustly hurt, would seek revenge. In our previous example, Lisa's need for revenge may be satisfied with breaking James's car antenna, while Kiddo's need for revenge requires the killing of the offender, Bill. Despite the supposedly universal urge for revenge suggested by Freud, we are still unable to evaluate the specific and unique acts of revenge performed by different people.

To complicate matters further, what at first seems to one person like justified revenge may later appear to the same person as unjustified. This is reflected in the relationship between Beatrix Kiddo and Elle. Elle, otherwise known as "California Mountain Snake" (another 'snake' in Bill's collection), is Kiddo's nemesis. Like Kiddo before her, she was sent to study martial arts with the Chinese master Pai Mei. Unlike Kiddo, who became a devoted follower of the grandmaster and obtained life-saving knowledge, Elle insulted the master who in response tore out one of her eyes. Elle has the same long blond hair as Kiddo, which makes her desirable to Bill, given his weakness for women with bright hair, yet Bill always preferred Kiddo. For these reasons Elle feels injured by Kiddo and seeks revenge. Kiddo, on the other hand, seeks revenge from Elle for her participation in the murder of Beatrix's fiancé and the attempt on her life.

Twice, in the middle of *Volume 1*, and in the middle of *Volume 2*, Elle attempts to kill Kiddo. In both cases, she suspends her attempts, not on account of a technical hitch—such as inadequate resources—but because at that moment she does not feel her acts would satisfy her sense of justice, nor quench her thirst for revenge. In her first attempt, Elle dresses up as a nurse and whistles her way to Kiddo's hospital bed. She is carrying a syringe loaded with enough poison to kill Kiddo. However seconds before administering Kiddo this dose of lethal poison, she decides (following a phone call from Bill) not to administer the poison to the unconscious Kiddo. A more satisfying experience of revenge would be achieved if Kiddo were aware of what was happening at the moment of revenge. Elle aborts her current attempt on Kiddo's life, but not her attempt to extract revenge. She still seeks revenge but she is determined to wait for better circumstances in which her desire for revenge would be better satisfied.

Elle's next opportunity arises when she finds out that Kiddo has been buried alive by Bud (Michael Madson), Bill's brother. She arrives at Bud's house where the following conversation takes place:

> **BUDD:** So, which "R" are you filled with?
>
> **ELLE:** What?
>
> **BUDD:** They say the number one killer of old people is retire-ment. People got a job to do; they tend to live a little bit longer so they can do it. I've always figured those war-riors and their enemies share the same relationship. So now that you're not gonna have to face your enemy no more on the battlefield, which "R" ya filled with? Relief or regret?
>
> **ELLE:** A little bit of both.
>
> **BUDD:** Horseshit. I'm sure you do feel a little bit of both. But I know damn well that you feel one more than you feel the other. And the question was: which one is it?
>
> **ELLE:** Regret.

Immediately after this encounter, she arranges for a black mamba to bite Bud, killing him. Over his death groans, Elle delivers a speech in which she informs him that her only regret is that Kiddo didn't get the death she deserved, but instead got to be killed by a low-life such as him. As Budd is taking his last breath, she discovers why the desired "R" is not *relief* (an expected result of a successful revenge) but *regret*.

Elle experiences regret because she does not feel that Kiddo got the death she deserved. Elle's justice "in the eye of the beholder" depends directly on her own view of the world. In an ironic twist, upon their next meeting, Kiddo snatches out Elle's remaining eye, thus depriving her of her sight and satis-fying at least on a symbolic level Elle's need for revenge. There is no more "eye of the beholder," hence there is no view of the world; so Elle need not worry anymore that her revenge won't be satisfactory.

The ever changing dynamic of revenge between Elle and Kiddo demonstrates the personal nature of revenge. In a Freudian reality, one point of view is not preferable to another because the sense of worthiness is private and subjective. Our argument so far leads to the conclusion that the inherently personal nature of revenge contradicts any notion of social dialogue on this issue. Nonetheless, our search for the meaning in seeking revenge must not come to an end here. Between these two polarities there must exist an area of shared ideas, which allows us to relate to identify with a desire for revenge.

A Kind of Wild Justice: The Normative Meaning of Revenge

The need for shared common ground as an immanent precondition for the determination of meaning is considered in depth by the philosopher Thomas Hobbes (1588–1679). For Hobbes a social-normative framework is a necessity since in its absence we are in a state Hobbes terms "the natural condition," a state that does not allow any sort of meaningful existence.

The natural condition is a chaotic mode, a "war of every man against every man" (bellum omnium contra omnes). The autonomous man is in constant struggle against his surroundings in a sphere devoid of any form of justice or government. In this state man's basic nature dominates, a basic nature, that according to Hobbes, is impulsive, animalistic, dynamic, and motivated by a constant need to gratify needs. Ultimately, in his natural condition, man will be driven to extinction since he ignores the (identical) needs of those surrounding him. In such a natural world, if it were possible, revenge would be taken exactly as Freud described it: a primal and animalistic aggregate of deterministic responses, uninhibited, but incapable of granting any meaning to human existence.

The "natural condition" is thus no solution. In spite of its natural charm (there is something very seductive in this "natural freedom" even in Freud's description of it), it must be abandoned if we are to continue existing. Hobbes's suggested solution to this impossible situation of constant war is the Social Contract:

> that a man be willing, when others are so too, as far forth as for peace and defence of himself he shall think it necessary, to lay

down this right to all things; and be contented with so much liberty against other men as he would allow other men against himself.[3]

The Social Contract takes into account the inevitability of giving up some rights in order to create a contractual relationship for the benefit of social order.

It is only within this framework, and not the private natural sphere that it is possible to speak of a meaningful revenge. Tarantino is well aware of this framework. In an interview he gave long before he directed the *Kill Bill* saga he said:

> As far as I'm concerned, if you're going to make a revenge movie, you've got to let the hero get revenge. There's purity in that. So you set it up: the lead guy gets screwed over. And then you want to see him kill the bad guys-with his bare hands, if possible . . . the minute you kill your bad guy by having him fall on something, you should go to movie jail. You've broken the law of good cinema.[4]

What Tarantino is saying here is that in order to make a revenge movie, you have to abide by the genre's rules. Moreover, those watching a revenge movie need to know that they are doing so, that is they have to have the ability to recognize such a film. They need to be able to identify the avenging hero, to identify the object of revenge, to differentiate between the avenging hero and the villain, to identify with the hero's suffering, and to internalize his sense of justice. The spectators need to be equipped with a set of shared tools that enables them to decipher the film in the appropriate manner. This set of tools, as Hobbes informs us, needs to be accessible to all in order to award meaning to shared endeavors.

The movie *Kill Bill* resonates with Hobbes's ideas in a manner that answers our first question, "Can revenge be meaningful?" in the affirmative. Tarantino has made a genre film with a typical, or indeed an archetypical avenging hero. Kiddo is a super-heroine—Bill even compares her to superman. The movie reaffirms our common understanding of the rules of the genre. Through the slow revelation of Kiddo's inner self (represented

---

[3] Thomas Hobbes, *Leviathan* (Oxford: Blackwell, 1957), Chapter 6.
[4] *Harper's* (August 1994), p. 22.

in her various names) Tarantino seduces the viewer to sympathize with Kiddo's pain and relate to her revenge, and in so doing he reminds us over and over again that the understanding of the desire for revenge is common to all of us. Tarantino's open exploration of the social understanding of revenge is apart from any legal or political discussion we might want to have about the best ways to regulate human conduct, and is thus artistically valid.

Freud is right to say that we are all driven, by our very natures, to avenge our injuries, yet living in the world of Hobbes's Social Contract, we have given up our right to take revenge in our own lives, at least in an unlimited way. Once in a while, however, we can acknowledge our primordial impulses, buried beneath layer upon layer of cultural mores. For moments such as these *Kill Bill* was created.

Tarantino invites us, with all due respect, to drag our feet into the darkness of a movie theatre and there, with a jumbo popcorn and super-sized soda, share in Kiddo's forbidden revenge. In so doing, we may relinquish our need to experience such extremes of vengefulness in our own lives.[5]

---

[5] Many thanks to Eliana Jacobowitz, Gideon Freudenthal, Ornan Rotem, and Orna Ben-Naftali.

To Think About

1. What's the difference between a criminal trial and an act of revenge? Are they mutually exclusive responses to an event? Can revenge be considered among the purposes of a criminal trial?

2. Gandhi has famously claimed that "an eye for an eye makes the whole world blind". What did he mean? Was he right?

3. What is the difference between revenge and resentment? Which of them is more dangerous in the long term?

4. How does one psychologically overcome the desire for revenge? Is forgiveness the only way to forgo the vindictive passions, or are there other, perhaps less morally ambitious ways to do so.

To Read Next

Francis Bacon. *The Essays or Counsels, Civil and Moral.* Edited with introduction and commentary by Michael Kiernan. Cambridge, Massachusetts: Harvard University Press, 1985.

Peter A. French. *The Virtues of Vengeance.* Lawrence: University of Kansas Press, 2001.

Thomas Hobbes. *Leviathan.* Edited with an introduction by Michael Oakeshott. Oxford: Blackwell, 1957.

Susan Jacoby. *Wild Justice: The Evolution of Revenge.* New York: Harper and Row, 1983.

Jerome Neu, ed. *The Cambridge Companion to Freud.* Cambridge: Cambridge University Press, 1991.

Robert Nozick. *Philosophical Explanations.* Cambridge, Massachusetts: Harvard University Press, 1982.

Take Five

How Should I Live My Life?

15

Pleasantville, Aristotle, and the Meaning of Life

ERIC REITAN

A Black-and-White Utopia?

With the help of a magical remote, David—a teen disillusioned by his life at the end of the twentieth century—escapes into his television set, dragging his sister Jennifer with him into an imaginary 1950s TV sit-com utopia. They find themselves thrust into the roles of Bud and Mary Sue, two wholesome teenagers growing up in the wholesome town of Pleasantville.

Thus begins *Pleasantville*, a richly-textured fantasy that dramatically plays out the clash of conflicting American values on a stage that gradually shifts from shades of gray to vibrant color. At the start of the film, Pleasantville is a literally black-and-white world where social and family roles are clearly defined, lives are framed by predictable routines, and the problems that exist can be neatly solved in half an hour. It is a world without divorce, without drugs, without teen pregnancy, homelessness, or violent crime. Since there is never a fire, the fire department exists solely for the purpose of rescuing cats from trees. In Pleasantville, clashing worldviews are unknown: every conflict is rooted in some temporary failure to remember the rules of polite behavior. The desperate cry of human anguish is missing, replaced by the cheerful hello. All is, in a word, pleasant. Unremittingly so.

As we watch the film, two paradoxical truths become increasingly apparent: first, Pleasantville has none of the problems that we tend to regard as impediments to happiness; second, David

213

and his sister have not landed in a world that anyone would really want to *live* in. While the film has numerous messages, the most important, perhaps, is this: a well-ordered life free from overt difficulties is not necessarily a life worth living. But what *does* make a life worth living? Put another way, what gives *meaning* to a human life? If we study the film carefully, we find an answer that, in many respects, resonates with the answer offered by the ancient philosopher Aristotle.

The Meaning of Color

The two displaced protagonists in the film bring conflicting perspectives to bear on the black-and-white world they find themselves in. David, who longs for a sense of belonging and security, sees Pleasantville as a utopian refuge, and, at least initially, is determined to see that it is preserved from any disruptive influences. The chief disruption he fears comes from Jennifer, who promptly renames the town "Nerdville" and complains bitterly about being thrust into this world just when everything in her life is going right: "I was getting really popular. Debbie Russell had transferred to another school, and my skin was really *great* since March. Mark Davis was finally starting to come around . . ." Pleasantville represents for her all the establishment values that, according to the rebel-cool image she seeks to cultivate, are worthy of nothing but contempt.

And so, in the name of being cool, she rebels. Her initial rebellion—carried out in a car on Lover's Lane with the captain of the high school basketball team—sparks a radical transformation of the town, shattering old patterns and ushering in a wave of conflict and changed relationships. With every change comes a splash of color, beginning with a single rose and gradually spreading to the people and places in the town. And Jennifer herself is not immune from this wave of change. As Pleasantville finds new life amidst the conflict of questioned values and changing relationships, Jennifer finds new life—and color—in books and academic study.

The spread of color through the town is met with sad bewilderment and confusion by some, with fierce resistance by others. Resistance becomes intolerance, which in turn becomes persecution. Signs appear in shop windows boldly proclaiming, "No Coloreds." As the infection of color spreads, persecution gives way to violence in the streets, as black-and-white mobs harass their colored neighbors and vandalize the newly colorful soda shop.

But the wave of color, once started, is unstoppable. By the end of the film Pleasantville is utterly transformed. It has become a messier place, a more unpredictable and dangerous place. Less pleasant, certainly—but also far more alive.

Pleasantville is a film about many things: the clash between community harmony and individual expression, the dynamics of social intolerance, the dangers of utopian ideals. But the spread of color is the symbolic heart of the film. And while the spreading colors are clearly linked to change and to emotional engagement with the world, color represents neither of these things alone—for not every change brings a wash of color, nor does every burst of emotion.

Jennifer is the key to understanding this symbolic significance of color in the film. At one point, as those around her are becoming colored while Jennifer remains stubbornly black-and-white, she expresses her confusion to her brother. As other teens begin to explore their sexuality, they burst into color. Why not Jennifer? "I've had, like, *ten times* as much sex as the rest of these girls!" she exclaims.

The answer, as David notes, is that color does not come just from having sex. Nor does it come merely from indulging one's passions in defiance of established norms. Jennifer refuses to be bound by the town's mores, indulging her desires without concern for stodgy rules—and yet, although her rebellion sparks others to become awash in color, she herself remains drearily black-and white. Her transformation comes only after she leaves behind her old rebel-cool script in favor of a night immersed in study and reading literature.

One might be tempted to say that color comes from this sort of change: abandoning old scripts in favor of new patterns. But change as such is not the hero of this story. When the angry mob shatters the colorful reclining nude painted on the window of the soda shop, when they burst through the shattered window and tear the soda shop apart, they have abandoned their old script of pleasant propriety. And yet they remain colorless. It is not change that brings color, but rather *meaningful* change. It is not passion *as such* that brings a rosy glow to pasty gray skin, but rather the passion that comes with living a *meaningful life*.

The Meaning of "a Meaningful Life"

But what, then, gives meaning to the lives of Pleasantville's inhabitants? To answer this question, we must step back and consider what we are asking. What do we mean by the phrase, "a meaningful life"? The quick answer is that, by "meaning", we mean "purpose." A meaningful life is one lived with purpose. This is surely right, at least in part. But more needs to be said.

In an essay scathingly attacking what he takes (wrongly, I think) to be the Christian understanding of the meaning of life, Kurt Baier offers a valuable distinction between two senses in which a life can be said to have purpose—what he calls "the purpose *of* life" and "purpose *in* life."[1] In the former, my life has a purpose if I am part of a cosmic order in which I have a designated role to fill—a role assigned me, perhaps, by God. Baier disparages this sort of "cosmic purpose" as unworthy of human dignity and autonomy, because it relegates humans to the status of mere cogs in a machine. To have a purpose in the cosmic sense, he says, is to be nothing more than a tool.

And yet even as he disparages cosmic purpose he insists that our lives *can* possess an uplifting sort of meaning, because there can still be a purpose *in* our lives even if there is no purpose *of* life. To have a purpose *in* life is to live in a goal-directed way— to set goals for ourselves and take action to pursue those goals. Purpose in this sense is consistent with our human dignity because it is generated by our own free choices about what goals to pursue. Thus, we can have a meaningful life even if there is no grand cosmic order. Our lives are meaningful, according to Baier, when we pursue goals that we have chosen for ourselves. This is basically an existentialist understanding of meaning: the meaning of a human life is determined entirely by the free choices of the person who lives it.

I suspect it is right to say that "cosmic purpose" is unworthy of us.[2] The writers of *Pleasantville* seem to agree. When David returns home from his adventures in Pleasantville, he finds his mother weeping at the kitchen table. She is weeping because

---

[1] Kurt Baier, "The Meaning of Life," in *Philosophy: Contemporary Perspectives on Perennial Issues,* fourth edition, edited by E.D. Klemke, A. David Kline, and Robert Hollinger (New York: St. Martin's Press, 1994), pp. 378–388.

[2] Although I am not convinced that his understanding of "cosmic purpose" is the only credible one.

she has lost what she had thought was the perfect life: the right home, the right car, the right husband. Everything had been, for one brief moment, the way it was supposed to be. But then it all fell apart (presumably with the end of her marriage). David listens with sympathy, and then utters what seems to be the moral of the movie: "Maybe there isn't a way things are *supposed to be*."

With these words, David is clearly rejecting the idea of a cosmic purpose, of some script for how life should be lived. And yet it also seems clear that David is not, in the same breath, denying the possibility of a meaningful life. What David has learned from his sojourn in Pleasantville is that meaning is found in something other than blindly following a scripted role.

Is the lesson of *Pleasantville*, then, the existentialist one offered by Baier?

I suspect not. While *Pleasantville* rejects cosmic purpose as the source of meaning, the positive alternative portrayed in the film is richer than Baier's. Baier seems to think that *any* purpose I choose for myself can give meaning to my life. But is this right? Imagine the man who, upon winning the lottery, sets as his life goal to watch television eighteen hours every day while consuming more beer than has ever before been consumed. Let's suppose that this man is highly intelligent and has an exquisite baritone singing voice—and that prior to winning the lottery he was considering a career in music education. But now, instead, he directs all of his financial resources towards the purchase of beer, and then proceeds to sit in front of the TV all his waking hours, slamming six-packs. He never sings, never uses his intellect, never engages others in conversation. He never falls in love, never has an enduring relationship with another human being. He just sits there and drinks, day after day, until finally he is found dead on the sofa from liver failure. By the number of empty beer cans piled around the sofa, there is good reason to believe that he succeeded in attaining the goal he set for himself. Would we say that this man has lived a *meaningful* life? Or would we be more inclined to call his life *wasted*?

And why is that? The reason is very similar to Baier's reason for disparaging "cosmic purpose" as a source of meaning: any purpose that is simply *handed to us* by the cosmic order (or by God) does not do justice to one of the most significant human properties—our capacity to make choices for ourselves,

undetermined by some blueprint for "the way things are supposed to be." Philosophers call this capacity *autonomy*. In a
life lived according to a cosmic purpose, our autonomy is
entirely irrelevant and may even be an impediment. But this
same underlying reasoning would render any number of
autonomously chosen purposes unworthy of our humanity as
well.

When we ask about the meaning of life, we are asking about
the meaning of *human* life—that is, a life characterized by certain distinctive properties such as rationality, creativity, and
autonomy. To say that a human life is meaningful is to say, in
effect, that these distinctive human powers are *of value* in that
life—that they are not simply allowed to rot, so to speak, but are
instead actively cultivated and used to their potential. A purpose
that makes our distinctive human abilities irrelevant is not just
unworthy of our humanity—it gives no *meaning* to our humanity. We might ask, "If my purpose is just to carry out some role
assigned to me in the cosmic order, then what is the function of
my autonomy? Why be autonomous at all?" Given such a purpose, a fundamental aspect of our humanity has no role, no relevance, no significance. In such a life, the *fullness of our
humanity* is squandered. But the very same thing can be said of
the beer-drinker's life, even though his purpose was
autonomously chosen. What we need in order to give life meaning is a purpose that fully engages our humanity.

Of course, that's not quite enough. Each of us is different,
with distinctive talents and abilities. What gives meaning to my
life can therefore be more precisely characterized as a purpose
that does not merely engage my humanity fully, but engages *me*
fully—in all my distinctness. A meaningful life is one lived
according to an autonomously chosen purpose that *engages my
powers* and *challenges me to actualize my potential*.

The point is this: While my choices play a vital role in giving
meaning to my life, not every choice I make will confer meaning. I can make bad or misguided choices that leave me feeling
as if my life has been, in a word, wasted. What makes for a bad
choice is determined by my human and individual nature—a
nature that renders some choices unworthy of who and what I
am. And this is why we regard the beer-drinker's life as wasted.
Had the lottery winner used his newfound financial freedom to
pursue his interests in music rather than sit on the couch and

drink, he would have done something meaningful with the money, and hence with his life. But instead, he pursued a goal that made no use of any of his talents, that rendered his unique abilities utterly irrelevant. The life that he chose to lead could as easily have been lived by a person with none of his talents—in fact, it could as easily have been lived by a pig.

Aristotle and the Flourishing Human Life

This view of what makes life meaningful is deeply indebted to the thought of the ancient philosopher Aristotle. Aristotle does not directly address the question of what gives meaning to life. His focus is on what makes for a *flourishing* human life. But his answer is clearly tied to the issue of meaning. For Aristotle, as human beings we flourish only when we actualize our potential.[3] Furthermore, we are animals characterized by a distinctive power that separates us from all other animals: the power of reason. We fully actualized our potential, then, only when we use this power and use it well—only when we become excellently rational.[4] Put another way, we flourish only when the things that make us human have a meaningful role to play in our lives.

In short, we flourish when our lives are meaningful in the sense spelled out above: To flourish is to live in a purposive way, where the purposes we live for are ones that fully engage and express who we are, as characterized by our most central talents and abilities. So long as Jennifer ignored her intellectual gifts in the quest to be cool, there was an important part of who she was that played no part in her life. When she discovered the joys of reading and academic study, she discovered a purpose that engaged her talents, that gave them a meaningful place in her life. Aristotle's philosophy holds that with such greater meaning comes greater personal fulfillment.

While Aristotle has nothing against pleasure—in fact, he thinks that the flourishing human life will be pleasant in many

---

[3] The Greek term used by Aristotle, translated as "flourishing" here, is *eudaimonia*—usually translated as "happiness." I think "flourishing" better captures Aristotle's intent, given the ambiguity of "happiness."

[4] See *Nicomachean Ethics* (from now on referred to as *NE*), Book I, Chapter 7, especially 1097b–1098a.

ways—pleasure is not the essence of a flourishing life. Only some pleasures are worth having—namely, those pleasures that come with living as fully actualized human beings.[5] We become self-actualized in two ways: first, by cultivating our intellects (what Aristotle calls *intellectual* virtue); second, by cultivating our emotional dispositions and desires so that they reflect and accord with reason (what Aristotle calls *moral* virtue).[6] In his discussion of moral virtue, it becomes clear that the flourishing life is neither self-indulgent nor self-denying. We do not flourish by simply doing whatever we want, nor do we flourish by suppressing our desires. Rather, we flourish when we cultivate the right kinds of desires—namely rational desires.[7] Even those who disagree with Aristotle's fixation on *reason* as the distinctive human power might nevertheless accept this general point: to flourish as a human being requires that we actualize our potential as a human being—which means that we cultivate and make use of our distinctive human powers in some goal-directed way, and have emotions and desires that both energize and achieve satisfaction from this very process of self-actualization.[8]

Put briefly, we flourish when we do something with our lives that we care about doing and that challenges us to achieve more than we thought we could. This is the aspect of Aristotle's thought that I think is mirrored especially well in *Pleasantville*.

---

[5] *NE*, Book I, Chapter 8, especially 1099a; and Book X, Chapter 5, especially 1176a.

[6] *NE*, Book I, Chapter 13.

[7] *NE*, Book II, Chapter 6.

[8] Stuart Hampshire, for example, has endorsed Aristotle's general principle about human flourishing while maintaining that Aristotle was too narrow in characterizing what is distinctive in human nature. For Hampshire, what distinguishes humanity is not reason narrowly conceived, but rather our endlessly inventive ability to express thoughtfulness in varied activities and ways of life—from the sporting arena to the music hall. We do not need to go to college or master the nuances of an academic discipline in order to live a life that makes rich use of our distinctive human powers. For Hampshire, while a meaningful human life must cultivate and express the human capacity for *thoughtfulness*, this capacity is paired with a creativity that allows thoughtfulness to manifest itself in many ways. See Stuart Hampshire, *Innocence and Experience* (Cambridge, Massachusetts: Harvard University Press, 1989), especially pp. 23–32.

The Requirements for Meaning

In a community like Pleasantville, where there are few challenges and everyone is handed a role that they live out faithfully, there may be little in the way of serious conflict. Life may, very well, be pleasant. But the pleasures will not be the ones worth having—the ones that come when we pursue a challenging goal we really care about, one that reflects our potential and inspires us to become more than we thought we could be. For that kind of life, two things are crucial. First, we can't simply follow a script handed us by others. We need to find out for ourselves how to live—not arbitrarily or by simply following whatever desires we happen to have, but through developing a real understanding of ourselves. Second, we must pursue goals that, given the circumstances in which we live, pose a challenge to our abilities, thereby inspiring us to develop those abilities fully.

In *Pleasantville*, David finds himself confronted with the fragmentation of his real life and seeks comfort in a 1950s fantasy where everyone has a clearly defined role or purpose. For a teenager disillusioned by the lack of coherence in his own life, by the frustrations of a single-parent home and the petty conflicts and posturings of high school, the Pleasantville fantasy seems to offer a meaningful alternative. The problem, of course, is that while the Pleasantville universe assigns every person a role, and hence a purpose, the creativity and autonomy of Pleasantville's inhabitants are stunted by their blind adherence to a purpose handed to them by their tiny cosmos. Furthermore, their emotions, wants, and desires are simply something to be ignored or suppressed in order to faithfully carry out their assigned roles. When Phil Johnson, the kindly proprietor of the local soda shop, first expresses dissatisfaction with his role, David (still faithfully trying to play the role of Bud) urges Phil to suppress those feelings to keep Pleasantville free from change: "Look, you can't always like what you do. Sometimes you just gotta do it because it's your job. And even if you don't like it, you've just gotta do it anyway."

Jennifer's rebellion against Pleasantville's roles represents an equally unsatisfactory alternative: it is autonomy without direction, where any old purpose will do so long as she chooses it for herself. *Pleasantville* exposes the inadequacy of each alternative. The rigid, role-governed life of Pleasantville may offer some semblance of order and predictability—it may hold off tragedy and despair—but it cannot provide genuine meaning. It imposes roles that leave no room for the people of Pleasantville to express their creativity and autonomy. The clockwork operation of those roles reduces Pleasantville to a world of endless routine, in which there are few challenges that can really engage human talents and abilities. Even basketball, a sport meant to challenge and inspire its participants to hone their physical strength, skill, and agility, is in Pleasantville a thing without challenge. No one on the high school team ever misses a basket. The team never loses a game—not because they have worked hard to attain excellence, but because nothing in Pleasantville requires effort.

Jennifer's rebellion against this world of roles and routines is equally incapable of engaging her full humanity. She may, in a sense, choose her own goals, but because her self-concept offers no way of distinguishing between appropriate and inappropriate desires, the ends she chooses are simply those that coincide with the desires she already happens to have. And these desires are not ones that she has cultivated on the basis of a clear self-understanding, but rather those that have been fashioned for her by her peer group: the desire for popularity, flawless skin, and a cool boyfriend. Just as there is nothing meaningful about blindly following a script even if it means suppressing our desires, there is nothing meaningful about doing whatever we happen to desire—especially when those desires, rather than springing from an appreciation of who and what we are, turn out to be just another kind of script written for us by others.[9] To actualize our potential, we need both understanding and discipline—the understanding necessary to appreciate our potential, the discipline needed to direct our abilities and our passions toward its actualization. Jennifer's rebel-cool self-indulgence is lacking in both, and turns out in the end to be just another empty role.

But somehow the clash between these empty roles—indulgence without discipline and discipline without challenge—

---

[9] Aristotle would describe Jennifer as a "slave" to her desires, in the way that he thinks non-rational animals are slaves to desire. He finds such slavishness unfitting human nature. See *NE*, Book I, Chapter 5.

generates a space for learning, for growth, and ultimately, for meaning. In the confusion created by Jennifer's rebellion, the inhabitants of Pleasantville are inspired, one by one, to re-evaluate who they are and take stock of what they are capable of. In the conflict that begins to embroil the town, they are challenged to develop their abilities in new ways. Jennifer, meanwhile, is driven to seek out some focus for her passions, some goal that can engage and challenge her. She finds that goal in the very place that Aristotle would urge her to look: the cultivation of her intellect. When 1990s teen rebellion crashes headlong into 1950s family values, Aristotle rises from the ruins to paint the world with vibrant colors.

Discovering Meaning: The Case of Phil Johnson

Perhaps the most striking example of such transformation comes with the character of Phil Johnson. As color begins to appear around him, Phil becomes aware of the emptiness in his own life. In one poignant scene, David/Bud finds Phil sitting on the floor in the back of the soda shop. "What's the *point*, Bud?" Phil asks. In the conversation that follows, Phil reveals that there is only one thing in his routinized existence that he really enjoys, that he genuinely looks forward to: painting the Christmas decorations in the soda shop window. It is the one thing he does that is different every year. David/Bud is at first impressed by the photo of Phil's artwork, but then quickly urges Phil to stop thinking about such things, perhaps seeing that this line of thought would threaten Pleasantville's role-governed harmony.

Once the idea has been planted, Phil cannot dispel it. As David himself becomes inspired by the burgeoning color around him, he finds himself moved by Phil's plaintive search for meaning. From a library whose books had previously contained nothing but empty page, David brings Phil a book of art masterpieces. Phil's mind begins to race with possibilities. He starts to explore his artistic side, discovering a real talent for painting in the very colors that have newly appeared on the streets of his town. Soon he has all but abandoned his former trade, forging for himself a new path—one that not only expresses his autonomy, but draws on the talents and powers he discovers in himself. His artistic creations become increasingly ambitious. And as the town turns against its newly colorful inhabitants—shattering the nude he painted on his shop window, imposing rules prohibiting the use of colored paint—Phil is inspired to the grandest project of all: to create a building-sized mural that tells the story of Pleasantville's transformations in every forbidden color.

It seems as if Phil has awakened from a long sleep, and in the passion of new life he throws himself into other passions as well, pursuing the love of Betty—the mother of Bud (David) and Mary Sue (Jennifer). Passion is such an important theme in *Pleasantville* that one might be tempted to think that color represents nothing more or less than passion itself. But this is not quite right. Human emotion is a vital part of the meaningful life—after all, how can we live a life in which we pursue a goal that challenges us and forces us to grow, unless we really *care* about that goal? But the anguish of Betty's cuckolded husband keeps the viewer from too readily romanticizing the passionate affair. Unrestrained passion is not the source of meaning. Rather, it is a forgivable by-product of liberation from those rules and roles that have for too long kept Pleasantville's inhabitants from living meaningful lives.

The end of the film does not leave us with a world of chaotic self-indulgence of the sort we would expect had Jennifer's teen rebellion become the norm. Roles and rules, rather than being abandoned, are put in their place. The right kinds of rules do not suppress our passions, but rather help to *shape* our passions so that they do not overwhelm us, but instead become an integrated part of a fully actualized human life.

Emotion and the Meaning in Virtue

Here we are led to one final Aristotelian dimension of *Pleasantville*. According to Aristotle, our emotional life contributes to our flourishing when it harmonizes itself with our reason. Emotion is not opposed to reason, as it seems to be in the Vulcan civilization of *Star Trek*. For Aristotle, emotion is a vital part of a flourishing life. But unrestrained emotional indulgence is not the source of human flourishing. Instead, we flourish when we come to feel those emotions when and to the extent that it is most rationally fitting—for example, when we become even tempered rather than short-tempered, feeling angry only when it is appropriate.

According to Aristotle, we develop the proper emotional dispositions through a process of habituation: we behave in an even-tempered way until the emotions follow suit and become internalized. The resulting habits, or emotional dispositions, are the moral virtues. Until these virtues are acquired, emotion and reason are at odds. A fully integrated human life, one that can express both reason *and* emotion, is possible only once moral virtue is achieved. But moral virtue is not dutiful adherence to external rules. Rather, it is doing *with feeling* the very things that our own reason and experience tell us are the right things to do.[10] We become like people with healthy lifestyles, who exercise and eat right because that is what they really want to do. For them, doing the right thing is not a chore but a pleasure.

This state of virtue does not come overnight. It does not come without struggle. It is a process in which there are growing pains, conflicts both internal and external. It is, in the words of Aristotle, the difficult effort to locate and live by a mean between the extremes of excess and deficiency.[11] This "mean" is not some mathematical middle point, but rather a point that is determined by reason, in the light of lived experience, to be fitting or appropriate.[12] For example, Aristotle endorses neither an absence of appetite nor a voracious appetite that knows no bounds. Instead, he endorses a healthy appetite that is directed towards and satisfied by what reason and experience teach us are the right kinds and amounts of food. When our entire emotional life is like this healthy appetite, we have acquired moral virtue. We are not without passion, but instead are guided by passions that are fully harmonized with our rational nature. What follows is a meaningful human life, in the sense that our most central human faculties are neither wasted nor suppressed, but are allowed to operate in harmony with one another.

In a way, *Pleasantville* is a dramatic portrayal of just this struggle towards moral virtue. In the beginning we have two extremes: In the town of Pleasantville (and in David's admiration of it) we see an external order that leaves no room for

---

[10] This is a summary of key themes developed in *NE*, Book II, Chapters 1–9.

[11] It is the very difficulty of finding and living according to this mean which, according to Aristotle, makes virtue a thing worthy of praise. See *NE*, Book II, Chapter 9.

[12] *NE*, Book II, Chapter 6.

emotional investment and is devoid of the satisfaction that comes from really caring about challenging goals. It is, in a word, *dull*. In Jennifer we see indulgence without direction, passion that is excessive precisely because it has no purpose but to fulfill the superficial expectations of her peers. Her life may not be dull—but its pleasures are empty. In the ensuing conflict we witness each extreme move in fits and starts toward the other, groping for the mean (and hence for meaning). As Phil bursts free of his routinized life of "grill the bun, flip the meat, melt the cheese," Jennifer leaves behind her superficial self-indulgence in order to cultivate her intellect. And we learn that this struggle towards self-actualization, for all of the occasional ugliness it engenders, is not nearly as bad as stagnation in the meaningless rituals of a pre-scripted existence. And so long as that struggle moves in the direction of virtue, it can be distinguished from mere chaos, from the universe of random meanings that Kurt Baier is in danger of recommending to us. In *Pleasantville* we see this distinctly Aristotelian alternative emerge—painted for us, stroke by stroke, in brilliant colors.

To Think About

1. What would it be like to live in a world without challenges, where every goal you set for yourself would be easy to achieve? Would you want to live in such a world? Why or why not?

2. How do you decide on the goals that you pursue in life? Do you let others choose them for you? Do you pick them out of a hat? How do you decide what goals are *worth* pursuing?

3. Are there any "roles" that you live out that have been created for you by your community? How do you feel about living out those roles? When and to what extent do assigned roles give us a sense of comfort and security? When and to what extent do they stifle our creativity and our ability to develop ourselves fully?

4. Consider the following claim: "Those who rebel against society are still letting society define them." Do you agree? Why or why not?

To Read Next

Aristotle. *Nicomachean Ethics*. New York: Penguin, 1955.

David Bostock, *Aristotle's Ethics*. Oxford: Oxford University Press, 2000.

Kurt Baier. The Meaning of Life. In E.D. Klemke, A. David Kline, and Robert Hollinger, eds., *Philosophy: Contemporary Perspectives on Perennial Issues*. Fourth edition (New York: St. Martin's Press, 1994).

Stuart Hampshire. *Innocence and Experience*. Cambridge, Massachusetts: Harvard University Press, 1989.

16

Of *Spider-Man*, *Spider-Man 2*, and Living Like a Hero

JONATHAN J. SANFORD

Peter Parker is leaning over the corpse of Uncle Ben, the man who took him in and raised him, gripped by a grief that quickly finds an outlet in a desire to capture and punish his killer. Off he races, modifying and perfecting his web-slinging technique of swinging down and through the urban canyons of New York. He finally beholds the face of the assailant in a dark warehouse, realizing with horror that he is the same thief that Peter, acting out of spite, let escape from the office of the wrestling promoter.

Peter suddenly realizes that if only he had heeded Uncle Ben's warning that "with great power comes great responsibility," he could have prevented his murder. Peter now knows that every failure to act with justice has negative consequences. This moment proves to be one of the transforming events in his life, serving as a constant reminder to never make the same mistake again. Soon after this Peter becomes the superhero Spider-Man, using his unique abilities to effect good in the world.

To be sure, Spider-Man is larger-than-life. Nevertheless, his predicament of finding himself with unique powers and facing the fundamental choice of how they are to be employed is by no means foreign to common human experience. In fact, he proves a model for our own lives, unapproachable in his uncommon abilities, but imitable in the moral quality of his actions and the end he serves. The moral teaching of *Spider-Man* and *Spider-Man 2* is that the way of the hero ought to be our own; that we too have unique and binding obligations, just like Peter,

"I'm Spider-Man, given a job to do"(*Spider-Man 2*); and that it is only through being faithful to these obligations—which is being heroic—that we live optimally meaningful lives.

But what makes a moral hero? What does it mean to choose the way of the hero? How can we do it? And, more fundamentally, why should we strive to be heroic? These questions amount to the core question of ethics: How ought one to live?[1] We'll look not just to Spidey, but to two of the greatest philosophers for help answering these questions. For Plato (428–348 B.C.) and Aristotle (384–322 B.C.), answering this last question and, more importantly, living that answer is the only life befitting a being who is capable of raising the question in the first place. That is, the very fact that we can ask how we ought to live our lives, a question that encapsulates in many ways what it means to be human, suggests that in asking and answering this question we find the key to the meaning of life.

One of the ways that both Plato and Aristotle suggest that this question can be answered is to look to those individuals whose lives shine forth as models for our own, the lives of heroes. Aunt Mae in *Spider-Man 2* suggests as much to Peter when he visits her while she is moving from her house. She, unaware of his full identity, tells Peter just what he needs to hear: that he should be heroic, like Spider-Man!

Plato presents a hero to us with his portraits of Socrates in the *Apology, Crito, Phaedo,* and other dialogues, and systematically lists the characteristics of a hero in Books V and VI of the *Republic*. Aristotle in his *Nicomachean Ethics* describes the individual of practical wisdom, who is the morally good individual of great soul. Such portraits both make the case for how one should live and inspire us to live in that way. The character of Spider-Man functions in a similar fashion as do these models, serving as both guide and inspiration for our own moral development. It's not so much that we are drawn to Spider-Man because we'd love to hang from ceilings, climb skyscrapers like they're stairs, and avoid rush hour from above (although we may want all those things!). Rather, what most draw us to Spider-Man are his outstanding moral feats, precisely those which we can and indeed want to imitate.

---

[1] See Plato, *Gorgias* 487e–488a, 500c; and *Republic* 344e, 352d.

Heroic models can perform their function only insofar as we recognize in them something we can imitate. This commonality between ourselves and these moral exemplars is threefold: a shared moral universe, similar moral capacities, and a common goal. *Spider-Man* and *Spider-Man 2* teach us that the meaning of life has much to do with living heroically, and such a life is our common vocation.

Spider-Man and Moral Exemplars

The Green Goblin has drugged Spider-Man and carried him to a high rooftop to tempt him to join forces, a scene reminiscent of Jesus Christ's third temptation. The Green Goblin explains that together they could do wondrous things, establishing domination over the whole city. Not only that, but the Green Goblin claims that they have a right to do this, since they are the exceptional types and the rest of humanity exists merely to do their bidding: "These teeming masses exist for the sole purpose of lifting those exceptional people on their shoulders" (*Spider-Man*). This is the same doctrine the character Raskolnikov formulates and tests—with disastrous consequences—in Fyodor Dostoyevsky's (1821–1881) *Crime and Punishment*, and that Friedrich Nietzsche (1844–1900) commends in *The Genealogy of Morality*: the exceptional few are entitled to everything and by virtue of their strength they are altogether beyond the moral law. One of the characters in Plato's *Republic*, Thrasymachus, similarly argues that for those who are strong enough, what is right is to exercise power over all and everything with a singular dedication to satisfying their desire to have it all. It is this same sort of doctrine that drives Doctor Octopus. The responsibility he once felt to use his knowledge to help humanity is perverted into an insatiable thirst for power: "The power of the sun in the palm of my hand!" (*Spider-Man 2*).

So why not join forces with the Green Goblin and his ilk? An answer to this can be found in Spider-Man's initial reaction to the Green Goblin's proposal: "But you're a murderer." To be a murderer is to be a usurper of the lives of others, which is to be the very opposite of a hero. The Green Goblin doesn't see the difference, or at least he pretends not to see the difference. He contends instead that they are not so different, for they've merely channeled their powers in different directions: "I chose my path. You chose the way of the hero." But to Spider-Man, it is precisely this choice that has made them contradictory moral types: the Green Goblin is dedicated to taking whatever he can whenever he wants it; he is dedicated to justice's opposite, greed. Spider-Man on the other hand is dedicated to using his powers in the service of others for a seemingly simple reason, a reason that Spider-Man voices when the Green Goblin asks him why he bothers to help those in need: "Because it's *right.*" Spider-Man sees that the direction in which we channel our efforts makes all the difference in the world.

In one sense, Spider-Man's reply is simple, for it indicates an uncomplicated orientation of his moral being towards one goal: the accomplishment of what is right. But when we examine what such an orientation entails, both on the side of the moral agent and on the side of the goal, we uncover a great deal of complexity. We will discuss some of this complexity in the sections to follow, but for now let's continue to examine the role of the moral exemplar in ethics.

Consider this counter-example: What would your reaction have been if instead of resisting the temptation of the Green Goblin, Spider-Man had been persuaded by him? This, of course, would not have happened immediately because that would have been too out of character. His resolve would have disintegrated in stages. Nevertheless, the final stage would have resulted in joining forces with the villain, so that Spider-Man himself would become a villain. What would your reaction have been to the first instances of Spider-Man's weakening? Would it be a disappointment bordering on a sense of personal betrayal? And would your reaction to the last stage in Spider-Man's moral collapse be to reject him as a hero altogether?

We find something like this to have almost happened in *Spider-Man 2*. Spider-Man does not turn into an arch-villain, but he does hang up, for a time, the whole hero business. One of the most painful scenes of the whole film is when Peter turns his back on the man being mugged in an alley. What was your reaction to this scene? The former Spider-Man fails to do what is minimally required of anyone seeing a person being mugged: at least to try to find help if you are unable to come to a victim's defense yourself.

But *why* would we have felt betrayed if Spider-Man had joined the Green Goblin? Why did we feel betrayed when Peter walks away from the mugging? Spider-Man never promised to other characters in the movies that he would be a superhero for them, nor did he make such a compact with the viewers. Nevertheless, the characters in the movie, and we the viewers, have expectations about what he should do. The greatest of expectations in fact, because we look to him as a model of the lives we ourselves are striving to live. Spider-Man is a hero, and heroes do what's right. We invest in him, and other moral exemplars, something of ourselves—a vision of the moral beings we hope to become—and it is for this reason that when a moral hero or exemplar fails we take it personally.

There is nothing psychologically unhealthy about this: it's not as though we're shirking our responsibility through identification with a moral proxy. Nor is looking up to heroes the type of thing that only kids should do. Plato and Aristotle, certainly mature thinkers, both recognized the need for heroic portrayal to draw us out of our own temptations of Green Goblinesque greed and into an unyielding orientation towards the right.

Moral Heroes and Determining What's Right

The main character in most of Plato's dialogues is Socrates, who was friend and mentor to Plato and many others and generally regarded as the first great philosopher. There appears to be a historical basis to one of the events in the life of Socrates that is related in the *Apology* as well as in Plato's *Letter VII*. In his defense against trumped up charges before a large Athenian jury Socrates tells of a time when he was ordered by a group of dictators in Athens to bring an innocent man to court on false charges. Socrates refused because, "death is something that I couldn't care less about, but . . . my whole concern is not to do anything unjust or impious" (*Apology*, 32d).[2] For Socrates, death is nothing compared to the horrors of doing wrong. The greatest of evils can only be self-inflected through a moral agent's own wrongdoing. This is a truth driven home at the end of *Spider-Man 2* with Doctor Octopus who in his right moral mind again realizes with dread what he has done and resolves not to die a monster but in striving to undo the havoc he produced.

---

[2] All quotations from Plato's works are taken from *The Complete Works of Plato*, edited by John M. Cooper (Indianapolis: Hackett, 1997).

Like Spider-Man refusing the offer of the Green Goblin, Socrates refuses to participate in evil-doing. Unlike Spider-Man, Socrates was eventually executed for his refusal to buckle to unjust injunctions, though Spider-Man is certainly persecuted for his way of life. Socrates accepted his execution despite being convinced that he had not done anything wrong (*Apology*, 37a), and despite being offered the chance to escape from Athens before his execution. He was convinced that it would be wrong to do harm to the laws of Athens by not enduring the verdict of the jury. In explaining this position to his friend, Crito, Socrates emboldens his friend, as well as readers, to dedicate ourselves to what is right no matter past or future harms:

SOCRATES: So one must never do wrong.

CRITO: Certainly not.

SOCRATES: Nor must one, when wronged, inflict wrong in return, as the majority believe, since one must never do wrong.

CRITO: That seems to be the case.

SOCRATES: Come now, should we mistreat anyone or not, Crito?

CRITO: One must never do so.

SOCRATES: Well then, if one is oneself mistreated, is it right, as the majority say, to mistreat in return, or is it not?

CRITO: It is never right. (*Crito*, 49b–c)

It is no easy matter to live this way. It can only be done through a high-degree of self-reflection, which is why it is no accident that Socrates is not only a man of great moral courage but also a great philosopher. Peter Parker may not be a great philosopher, but we do see him in reflective moments throughout both movies. *Spider-Man* is in many ways an extended self-reflection in which Peter Parker tells the story of how he has become Spider-Man, beginning with the question, "Who am I?", and concluding with the declaration, "I'm Spider-Man." *Spider-Man 2* picks up on the same theme, with Peter/Spidey attaining a more mature degree of personal unity through being unmasked on several occasions, and loved on at least two of them by the people on the train and by Mary Jane. He has become his true self, a transformation that included and will continue to include dedicating himself to fulfilling the responsibilities that fall to him.

Aristotle includes reference to the heroic individual in the very definition of virtue: "Virtue is then a state of choice, lying in a mean relative to us, this [mean] being determined by reason and in the way in which the man of practical wisdom would determine it" (*NE* II, Book 6, 1106b35–1107a2).[3] Virtue is an important term in both Plato's and Aristotle's ethics, for being virtuous implies being properly ordered, and acting virtuously implies doing the right thing for the right reason. Practical wisdom is that virtue of the intellect that accomplishes the subtle task of determining which actions are in fact right. This is often difficult, and not least because of the myriad possibilities that present themselves to us.

We see this intellectual virtue (and spider sense!) at work when the Green Goblin seeks to expose Spider-Man's weakness by forcing on him the choice of saving either Mary Jane or an elevator full of children (Spider-Man trumps the test by saving both, which may be good for a Hollywood production, though it weakens the force of the moral challenge he faces). But we also see it (and spider sense!) every time Spider-Man acts rightly. In the choices we face it is often difficult to determine just what course of action would be *right*. It's often necessary to look to a moral exemplar or hero for us to successfully determine what is right. We can ask ourselves, 'What would Spider-Man, or Socrates, or Maximilian Kolbe, or Mother Theresa or my mother do in this situation?', and use their example to determine what it would be virtuous for us to do. It is in this fashion that moral exemplars help us to determine what is right.

The role of moral exemplars or heroes is twofold: On the one hand they perform the general task of inspiring us to be like them, and on the other hand they serve as guides who help direct us to make the proper turns when determining what to do in the face of the nitty-gritty of our own particular circumstances. Now let's consider some of the features of the *right*.

Spider-Man, Virtue, and the Beauty of the Right

Spider-Man asserts that he does what he does because it is right, but what is meant by 'right'? For Plato and Aristotle this notion

---

[3]*The Complete Works of Aristotle*, Two Volumes, edited by Jonathan Barnes (Princeton: Princeton University Press, 1984). I have slightly modified the translation, and do so in a few other places as well.

has much to do with virtue. For both, a virtue is a matter of being excellent in some regard. Ethics is concerned with the question of how one ought to live, and an obvious, if broad, answer to that is 'excellently'.

In the *Republic* Plato emphasizes four virtues: wisdom, courage, temperance, and most importantly, justice (*Republic*, Book IV, 427e). These are often called the *cardinal virtues* because of their foremost importance. Each of these are the excellence or virtue of some part of the soul: wisdom, the excellence of the intellect whereby we determine what is right; courage, the excellence of the will and emotions which resolves us to hold onto and accomplish what we've determined to be right; and temperance, the excellence of our appetites which keeps us from being consumed by inordinate desire and drawn away from what's right.

Justice is the virtue that governs intellect, emotion, and appetite by enabling and sustaining the virtues specific to each sphere of the person and directing us as a whole towards the right (*Ibid.*, 433a–e, 443c–e). *Spider-Man* and *Spider-Man 2*, like the *Republic*, highlight the importance of wisdom, courage, temperance, and justice. Consider, for example, the last scene in *Spider-Man* in which Peter tells Mary Jane that he cannot offer her romantic love but only friendship. Since he was six years old Peter has wished for little more than a romantic relationship with Mary Jane. He has, however, used his *wisdom* (and spider sense!) to determine that it would not be right to become too close to Mary Jane, for by doing so he would endanger her life.

We see that same conviction in *Spider-Man 2,* and most poignantly when the unmasked Spider-Man and Mary Jane have their talk on the web and Spider-Man tells Mary Jane, "I will always be Spider-Man. You and I can never be." But this is an extremely difficult determination to put into practice because of his desire to be with Mary Jane. It takes a great deal of *courage* to stand by his determination not to become involved with her. It also takes *temperance*, a restraint especially of his sexual appetite, to be with her. *Justice*, insofar as it has to do with an overall orientation towards the right and enables Peter Parker to embody each of these virtues, makes his determination, resolve, and self-control all *right*.

Aristotle stresses these same virtues, although he also introduces some nuances to the notion of wisdom and places a greater emphasis on the habitual nature of virtue. For Aristotle, acting virtuously requires more than knowledge of the relevant virtue, it also requires that one already have acquired that virtue as a trait of character through repeated virtuous actions (*NE*, Book II:4, 1105a30–35). Learning to do what is right is a matter, then, of practice, for "it is by doing just acts that the just man is produced, and by doing temperate acts the temperate man. . . . But most people do not do these, but take refuge in theory and think they are being philosophers and will become good in this way" (*Ibid.*, 1105b9–14). Talk is cheap. A person must perform the types of actions a virtuous person would if he or she is eventually to become virtuous him or herself. This is why proper moral instruction—which includes the designation of moral exemplars like Spider-Man and encouragement to imitate them—is so essential for children: "It makes no small difference, then, whether we form habits of one kind or another from our very youth; it makes a very great difference, or rather *all* the difference" (*NE*, Book II:1, 1103b24–6).

In addition to knowing that some action is right, and acting out of a well-developed character, Aristotle also emphasizes that in order to act virtuously one must choose the virtuous action for its own sake and not for some further result. What is it about virtuous actions that make them appealing on their own terms? Plato and Aristotle both speak of virtuous actions as *kalon*, which is a Greek word that has no equivalent in English but is often translated as 'noble', 'fine', or 'beautiful'. For Plato, virtue is *kalon* in large measure because of its share in wisdom, and we ought to love virtue as we love wisdom.[4] Aristotle puts the matter pithily when he states: "Now virtuous actions are *kalon* and done for the sake of the *kalon*" (*NE*, Book IV:1, 1120a–23). It is the beauty and nobility of virtuous actions that call us forth to great deeds. This helps explain why we are drawn to moral exemplars in the first place: It is the nobility and beauty of Spider-Man's actions that attract us to him and inspire us to perform similarly *kalon* actions. To be sure, Spider-Man's acrobatics are beautiful, but the deeper attraction is to Spider-Man's unambiguously good interior and exterior moral acts; acts which we can do more than pretend to imitate.

---

[4]See, for example, *Republic* VI, 484a–487a; *Protagoras* 309c, 329c-d; *Gorgias* 506c-509c.

For Plato, Aristotle, and Spider-Man right action is virtuous action. We strive to do what's right because doing what's right constitutes living excellently, which is to live in such a way that we embrace the noble and beautiful. An understanding of this notion of the 'right' can be deepened by looking closer at its relation to our nature.

Spider-Man and Human Nature

The ethical approaches of both Plato and Aristotle rest upon a number of basic insights regarding human nature. It is because we are rational that we have the ability to raise questions, to consider them ourselves, to discuss them with others, to make choices about how we should live as individuals and as members of communities, to gain insight into the structure of reality, and to be sensitive to the beauty and nobility of truth and right action. It is towards a more full expression of this rational nature that Plato and Aristotle exhort us that we ought to live in such a way as to be all we can be (as the U.S. Army suggested, before we were exhorted to become an army of one). We should actualize our potential to live excellently.

Our potential is, of course, determined by our nature. Human beings have by nature a number of capacities, and it is the specifically human capacities that Plato and Aristotle argue are most relevant to ethics. But this presents a problem when we return to a consideration of Spider-Man. Is Spider-Man human? After he is bitten by a hybrid spider at Columbia University's Science Department we see the computer screen behind Peter Parker run through a DNA transfer and flash the words "New Species." And indeed, there is something other than human about the physical and sensory abilities that Parker discovers in the ensuing days. But these abilities, though more than human, do not prevent Parker from retaining the uniquely human features that Plato and Aristotle specify. For it is not so much our body or our abilities to sense and move that make us the moral beings we are. Rather, it is our ability to think about how we should live, and indeed this question is the central concern of Peter Parker throughout both movies.

This is not to say, however, that Peter's special spider abilities are irrelevant. If you or I attempted to jump from tall buildings in order to accost some thugs we would most likely be jumping to our deaths. Various fantasies notwithstanding, we just can't do what Spider-Man can (for he "does whatever a spider can"). The choices we make about what we *should* do are necessarily limited by what we *can* do, and for Spider-Man the perimeter of capacity is much wider than it is for ourselves. Only a Spider-Man could stop a Green Goblin or a Doctor Octopus, and it is because of Spider-Man's abilities that he is called to do the great things he does, a fact captured by the words of Uncle Ben that Peter Parker recalls at the close of the *Spider-Man*: "As long as I live I will never forget these words, 'with great power comes great responsibility'. This is my gift. This is my curse. Who am I? I'm Spider-Man."

It is because of Parker's human-spider hybrid nature that he has the responsibility to do the sorts of things that only he can. Nevertheless, insofar as Parker's actions can be analyzed as virtuous and right, insofar as they proceed from choice, and insofar as they lead to him becoming what he ought to become, we do see in them the essential ingredients of human actions. So even the most spectacular actions of Spider-Man bear the stamp of a human moral nature through and through. Moreover, it is important to recall that we are all gifted and cursed by our power—a fact Uncle Ben acknowledges insofar as he spoke those influential words without any knowledge of Peter's spider powers. Though we all share a common nature, no two of us find ourselves with exactly equivalent powers nor in exactly equivalent situations where obligations to others arise. Nonetheless, we are all called in common to utilize our unique gifts to carry through our specific responsibilities when they arise.

Although Peter tells us that his special power is a curse, we should be careful not to interpret this too literally. In a sense, Spider-Man is cursed by his power insofar as he is burdened with a wide scope of responsibility. We see this curse in full swing in *Spider-Man 2* with Peter failing to deliver pizzas on time, failing to make it to class on time, failing to make it to Mary Jane's performance of Wilde's play on time, all because he is repeatedly answering the call to help others in extreme danger. But on a deeper level this is no curse at all, at least if we accept the teachings of Plato and Aristotle, for it is precisely through fulfilling those responsibilities by right and virtuous action that Spider-Man can flourish as the human-spider hybrid he is; a fact he forcibly realizes in *Spider-Man 2* by tasting the alternative. The irony of human happiness is that our nature is so constituted that it is only by means of successfully shouldering the burden of responsibility to do what's right, and not by pursuing pleasure, that we can be happy. We can see, then, that Spider-Man shows us that the life of justice is to be preferred no matter what. Spider-Man is persecuted, suffers the loss of his uncle, the injury of his aunt, the hatred of his former friend, and (until the very end of *Spider-Man 2*) a romance with Mary Jane; and yet he *is* happy, even if that happiness is not without its touch of sadness. Obviously, this is not the sort of happiness that we expect to find in a Hollywood flick where at the end the hero gets the girl, unlimited wealth, and just about everything else. And, even though Peter does finally end up with Mary Jane, she does not give the gift of herself to him with the expectation that he should be anyone other than he is. Rather, in completing him with her love, and he completing her with his, she can serve as a further source of strength for his resolve to do what's right, as she does in the last words of the movie: "Go get 'em, tiger!". Spider-Man's happiness is true happiness, for his love for the beauty of the right has led him to become all he should be: Peter Parker and Spider-Man are one and the same person.

Spider-Man, Spider-Man 2, and the Meaning of Life

This brings us back to the scene in which the Green Goblin offers Spider-Man an opportunity to join forces with him so that together they can secure complete power and the satisfaction of their every desire. Spider-Man responds that to do this would not be right. Why? Because such a way of life is ugly and ignoble, and because the happy life, a life in which one is fulfilled, has actualized his or her potential, and flourishes cannot be one in which we are dedicated to an unbridled satisfaction of our appetites. Spidey notwithstanding, many do believe that that *is* what life is about, a point of view that is expressed in the 1980s banality "I want it all!", or in the titles of many a self-help book ("You *Can* Have it All, and I'll Tell You How!"), or in the central tenets—if they can be called that—of Scientology. But life is not about having it all, at least if by 'all' one means every object of desire, for we often desire things that are bad, ignoble, and ugly, and which cause us to fail to be the flourishing human moral beings we might. To spend one's life seeking to have it all is to live a tyrant's life, a life Plato describes as a living nightmare (*Republic*, Book IX, 571a–576c). It is to live the life of the Green Goblin, the projection of Harry Osborne's lust for power and control which has found a means to be realized.

Plato has Socrates teach us in the *Apology* that the unexamined life is not worth living (38a). To examine one's life, to be faithful to the Delphic oracle's mandate "Know Thyself," is to consider how one ought to live. When one begins to reflect upon this, he or she is already moving away from the way of the Green Goblin and Doctor Octopus, the way of the antihero, because such a lust for power cannot stand the light of rational reflection: it thrives only in the uncritical posture of obedience to one's appetites. This is skillfully depicted in *Spider-Man* by Osbourne's drunken conversations with himself in his study, and in *Spider-Man 2* by the dialogue between Octavius and his mechanical limbs. In saying yes to their darker desires, both Osbourne and Octavius become tyrants. Although these tyrants are wondrously cunning, they are at the same time hopelessly enslaved to their passions.

But such a way is not to be ours. When we reflect on who we are, what our capacities are, how they ought to be used, and towards what end we ought to be directed, and add to that our resolve to put our abilities to the service of the right, we begin to invest our lives with the meaning they are meant to have. This reflective appraisal of ourselves is aided through a consideration of moral heroes. We see in them a way to live that is noble and beautiful, a way of life truly worth living. Such heroes are often men and women who are close to us, but they can also be temporally or geographically distant. They can even be fictitious characters such as Spider-Man. We can indeed identify with Peter Parker's quest to become all he can be, to live like a hero, because we share with him a shared moral universe, a common moral nature, and a common goal: to live righteously and virtuously, which is to live worthily, meaningfully, and well.

To Think About

1. Can a person strive to be heroic? Does a real hero look for occasions to be heroic? Doesn't heroism arise from circumstance?

2. Is a hero really happier than a successful villain?

3. Is there a limit to what others can expect from a person's talents and abilities? Isn't there a part of a person's life that is distinctively their own?

To Read Next

Aristotle. *Nicomachean Ethics*. Translated by W.D. Ross, revised by J.L. Ackrill and J.O. Urmson. New York: Oxford University Press, 1980.

Viktor E. Frankl. *Man's Search for Meaning: An Introduction to Logotherapy*. Riverside: Simon and Schuster, 1997.

Plato. *Five Dialogues: Euthyphro, Apology, Crito, Meno, Phaedo*. Translated by G.M.A. Grube. Indianapolis: Hackett, 1981.

Plato. *Republic*. Translated by G.M.A. Grube, revised by C.D.C. Reeve. Indianapolis: Hackett, 1992.

Josef Pieper. *The Four Cardinal Virtues*. Notre Dame: University of Notre Dame Press, 1966.

17

So Tired of the Future: Free Will and Determinism in Spielberg's *Minority Report*

NIR EISIKOVITS and SHAI BIDERMAN

> Even if man really were nothing but a piano key, even if this were proved to him by natural science and mathematics, even then he would not become reasonable, but would purposely do something perverse out of sheer ingratitude, simply to have his own way. And if he does not find any means he will devise destruction and chaos, will devise suffering of all sorts, and will thereby have his own way. . . . If you say that all this, too, can be calculated and tabulated, chaos and darkness and curses, so that the mere possibility of calculating it all beforehand would stop it all, and reason would reassert itself—then man would purposely go mad in order to be rid of reason and have his own way!
>
> — FYODOR DOSTOEVSKY, *Notes from the Underground*

Mr. Marks, well-groomed, lackluster and middle-aged, suspects his wife is having an affair. As he leaves for work one morning, he sees her open the door of their Georgetown apartment for a younger man. He silently follows the two into the upstairs bedroom, slumping behind the bed as the oblivious lovers caress and fondle each other. A few seconds later he confronts them, wielding a pair of scissors. An instant before bloody revenge is had, a team of policemen smashes through the windows and apprehends the jealous husband for the double murder he is about to commit.

This "Cruise-Ex-Machina" is made possible through the good services of three "precogs"—mutants blessed (as long as you don't ask them) with the capacity to foresee impending murders.

Now in its sixth year, the crime prevention project, which employs these mutants, has turned a once violence-stricken city into an urban oasis. Relatives of murder victims appear on the ubiquitous ads sponsored by the "Precrime" initiative, reminding everyone of just how bad things used to be: parents living in fear of losing their children to school shootings, wives terrified that their husbands will get car-jacked and slaughtered on their way back from work, everyone forced to take a cab rather than walk home. Millions of people once enslaved by fear, now free. Or are they?

For one thing, Chief Anderton (played by Tom Cruise) has his men identify the future perpetrators, apprehend them, pronounce their guilt, and administer their sentence within the space of minutes. An unorthodox interpretation of the principle of the separation of powers to say the least.

But there is a more fundamental difficulty at play. As Marks is led away, he screams, "I didn't do anything." This is not a particularly shocking line of argument coming from somebody who is about to be put away for life. Nevertheless, in this case Marks is right. On the most obvious level, he didn't *do* anything because Precrime (appropriately abbreviated as PC from here on) got to him first. But we might be interested in a more fundamental question: *what is it to do something?* Does doing involve a choice? If so, can we really be said to choose to perform an action if someone else already knew when, how, and why we were about to undertake it? How could Marks choose to murder his wife and her lover if the precogs already knew that this was about to happen? After all, if they knew what Marks was going to do, his act was predetermined, and as such, could not have been voluntarily chosen!

Spielberg's film[1] conjures up a specter that has been haunting philosophers for ages. It raises what is perhaps the biggest of all "big questions": are we free? It certainly feels as if we are. We chose what to have for lunch, whom to marry, what line of work to pursue, where to live, where to go on vacation. Our actions are subject to moral judgment and punishment since we are assumed to have chosen to perform them.

---

[1] *Minority Report* is loosely based on a short story by Philip K. Dick, whose fiction also inspired the movies *Blade Runner*, *Total Recall*, *Impostor*, and *Screamers*.

In fact, life would be quite meaningless if we didn't choose how to live it. Think for a second about what we mean when we use the phrase "my life" ("I must have more excitement in *my life*," "I would like you to be a bigger part of *my life*," "Stay the hell out of *my life*"). There is a notion of ownership involved here. Our lives are *ours*. We own them. Perhaps not in the same way we own our Toyotas and Golden Retrievers, but in some significant way we do. Open any basic textbook in property law, and you will find that to own anything is to exercise control over it. We can speak of "our lives" because we can, to an important extent, decide what to do with them. If we couldn't, it would make no sense to use that expression. Life would cease to be "ours"; it would simply be something that keeps happening to us. Surely, such a description doesn't make sense! At least most of the time we feel that we make life happen, that we do live *our* lives.

Disturbingly enough, a careful look around raises some serious doubts as to the validity of this intuition. Challenges to the possibility of human freedom have emerged in both thoroughly religious and completely secular contexts. The postulation, by the three monotheistic religions, of an all-knowing, all-powerful god, capable of predicting our every action raises questions about our ability to chart our course independently.

More recently, the Scientific Revolution of the seventeenth and eighteenth centuries has transformed the ways in which we make sense of the world. We have moved from religious accounts to more systematic, materially based, and empirical explanations. Such accounts have recast questions about the possibility of freedom, rather than resolved them. The scientific emphasis on causal explanation has created both an aspiration and a fear that human behavior can be explained with the same degree of precision as the occurrence of other natural phenomena, like the boiling of water or the trajectory of falling balls. If human behavior can be accounted for through a chain of causes, the possibility of choosing one's actions evaporates. Our actions are not really up to us, according to this picture. They are, rather, the consequences of antecedent circumstances.

The accelerated development of psychology as an independent discipline has also compounded the concerns for human freedom. Whatever approach one chooses to concentrate on, it is clear that for psychologists our actions are largely determined by external factors, whether these be our childhood experiences or the various conditioning stimuli that operate upon us. Now let's look at *Minority Report* in greater detail, to illustrate how our religious beliefs, scientific achievements, and accounts of psychological development challenge the validity of our intuitive sense that we are free.

Mechanical Men: Scientific Determinism

Chief Anderton and Mr. Witwer (Colin Farrell) are standing on the opposite sides of a table. They don't like each other. Anderton thinks his guest is a nuisance, one of those "suits" sent by the federal government to snoop around. Witwer, on the other hand, is concerned that the Precrime team is getting dangerously close to playing God and questions the rationale behind capturing people for crimes they are yet to commit. In response Anderton hisses: "The fact that you prevented it from happening doesn't mean it wasn't going to happen."

To illustrate this point, he tosses a ball across the table, and the young FBI agent catches it an instant before it rolls off. Had he done nothing, the laws of motion and gravity would have caused the ball to drop. Witwer did not want this to happen. He stopped something from taking place that would have necessarily occurred without his intervention. Anderton's point is made: human behavior is subject, in principle, to the same kind of regularity as a moving ball. Given sufficient resources it is absolutely predictable. We are lucky enough to have found the pre-cogs who can do the predicting. Stopping crimes before they happen is no different from catching a ball before it hits the floor. In both cases, a certain event is bound to happen if no one intercedes.

Later, after the precogs have identified him as a future murderer, a distraught Anderton locates Dr. Hinerman (Lois Smith), the scientist who first discovered the precogs' abilities. With desperation and hysteria commingling in his voice, Anderton tells her that the prediction pointing to him as a murderer has to be wrong. He simply couldn't. He'll stay away from the victim, stay away from the scene. He'll stop it. The pleasant looking old lady, who has graduated from generating mutant humans to creating twisted, psychotic plants, briefly looks up from her gardening: "A chain of events has started," she says, "that will inexorably lead you to it." That simple. That Anderton will kill is as sure as water freezing at zero degrees centigrade, as certain as exhaling must follow inhaling. A simple matter of cause and effect, action and reaction.

These assumptions regarding the predictability of human behavior can be traced back to the seventeenth and eighteenth centuries. In the space of two hundred years, everything we knew about the world was stood on its head. Until then, natural phenomena were assumed to have purposes. The rain fell so the grass could grow; acorns aspired to become fully grown oak trees. Religion provided a second mode of explanation, which at times completed and at others competed with the former one. Theistic understandings of nature posited specific superhuman forces as the causes of all events. A boy dies at the age of three because God doesn't like children born out of wedlock; a little girl trembles and foams at the mouth because the devil speaks through her.

As the methods of the natural sciences gained currency, the world was slowly emptied of purposes and super-human intentions. Gradually, we became convinced that everything around us is subject to the same set of basic natural laws. This, in turn, led us to believe that given enough time and patience no real mysteries would remain. We were to become, as René Descartes so grandly pronounced in his *Discourse on Method*, the "masters and possessors of nature."[2] Rain has no purpose, really. It is simply the effect of a certain level of condensation of water at a certain height. Acorns don't really want to become oak trees; they just develop as a result of sufficient nourishment and light. God didn't kill the boy. He died at the age of three because he was born with a defective heart, incapable of pumping enough blood to sustain his vital organs. The devil did not employ the little girl as a spokesperson. She trembled and foamed at the mouth due to an anomaly in electric conductivity between different parts of her brain.

In 1726 Isaac Newton published his *Philosophiae Naturalis Principia Mathematicai,* in which he articulated three basic laws purportedly governing the motion of all bodies. They were: 1) Every body continues in its state of rest or of uniform motion in

---

[2] René Descartes, *Discourse on Method* (Indianapolis: Hackett, 1999), Part VI.

a straight line, except insofar as it may be compelled by force to change that state. 2) Change of motion is proportional to force applied, and takes place in the direction of the straight line in which the forces act. 3) To every action there is always an equal and contrary reaction.

These three rules of motion create a world in which bodies act on each other according to fixed laws, very much like the wheels in a great mechanical clock. In Newton's brave new world, humans, animals, and plants do not differ in any essential way. We are more complicated than cacti, not because some abstract idea of what it is to be human is superior to the notion of "cactusness." Rather, our parts are more numerous and complex, thus increasing the number of interactions that must be understood in order to decipher how we operate.

It's not difficult to see why such mechanistic explanations are incompatible with the idea of human freedom. Machines function with stringent regularity. One wheel moves another, which pulls back a spring, which cocks back a hammer, and so on. Freedom represents a gap in the causal chain, a disjunction before which confident, smooth predictability must grind to a halt. To say that our actions are governed by a strict set of rules is to hold that they are not governed by us; it is to claim that we are *pre-determined* rather than *self-determined*. In other words, if everything we do results from a prior cause, nothing we do can be free.

Anderton justifies Precrime by assuming that people have no more choice than rolling balls. Dr. Hineman's statement claiming that he will necessarily become a killer rests on the same presumption. Both are convinced that everything we do is, in principle, predictable. As Laplace puts it in his *Philosophical Essay on Probability*:

> Given for one instant an intelligence which could comprehend all the forces by which nature is animated and the respective situation of the beings who compose it—an intelligence sufficiently vast to submit these data to analysis—it would embrace in the same formula the movements of the greatest bodies of the universe and those of the lightest atom; for it nothing would be uncertain and the future, as the past would be present to its eyes.[3]

---

[3] P.S. Laplace, *Philosophical Essay on Probability* (New York: Springer-Verlag, 1999), Chapter II.

Anderton adheres to this model only as long as it does not apply to him. As soon as the red ball engraved with his name rolls down the pipes, the tough-minded determinist becomes a staunch believer in free will. Perhaps this instinctive rejection of Newtonian mechanics when it hits close to home, when it is *about us*, teaches us something about what it is to be human that the laws of motion can't. Perhaps it indicates that while scientific determinism can help make sense of our environment, it renders our own everyday experience meaningless.

In the twentieth century, Einstein's theory of relativity and later quantum theory partly displaced Newtonian explanations. Though new and exciting, these developments did not carry any great news for human freedom. Relativity, though it does away with the traditional Euclidean assumption of three-dimensional space, is still considered to be deterministic by most philosophers of science. Many interpreters of quantum theory claim that the indeterminacy the theory implies about the behavior of subatomic particles does away with determinism. Even if this were true (the conclusion is problematic as it arises from the theory's most controversial part—its account of measurement processes), it would not pave the way for freedom. Indeterminism and determinism are equally incompatible with it. There is no more choice under conditions of absolute chaos than there is under absolute order. In the former, it is impossible to predict the outcomes of your actions, and choice becomes meaningless. In the latter, the outcomes of actions are governed by a regularity so absolute that it makes choice superfluous. Neither robots nor madmen are free. The former proceed according to some preset algorithm. The latter cannot set goals. They do not proceed at all.

Cogs in God's Plan: Religious Determinism

Chief John Anderton believed Precrime was flawless. Unfortunately for him, the program was not yet established when his only son, Sean, was snatched while playing at a public pool. Blaming himself for this loss, John slowly retreated into himself, divorced his wife, and married his job. His days were spent hunting future murderers. His nights were a narcotic cocktail of running and reminiscences. There were no reasons to think anything could break this surreal routine. But PC file 1109 turned the dedicated career officer from hunter into prey: the red ball rolling down the tubes at headquarters was engraved with his name.

With PC file 1109 Anderton's world comes crashing down. He is designated as the future killer of a certain Leo Crow (Mike Binder) by a system to which he is completely devoted. He has never met Crow, so how could he possibly intend to kill him? But if he isn't about to murder anyone, then the pre-cogs are wrong and the project is terribly flawed! He knows he can't kill. It goes against everything in him. But he also knows that the pre-cogs can't be wrong. They are the closest things in Anderton's world to God. The program is a source of hope, hope for the existence of the divine. And Gods never err. The resulting disjunction is grim: either Anderton's life is meaningless because he has no control over what he is about to do, or it is meaningless because it has been devoted to a farce. Either his gods have abandoned him, or there are no gods at all.

So Anderton begins to run: from his colleagues, his prophesied future, everything he came to believe in the previous six years. His is a crisis of faith, a moment in which the most basic assumptions about how the world is arranged collide.

A similar conflict of assumptions has haunted Christianity from time immemorial. The basic problem, recast in theological terms, is this: we think God cares about us personally. He exercises personal providence over us, punishing us for sins and rewarding our good deeds. Such personal providence presupposes freedom and choice, since it only makes sense to praise or blame someone for what they did willingly. But we also think God is all knowing. If he is, he must know in advance what we are about to do. But if that is the case, there is no way for us to do anything *freely*. As Evodius poses the question in Saint Augustine's *On the Free Choice of the Will*:

> I very much wonder how God can have foreknowledge of everything in the future, and yet we do not sin by necessity. It would be an irreligious and completely insane attack on God's foreknowledge to say that something could happen otherwise than as God foreknew. So suppose that God foreknew that the first human being was going to sin. Anyone who admits, as I do, that God foreknows everything in the future will have to grant me that. Now . . . since God foreknew that he was going to sin, his

sin necessarily had to happen. How, then, is the will free when such inescapable necessity is found in it? [4]

Some theologians tried to resolve this conflict by eliminating one of its sides. Embracing the notion of predestination, they claimed that whether we become vicious or good is decided in advance. Freedom does not exist according to this view. Rewards and punishments are not carrots and sticks for good and bad choices, but, rather, indications or divine signs pointing towards the decisions God has already made about us and for us.

Others have chosen to eliminate the opposite side of the conflict, by foregoing providence. On this understanding, God does not care about us personally, he does not hold us individually responsible for our actions, and he does not intervene in history. This position conceives of a philosophical, rather than a personal divinity, an entity that must exist as a first cause or some other logical condition, but does not strive for any specific involvement in this world.

The most famous attempt at reconciling freedom and God's omniscient nature is associated with St. Augustine. It makes little sense, Augustine argues, to attribute foreknowledge to God, as if he is subject to our linear understanding of time in which there must be "before" and "after." For God past, present, and future are merged. He doesn't come to know the world under the same restrictions and conditions that we do. He is not bound to perceive events through a fixed order. All is present to him simultaneously. Hence, it is incorrect to say that God has foreknowledge of anything. But even if we were to insist on using this terminology, Augustine tells us that the free operation of our will is among the things foreknown; that God knows in advance how and when we will act freely. The point underlying this argument seems to be that knowing in advance does not imply determining in advance. To illustrate this point, consider the following questions: 1) If I fast-forward *Minority Report* in double speed, I will know at 9:00 what you, who watches the film in regular speed, will only know at 10:00. But does this mean that I have, in any way, determined what you are about to see? 2) If you are watching a recorded World Cup soccer match that I had tuned into the night

---

[4] Augustine, *On The Free Choice of the Will* (Indianapolis: Hackett, 1993), Section 3.2.

before, does my foreknowledge of the end result determine, in any way, your hopes and aspirations or how you experience the competition (assuming that you are ignorant of the game's outcome)? In other words, it does not seem that knowledge of the future and the course it takes are causally linked.

Another, more famous claim, associated with Augustine ties human freedom to the existence of evil. He asks: If God is all good and all powerful, how does he allow for so many bad things to happen? The only explanation for this, according to Augustine, is that humans are free to act wickedly or beneficently. Freedom is part of our essence, and evil is its cost. Simply put, there cannot be evil without freedom, and the existence of evil is the strongest proof for the fact that we are free.

Anderton's distress mirrors these theological concerns very closely. He believes the pre-cogs are infallible (and therefore god-like). To his dismay, a set of circumstances arises in which that infallibility implies that he is not a self-determining agent. Anderton clings to the minority reports, understanding that they represent his only way to maintain a sense of freedom. But with the discovery of these reports, his dreams regarding the divine nature of Agatha (Samantha Morton) and her two comatose colleagues, suffer shipwreck. Gods do not make mistakes; humans do. For Anderton there is no happy Augustinian solution maintaining both our secure, happy attachment to God and our sense of freedom.

As the film progresses, one gets the sense that Spielberg is more concerned with the relationship between freedom and evil than he is with that between freedom and foreknowledge. For Augustine, evil proves that we are free, not that God does not exist. Washington, D.C., under Precrime is significantly cleansed of the evil that is murder. But as we delve deeper into the plot, we understand that freedom has been eliminated with it. If Anderton's journey tells us anything at all, it is that trying to empty the world of risks, trying to purify it from anything malignant, ends up draining it of human content. It leaves us with a picture perfect aquarium in which none of us would like to live.

The Child Is Father of the Man: Psychological Determinism

Ever feel that your buttons are being pushed? That someone says or does something at a certain time, in a certain way, and whether you like it or not, you just lash out? Maybe it's your father asking if there is beer left in the refrigerator, when what he really wants is for you to get him one. Maybe it's your husband leaving his socks next to the shower stand, as if a dedicated platoon of fairies were standing ready to collect them.

Lamar Burgess was pushing John Anderton's buttons. He knew that Sean's abduction would motivate the younger officer, so he recruited him to head Precrime. He also knew that an encounter with his son's killer was the one thing that could move John to become a murderer. So when Lamar felt that the dark secret at the root of his project was about to be uncovered (the murder of Agatha's mother), he staged just such a meeting.

When they know us well enough, others can often predict what we are about to do. Familiarity with our personal make-up, with our character traits, allows them to 'play' us. Even more frightening, though, is the fact that these traits don't really depend on us. They are ours, but we don't create them. Anderton did not choose to become the kind of person to be driven half mad by feelings of guilt, nor did he elect to be someone who deals with loss by plunging himself into work or narcotics. If asked in the abstract, he would have probably wanted to process his tragedy differently. He would have liked to stay off drugs, to remain married. Like the rest of us, he did not mold his own personality. He was, rather, cast into a set of circumstances that made him discover it.

This frightening realization, that most of what we do springs from a personality we are not responsible for shaping, is Sigmund Freud's most lasting legacy. Psychoanalysis asks us to reorient our expectations. It replaces self-determination with self-discovery as the best we can hope for. Our conscious activity is described as "the tip of the iceberg", the small visible portion of a largely submerged, unconscious existence. Furthermore, these discernable activities of ours are largely determined by our more significant "sunken" part.

Freud tells us that we are homeostatic stimulus-response systems. In simpler terms, we have to react to anything we encounter in our environments. But, the ways in which we react are shaped by the feedback we get from our surroundings. A child is frustrated when her mother takes away a toy. In response to the child's anger, the mother is deeply offended and for the next few hours keeps her distance. The child learns that anger cannot be expressed directly. Thus future expressions of anger are disguised, they become less overt (for example, through complaining of sickness more frequently, or through damaging something that belongs to the parents). The idea is simple enough: by means of our early interactions with the environment, a kind of sorting system or filter develops, which disguises our responses into a form that will be accepted by those around us. It is this sorting system, which is called the "pre-conscious" in Freud's earlier writings, and the "Super Ego" in his later work that shapes how we actually behave. The differences between peoples' behaviors *are* the differences between their filters. But the shape these filters take does not depend on us. They are designed early on by our interaction with our close environment. The patterns in which we end up behaving, what we end up doing, essentially who we end up being, is not really up to us. We are, for the most part, determined by our early history. It is in this sense that the child in everyone of us is the "father" of the grown person.

On a Freudian account, Anderton could not have chosen to react differently to the crisis he underwent. When calamity struck, the patterns of his behavior had already been set. Similarly, Agent Witwer could not have declined to pursue the truth about Precrime once it suggested itself. His own disposition for critical inquisitiveness was engraved long before. By the time we are conscious, the ways in which we react to the world are largely fixed. They cannot be completely erased and recast, as this would be tantamount to erasing ourselves. If we are lucky enough to find a competent therapist, and if we are even luckier to be able to pay her, we can recognize the structure of our own pre-consciousness. Rarely, we might even be able to slightly modify some of our patterns, to make a slight dent in our ways of response. But that's as good as is it gets.

Significant self-knowledge?—perhaps. Complete self determination?—not by a long shot. If Anderton's life has any meaning, it is to be found in understanding why he behaves as he does: why he joined Precrime, why he can't let go of Sean's memory. Similarly, Witwer's life becomes significant not because of what he does, but by understanding why he does it.

Our Need for Freedom

In his *Treatise of Human Nature*, the famous Scottish philosopher David Hume points out that we consistently fail to explain some of the most basic ideas that underlie everyday experience. We cannot provide a coherent account of our own personal identity over time, yet we know there is a continuum between who we are now and the baby that emerged from our mother's womb. We fail to explain the relation of cause and effect (afterall no one has actually *seen* causality itself, only the constant conjunction of two events), yet we know that heating water to one hundred degrees centigrade *causes* it to boil.

For those of us who are bent on rationally understanding every aspect of the world these failures can be disturbing and disorienting. They can lead to the kind of depressing skepticism that makes you think that life doesn't make sense. For the rest of us, these gaps in explanation point to the limitations of our ability to know. We do our best to clarify things to ourselves, and some of the things we can't, we just take on faith. After all, what are we to do? Deny our own existence? Stop making tea?

Our Freedom is one of these things. Science, religion, and psychology undermine it. Careful systematic thinking casts grave doubts over it. And yet, the intuition cannot be extinguished. Choice is required to makes sense of what we do everyday; it is required to make life meaningful. Between a philosophy that empties our experience of content and a form of experience that cannot be fully accounted for philosophically, we choose the latter. As Hume warns us:

> Indulge your passion for science . . . but let your science be human, and such as may have a direct reference to action and society. Abstruse thought and profound researches [nature] prohibit[s], and will severely punish, by the pensive melancholy which they introduce, by the endless uncertainty in which they involve you, and by the cold reception which your pretended discoveries shall meet with, when communicated. Be a philosopher; but, amidst all your philosophy, be still a man.[5]

---

[5] David Hume, *Enquiry concerning Human Understanding* (Indianapolis: Hackett, 1993), Section I.4

Minority Report shows us what happens when we don't make sure our science remains human: we find ourselves in a world where our most basic intuitions are negated, where "freedom" is secured by its own denial. We should probably keep this in mind next time we are so impressed with the immanent possibility of human cloning or with advances in artificial intelligence research. Go to sleep with Lamar Burges and you just might wake up in John Anderton's world.[6]

---

[6] We would like to thank Maria Granik for her invaluable help.

To Think About

1. What do you think is meant by the Precrime slogan "That which makes us safe is that which makes us free"? Is there anything dissatisfying about that kind of freedom? Are there any other conditions we require in order to be free except safety?

2. How does Newtonian mechanical science eliminate the possibility of freedom? How do Freud's insights curtail it? How would you defend freedom against them?

3. If the determinists are even partially right, how can we justify our everyday activities of punishing and making moral judgments?

4. Some thinkers have claimed that freedom is possible inside a solitary confinement cell and even at gunpoint. How is this possible?

To Read Next

Augustine. *On The Free Choice of the Will*. Indianapolis: Hackett, 1993.

Isaiah Berlin. Two Concepts of Liberty. In Isaiah Berlin, *Four Essays on Liberty* (Oxford: Oxford University Press, 1990.

Gerald Dworkin, ed. *Determinism, Free Will, and Moral Responsibility*. Oxford Readings in Philosophy Series. New Jersey: Prentice Hall, 1970.

Thomas Nagel. *What Does It All Mean? A Very Short Introduction to Philosophy*. New York: Oxford University Press, 1981. Chapter 6, "Free Will", pp. 47–58.

Jean-Paul Sartre. *Existentialism and Humanism*. London: Methuen, 1948.

18

Grace, Fate, and Accident in *Pulp Fiction*

MICHAEL SILBERSTEIN

"If my answers frighten you then you should cease askin' scary questions," proclaims the morally awakened Jules (Samuel L. Jackson) to the doubting Vincent (John Travolta).

Pulp Fiction (1994), directed by Quentin Tarrantino, is a buzzing, blooming confusion, presenting a variety of subcultures, races, ethnicities, lifestyles, religious and non-religious worldviews, and moral perspectives. Given such a world, how are we to figure out what is right and what is wrong? How could there exist any universal moral truths or values? And if universal moral truths or values don't exist, how can we agree upon how we should live our lives, much less whether or not these lives are meaningful?

Do life and existence have a universal and objective meaning or purpose? Are the events of our lives and the events that make up existence meaningfully connected in some way—is there some purpose, plan, pattern, ultimate end or grand narrative that connects all these events? In the words of Leo Tolstoy in his essay *My Confession*, "what's the point of it all?" Questions about the nature of meaning and morality are, unlike many others, philosophical questions that deeply concern us all. In the words of the great existentialist philosopher Camus, "the meaning of life is the most urgent of questions . . .judging whether life is or is not worth living is the only serious philosophical problem."[1] (*The Myth of Sisyphus*, 1955, p. 3).

---

[1] Albert Camus, *The Myth of Sisyphus* (New York: Vintage, 1955), p. 3

Pulp Fiction presents us with a conversation between nihilism and relativism, on the one hand, and meaningfulness and universalism on the other. *Nihilism*, literally, a belief in nothing (*nihil* in Latin), suggests that there are no values or truths, moral or otherwise; at the very least, we're certainly not justified in believing in any of these truths.[2] According to the nihilist, the universe is a cosmic Rorschach print, a morally blank canvas onto which we project meaning, values, and purpose. *Moral nihilism* holds that moral claims are meaningless and *meaning* or *purpose nihilism* holds that life is without any objective or universal meaning—life is pointless. *Relativism*[3] is the related view that certain facts or truths are not universal and objective, but *relative* to individuals, cultures, or other groups. By contrast, *moral universalism* is the claim that moral facts or truths are the same *everywhere* and *every when*, while *moral objectivism*[4] holds that moral facts are real and independent facts given by the universe and not merely subjective human projections or conventions.

These questions about morals and meaning are inseparable. For example many people of radically different philosophical persuasions have felt that only the existence of God could

---

[2] "Most contemporary discussions of nihilism arise out of a consideration of Friedrich Nietzsche''s remarks on nihilism, especially in *The Will to Power*. Nihilism can also be described as an extreme form of *existentialism* or *pessimism* which holds that life has no meaning and that even if you try to achieve your goals, in the end your life must necessarily come to nothing— thus nihilism is similar to *fatalism*. Sometimes, nihilism is worse than fatalism because nihilists don't usually say that life comes to zero but to less than zero, since they hold that life really just consists of one thing: pain. See the Stanford Internet Encyclopedia of Philosophy for more details.

[3] The doctrine of moral relativism goes back to the Sophists, such as Protagoras, who argued against Socrates's moral objectivism in Plato's dialogues. Sophists would also invoke cultural relativism in these debates which they learned about in detail from the historical works of Herodotus. See the Stanford Internet Encyclopedia of Philosophy for more details.

[4] The origins of moral objectivism and universalism also go back to ancient Greece. Plato himself defends a kind of objectivism grounded in the forms and a type of objectivism known as the Divine Command Theory. The theory holds that moral facts are determined by God's will. The Ten Commandments for example are often thought to be the manifestation of God's will. See the *Stanford Internet Encyclopedia of Philosophy* for more details.

ground universal and objective moral facts and objective purpose or meaningfulness. If God does not exist it is hard to see
how meaning and morality can be anything but the interpretation or projection of various individuals. As the famous existentialist[5] philosopher Sartre put it: "The existentialist thinks it
very distressing that God does not exist and that we have to
face all the consequences of this. Because all possibility of finding values in a heaven of ideas disappears along with him.
Indeed, everything is permissible if God does not exist."[6]

If God exists then it is possible that the events of our lives
are meaningfully connected and that through God's *grace* our
suffering is not a random and meaningless *accident* but rather a
necessary vehicle of moral and spiritual transformation. If God
exists to give us guidance and also freedom, then it is possible
the future is open in such a way that there is fate without *fatalism* and we have the choice to accept or reject God's grace. As
we shall see the existentialist philosopher Kierkegaard thinks
that the resolution to the problem of meaning and morality can
only be resolved by a "leap of faith."

At first glance, *Pulp Fiction* appears to be nothing more than
an innovative take on *film noir*, and a sympathetic meditation
on relativism. The non-linear structure of the movie forces us to
consider how, if at all, the five seemingly unrelated 'episodes'
within the film are meaningfully connected. The very structure
of the film raises the question as to whether or not there is any
temporal, narrative, and moral order in this pulp world. At every
key point in *Pulp Fiction* we are faced with a turn of improbable events that begs the question: Was it fate, grace or accident?
Consider the following examples:

---

[5] Existentialism was a philosophical movement that had its roots in the late
nineteenth century but really blossomed in the mid-twentieth century. In addition to Sartre, Camus and Nietzsche, some of the great figures in existentialism
include Kierkegaard, Heidegger, and Jaspers. While part of the same movement (or better yet anti-movement) there was as much disagreement as agree-
ment among the existentialist philosophers. For example, some existentialist
thinkers such as Kierkegaard thought that the belief in God was necessary to
ground meaningfulness, whereas others such as Sartre disagreed. See the
Stanford Internet Encyclopedia of Philosophy for more details.

[6] Jean-Paul Sartre, *Existentialism* (New York: Citadel, 1947), pp. 25–27.

1. Vincent and Jules escape death at point-blank range.

2. Shortly thereafter Marvin inexplicably gets his head blown off when Vincent's gun misfires.

3. Vincent and Butch happen to meet in Marsellus's bar and take a disliking to each other before Butch kills him.

4. Vincent and Mia have a lot in common, both having unknowingly spent time in Amsterdam at the same bar with the same people.

5. Mia mistakes Vincent's heroin for coke and thereby overdoses. If that had not happened they might have had sex together with dire consequences for both.

6. Fabian, Butch's girlfriend, forgets his watch at the apartment.

7. Butch runs into Marsellus while escaping from his apartment.

8. Butch and Marsellus end up in the Mason-Dixon Pawnshop.

9. Vincent and Jules find themselves near Jimmie's house when they are in need.

10. Vincent and Jules encounter Pumpkin and Honeybunny at the coffee shop.

Is there any moral and purposeful order in these events? At the beginning, *Pulp Fiction* feels like pulp—a soft, moist, shapeless mass of matter, but by the end of the movie we can see its meaningful shape. In contrast to its title, it's much more than a lurid tale filled with rough characters and unfinished thoughts, it's a movie that is alive with the possibility of meaning and salvation.

Relativism with a Vengeance

If relativism endorses the general claim that certain facts or truths are not universal or objective, but relative to individuals, cultures, or groups, *moral relativism* is the normative claim that moral truths are relative to cultures or individuals. *Cultural relativism* is the simple descriptive claim that different cultures have different values and practices. Moral relativism is a normative claim—it makes a value judgment, whereas cultural relativism is an indisputable factual claim—it is just a fact that human sacrifice was practiced by some cultures but to claim that such sacrifices were not immoral in such cultures is a relativist value judgment. *Pulp Fiction* flirts with moral relativism by getting us to sympathize with its main characters who are, after all, criminals and thugs.

In a modern streetwise version of a Platonic dialogue, the main characters Jules and Vincent engage in conversation about cultural and moral relativism.

> **JULES:** Okay now, tell me about the hash bars? [Vincent has just returned from Amsterdam]
>
> **VINCENT:** What do you want to know?
>
> **JULES:** Well, hash is legal there, right?
>
> **VINCENT:** Yeah, it's legal, but it ain't a hundred percent legal. I mean you can't walk into a restaurant, roll a joint, and start puffin' away. You're only supposed to smoke in your home or certain designated places.

The conversation continues in the same vein, drifting from Vincent informing Jules of various rules and regulations regarding hash bars in Amsterdam to other cultural differences between Europe and America, such as beer being served in the movie theaters in Amsterdam, mayonnaise being served on fries in Holland, as well as various complications with the metric system. Their dialogue turns explicitly to ethics when they debate the fate of Antwan Rockamora, whom they believe was thrown out of a four-story window by Marsellus (Ving Rhames) merely because he gave Mia (Uma Thurman) a foot massage.

> **JULES:** Look, just because I wouldn't give no man a foot massage, don't make it right for Marsellus to throw Antwan off a building into a glass-motherfuckin-house, fuckin' up the way the nigger talks. That ain't right, man.
>
> **VINCENT:** I'm not sayin' he was right, but you're sayin' a foot massage don't mean nothin', and I'm sayin' it does. I've given a million ladies a million foot massages and they all meant somethin'. We act like they don't, but they do. That's what's so fuckin' cool about 'em.

We begin to see a moral universe emerge. Vincent and Jules each operate with competing codes of morality. Vincent personifies an ethical perspective that holds that the rightness or wrongness of an act is determined primarily by the intentions and feelings of the agent. Because Vincent thinks that the real intention behind a foot massage is seduction motivated by lust, he concludes that a foot massage can constitute an act of sex. By contrast, Jules seems to think that a foot massage is not a sexual act because the foot is not a sexual organ. For Jules it is not the intention of an act that determine the act's rightness or wrongness, but whether or not one's actions adhere to standard normative practices.

Old versus New

The previous conversation takes place right before Vincent and Jules are about to enter an apartment and execute several young men. Ironically it never occurs to either of them to discuss whether or not murder is wrong. They both feel that the young men who are about to get capped deserve to be killed because they have wronged Marsellus by stealing his briefcase. Jules accuses the young men of trying to "fuck Marsellus like a bitch," effectively equating their act of theft with the immoral act of rape. This harsh moral judgment may have something to do with the value of what is in the case (the contents are never revealed). There does seem to be a code of ethics at work here, which is based upon the principle of "honor among thieves."[7]

This principle amounts to an Old Testament "eye for an eye" morality that is rooted in revenge. In the Old Testament, God frequently doles out a fire and brimstone brand of justice, which amounts to vengeance or retribution. By contrast, in the New Testament, God in the form of Christ urges us to repay hate and violence with love and passivity. Throughout *Pulp Fiction*, we will see that the main characters who move away from Old Testament morality towards New Testament morality will end up faring much better than their more morally recalcitrant peers. By the end of the movie, one of the characters, Butch the boxer

---

[7] One can find the same theme in Tarantino's film, *Reservoir Dogs*.

(played by Bruce Willis), rides to freedom on a chopper named "Grace," suggesting that he was saved by the grace of God. The very notion of God's grace only makes sense from the point of view of the New Testament in which God does not engage in well-deserved retribution, but rather acts with compassion and forgiveness.

Jules and Vincent believe that the young men were aware of the code and the consequences for transgression; therefore, they deserve to be executed. Interestingly, Brett, the young men's apparent leader, tries to defend their actions by saying, "When we entered into this thing, we only had the best intentions . . ." But before Brett can finish his thought, Jules retorts:

> Yes ya did Brett. Ya tried ta fuck 'im. You ever read the bible Brett? There's a passage I got memorized, seems appropriate for this situation: Ezekiel 25:17. "The path of the righteous man is beset on all sides by the inequities of the selfish and the tyranny of evil men. Blessed is he who, in the name of charity and good will, shepherds the weak through the valley of darkness, for he is truly his brother's keeper and the finder of lost children. And I will strike down upon thee with great vengeance and furious anger those who attempt to poison and destroy my brothers. And you will know my name is the Lord when I lay my vengeance upon you."

Jules always recites this passage right before he "blasts a cap in somebody's ass." The passage is in fact a contrived version of Ezekiel's prophecy against the Philistines. The actual text of Ezekiel 25:17 reads as follows: "And I will execute great vengeance upon them with furious rebukes; and they shall know that I am the Lord, when I shall lay my vengeance upon them" (King James Version). Jules's tweaked version conveys both Old and New Testament moral sensibilities, which signifies his struggle to ultimately embrace New Testament morality.

While Vincent and Jules are career criminals, they're not amoral sociopaths, for each of these characters operates out of his own idiosyncratic moral code. Vincent and Jules exhibit the virtues of professionalism, loyalty, and honor. After all, they only kill people in self-defense, or when someone has dishonored them, their family, or their boss. The movie's main characters engage in immoral acts—murder, robbery, drug dealing—but they also exhibit virtues such as loyalty, honesty, diligence, and integrity. If the moral relativist is right, then it may be that this cast of criminals are, in the end, morally decent. At the very least, they would be able to justify their actions by invoking their individualized moral codes of conduct or those of their criminal caste.

Virtue among Thieves

Now let's consider the following scene in which Vincent's value system is put to the test. After the discussion of what happened to Antwan Rockamora for giving Marsellus's wife Mia a foot massage, Vincent finds himself in the unenviable position of being ordered by Marsellus to take Mia out for the evening while he is out of town. As we watch Mia and Vincent flirt and dance barefoot with one another, we can't help but recall Vincent's earlier remarks about foot massages. Dancing can certainly be regarded as a surreptitiously sensual act. Mia is beautiful, sexy, smart, and has much in common with Vincent. Vincent's attraction to Mia, plus the ribbing he has received from his peers about the date with his boss's wife, makes him very nervous. While washing his hands in Mia's bathroom at the end of the evening, Vincent tries to psyche himself up to practice restraint:

> One drink and leave. Don't be rude, but drink your drink quickly, say goodbye, walk out the door, get in your car, and go down the road. It's a moral test of yourself, whether or not you can maintain loyalty. Because when people are loyal to each other, that's very meaningful. So you're gonna go out there, drink your drink, say "goodnight, I've had a lovely evening," go home, and jack off. And that's all you're gonna do.

It is clear from Vincent's thoughts that the virtue of loyalty is truly important to him. He feels a real duty toward Marsellus, and he is not avoiding cheating with Mia merely because he fears the possible consequences.

After having recovered both Marsellus's briefcase and Marvin, Vincent accidentally blows off Marvin's head while driving around L.A. With Marvin's brains splattered all over their car, Vincent and Jules find a port in the storm in the home of Jules's old partner Jimmie (played by Quentin Tarrantino).

Jimmie wants to help them to dispose of the body but he's worried that his wife will come home and find the gangsters and the headless corpse. Even though Jules's ass is on the line we see him exhibit the virtue of friendship.

> **JULES:** Well, we ain't leavin' til we made a couple phone calls. But I never want it to reach that pitch. Jimmie's my friend and you don't bust in your friend's house and start tellin' 'im what's what . . . Don't forget who's doin' who a favor.

In another scene, when we first encounter Butch (Bruce Willis), he is not a very sympathetic character. He is, at Marsellus's order, agreeing to throw an upcoming fight.

> **MARSELLUS:** Boxers don't have old timers' day. You came close, but you never made it. And if you were gonna make it, you'd a made it before now. Now, the night of the fight, you may feel a slight sting, that's pride fuckin' wit ya. Fuck pride! Pride only hurts, it never helps. Fight through that shit. Cause a year from now when you're kickin' it in the Caribbean you're gonna say, Marsellus Wallace was right.
> **BUTCH:** I got no problems with that.
> **MARSELLUS:** In the fifth, your ass goes down. Say it!
> **BUTCH:** In the fifth, my ass goes down.

When next we meet Butch, he is escaping from Marsellus after having inadvertently killed the boxer to whom he was supposed to throw the fight. Apparently Butch took the money Marsellus paid him to throw the fight and bet it on himself to win. Here he explains to the cabdriver, who functions as his get away driver, how he feels about having killed the other man:

> **ESMARELDA:** I want to know what it feels like to kill a man—
> **BUTCH:** —I couldn't tell ya. I didn't know he was dead 'til you told me he was dead. Now I know he's dead, do you wanna know how I feel about it?
> **ESMARELDA:** Yes.
> **BUTCH:** I don't feel the least little bit bad. You wanna know why, Esmarelda?

ESMARELDA: Yes.

BUTCH: Cause I'm a boxer. And after you've said that, you've
said pretty much all there is to say about me. Now maybe
that son-of-a-bitch tonight was once at one time a boxer.
If he was, then he was dead before his ass ever stepped
in the ring. I just put the poor bastard outta his misery.
And if he never was a boxer—That's what he gets for
fuckin' up my sport.

First impressions can be tricky. Initially we think that Butch is
all too happy to sell his soul and compromise his profession for
money. Having agreed to throw the fight, and then welch on the
deal seems even more reprehensible. He seems heartless about
having unintentionally killed his opponent. But the preceding
dialogue between the cab driver Esmarelda and Butch shows us
that Butch was under duress when he agreed to throw the fight.
It was his sense of pride, his honor, and his love of the sport
that drove him to give it his best shot. Butch no doubt rational-
izes that since Marsellus was forcing him to throw the fight that
it would be okay to break his promise and thereby profit from
the deal. Butch feels little sympathy for Marsellus because he
has no respect for the sanctity of boxing. As for his deceased
opponent, Butch reasons that if he was once a true boxer then
the fact that he was selling out meant that his soul was already
dead and thus Butch was doing him a favor by killing him. On
the other hand, if he was not ever really a boxer then he got
what he deserved for disrespecting the sport. Here it appears
that even the initially unlovable Butch is operating according to
some sort of moral code.

Judge Not Lest Ye Be Judged

There is an obvious tension between the relativist bent of the
film, the relativist pattern of rationalization used by the criminals
to justify their actions, and the universalist "eye for an eye" ethic
prescribed by the Old Testament that Jules, Vincent, and Butch
use to justify their violent retribution. No doubt Jules and Vincent
do not view themselves as nihilists or moral relativists but rather
as acting according to some universal principles. However from
the perspective of the viewer, much of the justification that the
gangsters give for their violent criminal behavior rings as hollow

rationalization. We feel that only the truth of moral relativism could redeem these characters, just as the dialogues at the beginning of the film tacitly suggest. These moral tensions are eventually resolved one way or the other for each of the main characters, depending on their capacity for a change of heart and, if you will, the grace of God.

After Jules and Vincent "miraculously" escape being shot by the .357 magnum "hand cannon" unloaded at them at point blank range, Jules sees it as an act of God and decides to quit the criminal life: "That's it for me. From here on in, you can consider my ass retired. I'm tell'in' Marsellus today I'm through." To the best of our knowledge Jules lives out the rest of his natural life walking the Earth and searching for God "like Caine in Kung Fu."

When Pumpkin (Tim Roth) threatens Jules at gun point for his wallet and Marsellus's briefcase in the coffee shop, Jules gets the drop on him and could easily kill him. Instead, he turns the other cheek.

JULES: . . . I'm givin' you that money so I don't hafta kill your ass. You read the bible?

PUMPKIN: Not regularly.

JULES: There's a passage I got memorized. Ezekiel 25:17 . . . And if you ever heard it, it meant your ass. I never really questioned what it meant. I thought it was just a cold-blooded thing to say to a motherfucker 'fore you popped a cap in his ass. But I saw some shit this mornin' made me think twice. Now I'm thinkin', it could mean you're the evil man. And I'm the righteous man. And Mr. .45 here, he's the shepherd protecting my righteous ass in the valley of darkness. Or it could mean you're the righteous man and I'm the shepherd and it's the world that's evil and selfish. I'd like that. But that shit ain't the truth. The truth is you're the weak. And I'm the tyranny of evil men. But I'm tryin'. I'm tryin' real hard to be a shepherd.

Jules remains true to his moral epiphany, letting Pumpkin and Honeybunny (Amanda Plummer) go in peace with his fifteen hundred dollars. Maybe Jules has come to realize that both his relativistic posturing and proclamations of Old Testament vengeance were little more than rationalizations for his immoral behavior. Jules has stopped deceiving himself about his actions. He now realizes that he has been leading an immoral life and he must change his ways or truly lose his soul.

Vincent, by contrast, sees nothing divine or meaningful in the fact that all of the bullets missed them when they were surprised by an attacker with a .357 magnum. He sees it as merely an improbable event; they were lucky and that is all. Vincent is still morally and spiritually asleep and he pays the ultimate price for it shortly thereafter when he is shot by Butch with his own gun while walking out of Butch's bathroom holding a copy of *Modesty Blaise*. Vincent was waiting in Butch's apartment to do unto him what Butch did first.

Shortly after Butch escapes death at the hands of Vincent, he is presented with his own critical moral test. The only reason Butch risked his life by going back to his apartment was to retrieve his father's gold watch that had been passed down through several wars and generations of family soldiers. For Butch the gold watch symbolizes honor, familial piety, respect, bravery, and courage. In short, the watch symbolizes everything that is moral and meaningful to Butch. As he tells himself:

> This is my war. You see, Butch, what you're forgettin' is this watch isn't just a device that enables you to keep track of time. This watch is a symbol. It's a symbol of how your father, and his father before him, and his father before him, distinguished themselves in war. Using that perspective, going back for it isn't stupid. It may be dangerous, but it's not stupid. Because there are certain things in this world that are worth going back for [i.e., worth dying for].

Butch, speeding away from his apartment, is quite proud and happy with himself after killing Vincent. To himself he says: "That's how you're gonna beat'em, Butch. They keep underestimatin' ya." Just when Butch thinks he has gotten away free and clear, he quite unexpectedly encounters Marsellus in the street. A struggle ensues and out of rancor they try to kill one another.

Both Butch and Marsellus find themselves in the Mason-Dixon Pawnshop and just as Butch is about to shoot Marsellus in the head, the owner of the shop (the redneck Maynard) knocks Butch out. When next we see both Butch and Marsellus tied up, beat up, and gagged in Maynard's S&M hillbilly dungeon below the pawnshop, we are reminded of Marsellus's earlier speech to Butch about pride. Both men are indeed learning the hard way that "pride cometh before a fall." As Maynard and Zed are avariciously deciding who to rape first, we see Butch and Marsellus look at each other, all traces of hostility gone, replaced by a shared terror.

Unsurprisingly the two rednecks pick Marsellus to rape first. Butch manages to escape, but just as he is about to leave the pawnshop and thereby abandon Marsellus to his fate, his conscience kicks in. Listening to the two rednecks have their way with Marsellus, Butch decides he cannot leave anybody in such a hellish situation and begins rooting around in the pawnshop for a weapon. He tries several weapons on for size, a big hammer, a chainsaw, a Louisville slugger, but then he sees the perfect weapon hanging on the wall above a neon sign that says "Dad's Old-Fashioned Root Beer." The weapon is a samurai sword, a katana, the ultimate symbol of honor, duty, and the Bushido warrior code.

Ironically, Butch cannot abandon Marsellus for the very same reason he could not throw the fight. Butch frees Marsellus ending the feud between them: Butch rides away a free man, having passed his moral and spiritual test. Butch and Marsellus crossed the Mason-Dixon Line, both becoming slaves to and allies against a common enemy: rednecks who rape, torture, and kill their victims just for fun. Only the humility of cooperation and the Golden Rule can deliver these two from the bondage of truly evil men.

Epilogue: From Nihilism to Redemption

As we saw earlier, philosophical questions about meaning and morality are inextricably connected. Recall that Vincent thinks it is loyalty that gives life meaning hence his demeanor toward Mia and it is Butch's belief that honor and respect for his father are worth dying for that sends him back for the watch.

Let's take a look at the debate that breaks out between Jules and Vincent regarding their Near Death Experience brought on by the .357's being unsuccessfully unloaded in their face:

JULES: We should be fuckin' dead right now.
VINCENT: Yeah, we were lucky.

JULES: That was . . . divine intervention. You know what divine intervention is?

VINCENT: Yeah, I think so. That means God came down from Heaven and stopped the bullets.

JULES: Yeah man, that's what it means. That's exactly what it means! God came down from Heaven and stopped the bullets.

VINCENT: Ever seen that show "COPS?" I was watchin' it once and this cop was on it who was talkin' about this time he got into a gun fight with a guy in a hallway. He unloads on this guy and he doesn't hit anything. And these guys were in a hallway. It's a freak, but it happens.

JULES: If you wanna play blind man, then go walk with a shepherd. But me, my eyes are wide fuckin' open.

VINCENT: I guess it's when God makes the impossible possible. And I'm sorry Jules, but I don't think what happened this morning qualifies.

JULES: Don't you see, Vince, that shit don't matter. You're judging this thing the wrong way. It's not about what. It could be God stopped the bullets, he changed Coke into Pepsi, he found my fuckin' car keys. You don't judge shit like this based on merit. Whether or not what we experienced was an according-to-Hoyle miracle is insignificant. What is significant is I felt God's touch. God got involved.

Jules has had a religious existential experience. He decides to make a leap of faith based on a personal subjective experience. The Danish philosopher Søren Kierkegaard (1833–1855) talked about the true leap of faith whereby, through the sheer force of passion, the individual rips himself out of his old form of existence and throws himself into a new existence where he will hold himself responsible to the will of God. This new life represents a commitment to self-perfection and other human being's welfare. For Kierkegaard what is essential about such a leap of faith is that it is beyond reason and empirical justification.[8]

Jules and Vincent are faced with the same question we all are, how to interpret our experience? Whereas Jules sees a moral, spiritual and meaningful order in existence (fate without

---

[8] See for example Kierkegaard's *Fear and Trembling*.

fatalism and the grace of God), Vincent sees only chance and accident when he reflects on the recent events that comprise the film. Just as Jules and Vincent cannot resolve their philosophical differences with any certainty—in the end an inductive leap is unavoidable when choosing a worldview or interpretation of experience—we the viewers cannot know with certainty how best to interpret this film. Based on the ultimate fate of the characters (those who refuse to listen to the angels of their better nature are laid to waste) and based on the highly improbable chain of events that comprise the film, my conclusion is that Tarantino's worldview is closer to that of the transformed Jules.

Finally, consider the fate of Butch. After rescuing Marsellus he rides away into freedom on a chopper named "Grace," perhaps suggesting that he is literally being carried away by the grace of God. Earlier events in *Pulp Fiction* foreshadow this eventuality. The viewer notes earlier in the film that the partially burned out Killian's Red Beer neon sign in the pawnshop reads "kill ed" and that Zed's key chain for Grace is a large gold metal "Z." Add the Z to the sign and you get "Kill Zed." Is this mere coincidence or a meaningful synchronicity foretelling the future? We can never know with certainty but we do know Butch escapes on Zed's chopper Grace, leaving each of us to decide for ourselves whether or not to make the leap of faith in this apparently pulp world.

TO THINK ABOUT

1. How do the ethical perspectives of Jules and Vincent differ? Can you think of specific examples?

2. Some people believe that relativism is better because it encourages toleration of others' beliefs; however some claim relativism is bad because "all is permitted." Which do you think is right?

3 Can life be valuable even though it lacks meaning?

4. Can meaning or morality be subjective or grounded in human experience without implying nihilism?

TO READ NEXT

Albert Camus. *The Myth of Sysiphus*. New York: Vintage, 1955.

Walter Kaufmann. *Existentialism from Dostoevsky to Sartre*. New York: Meridian, 1975.

Jack Meiland and Michael Krausz, eds., *Relativism, Cognitive and Moral*. Notre Dame: Notre Dame University Press, 1982.

Kai Nielson. *Ethics Without God*. London: Pemberton Press, 1973.

James Rachels. *The Elements of Moral Philosophy*. Third edition. New York: McGraw Hill, 1999.

Leo Tolstoy. *My Confession*. New York: Norton, 1996.

19

What Nietzsche Could Teach You: Eternal Return in *Groundhog Day*

JAMES H. SPENCE

> What if some day or night a demon were to steal after you into your loneliest loneliness and say to you: "This life as you now live it and have lived it, you will have to live once more and innumerable times more; and there will be nothing new in it, but every pain and every joy and every thought and sigh and everything unutterably small or great in your life will have to return to you, all in the same succession and sequence, even this spider and this moonlight between the trees, and even this moment and I myself. The eternal hourglass of existence is turned upside down again and again, and you with it, speck of dust!"
>
> — FRIEDRICH NIETZSCHE, *The Gay Science*

Nietzsche and Eternal Return

In *Groundhog Day* a weatherman must relive the same day over and over again, with no hope of escape. Only when he begins to live for the present (despite the fact that it is always the same day) is he released from this curse. The story beautifully illustrates Friedrich Nietzsche's thoughts about eternal return and how we perceive the importance of the future, and we will see how Nietzsche was able to offer an alternative to the Christian view of the meaning of life.

Any discussion of the meaning of life quickly invites one very difficult question: Is that meaning self-created and self-imposed or is life meaningless without some form of validation from outside itself? Traditionally, in western societies, the prevailing view has been that the meaning or purpose of this life is determined by something external to and greater than us, and that this life is, purely in and of itself, really not all that meaningful. What is truly of value, spiritual union with God, is available only after our deaths.

Christianity has a linear view of time and it is the future (when we will be in heaven) that gives value to the present. According to Nietzsche, this aspect of Christianity is essentially life-denying, and for this reason corrupts our view of our time here on Earth. His alternative involves rejecting the linear conception of time. Rather than moving on to a better (or worse, if we are bad) place after this life, we would relive our life over and over again, exactly as we had before. This possibility has been called *eternal return*.

This Is the *Last* Time I Will Do the Groundhog Day Festival

Groundhog Day provides a wonderful means of presenting Nietzsche's ideas about eternal return. In it Bill Murray stars as Phil the weatherman who has worked for the same station for several years and is hoping to move on to a job at a larger station in the near future. In the opening scene, Phil is doing his forecast for the evening news and it is clear that he is intelligent, funny, unhappy, and bored. He seems disconnected from what he is doing, as if he had done it thousands of times before (which presumably he had).

We quickly learn that he is about to cover a Groundhog Day celebration, in the small town of Punxsutawney, for the fourth year in a row, and he is especially unhappy about it. He is expecting to move on to something better soon, leaving this station, and the Groundhog Day festival, behind him. "This will be the *last* time I will do the Groundhog Day festival," he proclaims. This thought pleases him, since he dislikes the people around him ("People are morons" he claims at one point) and the festival itself ("same old shtick every year").

Unfortunately for Phil, the weather is worse than he predicted and he is forced to spend another night in Punxsutawney. Even worse, when he awakens he finds himself reliving Groundhog Day all over again, and again, and again. *Groundhog Day*, then, is the story of a man who must come to grips with the bleak prospect of having no future, who must relive the same day over and over again among people he disdains in a town he dislikes. It is also the story of a man who comes to appreciate and love his life as it is rather than dreaming of a better future while detesting his present.

The Greatest Weight

Nietzsche thought the Christian belief in Heaven caused negative attitudes towards the present. If we believe this world is inhabited by Satan, that the end is truly near and will be followed by something far better, then this life will be seen as a burden, to be merely endured until something better arrives. Nietzsche thought that this life-denying future orientation was especially attractive to the least powerful members of society, giving them hope for a better time to come, and helping them endure a situation that they could not change. Consider the following lyrics to an old spiritual:

> I'll see Jesus, hallelujah, when I lay my burden down,
> I'll see Jesus, hallelujah, when I lay my burden down
>
> I'm goin' home to live in glory, when I lay my burden down
> I'm goin' home way over in heaven, when I lay my burden down[1]

Or the following:

> One glad mornin', when this life is over
> I'll fly away, to the sky[2]

These lyrics help illustrate why Nietzsche thought that Christian doctrine leads to a denial of the importance of this life, and a rejection of much of what this life has to offer. Death is presented as something to be welcomed because this life is a burden, an unpleasant prelude to the good stuff that we will experience later. It will be a glad morning when the burden of this life is finally cast aside, so that we can fly away to a better

---

[1] Alan Lomax, *The Land Where Blues Began* (New York: Pantheon), p. 34.
[2] Lomax, p. 105.

place. It is our future in heaven that matters, and this explains why early Christians shunned the pursuit of worldly goods such as fame, wealth, and power. That there is something better than this world, and that this "vale of tears" is something to be tolerated temporarily, a burden to be endured, is an enduring Christian theme.[3]

Nietzsche thought most people would be depressed by the thought that there was no God, no heaven, no life after death. It would be a depressing and terrible thought because these beliefs provide us with comfort and strength and help us persevere in difficult times. Indeed, Nietzsche thought Christianity was so popular because it provided ordinary people a way of giving meaning to a life that involves pain, sadness, and death. This is why the passage introducing the idea of eternal return is titled "The Greatest Weight"—the knowledge that there is nothing better than this life would be a terrible burden, an enormous weight upon our minds.

In place of the Christian linear conception of time, with its emphasis on future reward, Nietzsche asks us to consider a radically different possibility. What if this life is all that we have? What if, rather than death being a chance to enter Heaven, we relive this life again and again? What would you do if you learned that there were no after-life, and that you were doomed to live this life over and over again, exactly as you have this time?

> Would you not throw yourself down and gnash your teeth and curse the demon who spoke thus? Or have you once experienced a tremendous moment when you would have answered him: "You are a god and never have I heard anything more divine." If this thought gained possession of you, it would change you as you are or perhaps crush you. The question in each and every thing, "Do you desire this once more and innumerable times more?" would lie upon your actions as the greatest weight. Or how well disposed would you have to become to yourself and to life to crave nothing more fervently than this ultimate confirmation and seal?[4]

---

[3] Consider, for example, the popularity of the *Left Behind* series of books, or the common Christian reaction to a tragic death: "He's in a better place now."
[4] Nietzsche, *The Gay Science* (New York: Vintage, 1974), Section 341.

The difference, as Nietzsche saw it, is the difference between a metaphysics that lends itself to life affirmation and a metaphysics that lends itself to life denial. Will we embrace a linear view of time, and turn away from this life while hoping for a bigger prize? Or will we embrace the thought that there is nothing more than this life, and we will have to endure it again and again? The alternative to the Christian ideal of a person who successfully evades the temptations of this life for future reward is:

> the ideal of the most high spirited, alive, world affirming being who has not only come to terms and learned to get along with whatever was and is, but who wants to have what was and is repeated into all eternity, shouting insatiably *da capo* [again, from the start]—not only to himself but to the whole play.[5]

It is a person who loves himself and life because it gives him a chance to choose an ideal and work to perfect himself according to that ideal. Unlike the Greeks who thought life was a matter of becoming who you truly are, Nietzsche thought that this ideal is freely chosen. "We must overcome even the Greeks!" he claims. The Greek motto, "Become who you are!" should be replaced with "Invent who you are!" The challenge presented by the thought of eternal return, then, is this: Are you strong enough to freely choose and live according to an ideal, an ideal that is appropriate for you as an individual (and therefore not appropriate for everyone) and that has no metaphysical basis (such as God or heaven)?

Eternal return, then, should not be understood as another metaphysical view. Nietzsche is not simply suggesting that we adopt his view of the universe (eternal return) instead of the Christian view (linear time). We can distinguish eternal return as a metaphysical thesis (we actually will live the exact some life over and over again) from eternal return as a "what if?" intended to provoke us into thinking about alternative ways of understanding our time on this earth. It is as a provocative "what if?" that eternal return has value, not as a metaphysical thesis. What if there is nothing more than this life? How would you live?

---

[5] Nietzsche, *Beyond Good and Evil*, (New York: Vintage, 1989), Section 56.

What Would You Do if You Were Stuck in One Place, and Every Day Was Exactly the Same, and Nothing You Did Mattered?

Phil the weatherman is faced with a situation very similar to the one envisioned by Nietzsche. It is not exactly eternal return, because Phil relives one day rather than an entire lifetime and (more importantly) he learns from his experience and alters his behavior accordingly. But since eternal return is not a metaphysical thesis, these differences are of little importance. Phil is directly confronted with the possibility that he has no future, that he must relive an ordinary day over and over again, and this is why *Groundhog Day* s helps to illuminate Nietzsche's ideas. Phil does not appear to be a religious person, but he does live for tomorrow in a way that devalues today. He is forced to relive the same day over and over again, with no hope of a better future. When Groundhog Day begins its eternal return, he feels his "greatest weight" because he must relive over and over again a day he detests.

When Phil tries to escape Punxsutawney, he is prevented by a police officer who informs him that a blizzard is coming. "You can go back to Punxsutawney or you can freeze to death!" the officer shouts at Phil, neatly summing up his life. He can come to grips with the fact that Punxsutawney, the Groundhog Day festival, and the people he disdains *are* his life, or he can further withdraw from his actual imperfect life, thinking of a time when things will be perfect. Phil chooses to go back to Punxsutawney, and is forced to relive Groundhog Day until he no longer lives for tomorrow.

How does Phil react to being trapped in a time and place he despises? At first he is disoriented and confused. While drinking beer with a couple of locals, he asks, "What would you do if everything you did was the same and nothing you did mattered? One friend responds "That about sums it up for me"; the other looks and him and says: "Some guys would look at this glass and see it as half full. Others would see it as half empty. I see you as a half empty kind of guy," which seems an accurate description of Phil up to that point. Phil then asks, "What if there were no tomorrow?" One of his friends responds, "Then there would be no consequences, no hangovers, we could do whatever we wanted!" Phil agrees, and decides to begin seeing his cup as half full. He starts driving wildly, "I'm not gonna live by their rules any more!" The thought that there is no tomorrow has given him a sense of freedom to reject conventional norms.

How does Phil use his freedom? He attempts to seduce a woman. He spends day after day learning about a woman so he can manipulate her into sleeping with him. At first it is Nancy, one of the residents of Punxsutawney. She turns out to be relatively easy to manipulate, and Phil loses interest in her. Rather than recognizing that a casual sexual relationship is not really an adequate purpose for his life, Phil turns his attention to his co-worker, Rita. Rita is very different from Phil and Nancy. She is honest and kind and happy with her life. She is also not interested in a superficial relationship with Phil, so spending the night with her turns out to be a serious challenge. Phil spends days (weeks? years?), trying to attain his goal of spending the night with Rita.

At this point in the movie, Phil is no more interested in his present day life than he was prior to Groundhog Day. He has simply changed goals. Previously, he looked forward to a better job at a better station and disregarded the importance of his actual life. Now he pursues a woman who is not really interested in him. He plays a part (fun loving, interested in French poetry, interested in *her*) for no other reason than to advance towards a future goal. In doing so, however, he is casting away whatever value his daily life actually has. He still values the future over the present.

When it becomes clear that he is not going to achieve his goal, Phil once again perceives his life as hopeless, and he is clearly overwhelmed and worn out by his experience. He smashes his alarm clock each morning. At one point he steals a car and the groundhog and drives over a cliff. He steps in front of a truck, jumps off of a ledge and takes other drastic actions to end his ordeal. Each attempt fails. These actions are *understandable*. It's not difficult to see how someone could be driven to such extreme behavior if he perceived life to be meaningless, and it's not difficult to understand why Phil now sees his life as meaningless. It is not an admirable response to his situation. It suggests life has handed him more than he can handle; it suggests weakness.

Eventually, Phil comes to grips with his situation. Rather than substitute some new goal for the old goal of getting a better job, rather than acting with reckless abandon, Phil relaxes, and makes the best of his situation. He helps change a stranger's tire; he tries to help an old man, though the man dies. Even though his actions are different from what might be expected of the "old Phil" he is still more himself than he was when he was pursuing Rita. Previously he would laugh and start playful snowball fights, but it was all very contrived. He did not enjoy the snowball fight, he valued it only for what it might bring him in the future. Now he rescues a boy from falling every day, at the same time and the place, calling the boy a "little jerk" for failing to thank him. He is sincerely Phil in a way he was not while pursuing Rita. Phil explains his situation to Rita and she (finally) spends the night with him to see what will happen when morning comes. They spend their time flipping cards into a hat, prompting Rita to ask him "Is this how you spend eternity?" At one point she looks at him and says, "I don't know Phil, maybe it's not a curse. It just depends on how you look at it." Phil smiles, but his expression reveals that things are not quite that easy. He has fully embraced his situation, but he has no illusions about it. When he wakes up, Rita is gone and he must relive Groundhog Day once again. But this time, when he gives his Groundhog Day performance, he concludes by saying, "standing here in Punxsutawney. . . . I could not imagine a better fate" and he is finally released from his curse.

"What? A Great Man? I Always See Only the Actor of his Own Ideal"[6]

We are offered different perspectives on Phil's situation throughout the movie. "What if there were no tomorrow?" "What if nothing you did mattered?" "How should you spend eternity?" There is an interesting contradiction in the following fact: there seems to be something right about each of these three ways of characterizing Phil's situation, but they are mutually incompatible. It can't be the case that there will be no tomorrow *and* we must decide how to spend eternity. It can't be the case that nothing I do matters and I have a grave responsibility with respect to how I spend my time. It can't be the case that despair and exhilara-

---

[6] *Beyond Good and Evil*, section 97.

tion are both appropriate responses to the situation. If each of these three incompatible ways of conceiving the situation captures something true about it, then we are not facing an intellectual choice. We are not deciding which option most closely approximates the truth. It is in an important sense a moral choice, a choice about who we want to be and what sort of life we are going to live. Rita is right, then, at least in part. We do have to make a choice regarding how we will conceive of our situation, and it is a choice that matters.

How should we choose? Nietzsche thought that resignation and resentment were the responses of a weak person. The moral choice we must make regarding how we will see our situation should express strength. We should choose to see our lives as an opportunity to become uniquely full of life, as an opportunity to choose an ideal to strive for. This ideal should be set high, to provide a real challenge for us. This life, with all of its pains and sorrows, provides us with worthy challenges, and an opportunity to perfect ourselves according to our own ideal. This ideal will then "negate" (to use Nietzsche's language) other ways of living insofar as they are incompatible with the ideal. But, unlike future oriented perspectives, it is not *essentially* a negation. It is not a loud "No!" to life. To embrace eternal return is to embrace all of life.

Modern Americans, including most Christians, do not need Nietzsche's help in renouncing an ascetic lifestyle. Convents and monasteries are not overfull and turning people away. But Nietzsche does help us understand our alternatives. He draws our attention to the fact that how we conceive of life and its meaning dramatically affects how we live. We should not, however, merely define ourselves negatively. To do so leaves a hole where our ideals should be. Also, we should not be overly reliant on any metaphysical view to give meaning to our life. We should not, in other words, look outside of ourselves for meaning. To look for meaning outside of our actual life is to adopt a metaphysical crutch when we should rely on our own strength.

If Nietzsche is correct, Christianity as practiced by most Christians is problematic because its ideals and norms are not freely chosen. Instead, they result from social pressures and for this reason will reflect a "lowest common denominator." They will be ideals suitable for everyone in general and no one in particular. So, while originally Christianity may have provided a set of challenging ideals, those ideals now require little of us. John Stuart Mill makes a similar same point in *On Liberty*. According to Mill:

> All Christians believe that the blessed are the poor and humble, and those who are ill-used by the world; that it is easier for a camel to pass through the eye of a needle than for a rich man to enter the kingdom of heaven; that they should judge not, lest they be judged; that they should swear not at all; that they should love their neighbor as themselves; that if one take their cloak, they should give him their coat also; that they should take no thought for the morrow; that if they would be perfect, they should sell all that they have and give it to the poor. They are not insincere when they say that they believe these things. They do believe them, as people believe what they have always heard lauded and never discussed. But in the sense of that living belief which regulates conduct, they believe these doctrines just up to the point to which it is usual to act upon them.[7]

Mill continues:

> But any one who reminded them that the maxims require an infinity of things which they never even think of doing would gain nothing but to be classed among those very unpopular characters who affect to be better than other people. The doctrines have no hold on ordinary believers—are not a power in their minds. They have an habitual respect for the sound of them, but no feeling which spreads from the words to the things signified, and forces the mind to take them in, and make them conform to the formula. Whenever conduct is concerned, they look round for Mr. A and B to direct them how far to go in obeying Christ.

Christianity as practiced, Nietzsche maintains (and Mill seems to agree), amounts to living in accordance with undemanding negative standards set by other people. Is he right? Consider how many Christians today believe that Christians must oppose abortion, should speak out against homosexual marriage, and should decry the absence of God in public places. Just how demanding are these standards? How challenging is it for the typical male to live a heterosexual life without abortions, while occasionally complaining about a court decision?

---

[7] John Stuart Mill, *On Liberty* (Indianapolis: Hackett, 1978), Chapter 2.

The point is not that Christians are wrong on these issues, or that these issues are unimportant. Furthermore, the point is not that living as Jesus lived would be easy. To the contrary, it would be very challenging. Turning the other cheek, giving more than is asked of us, and willingly sacrificing ourselves for what we believe in are all very demanding. The point is that these are not central to Christianity as practiced, despite being important Christian themes. The hard edges of Christianity have been knocked off, so to speak, to make the religion more acceptable to everyone. (When was the last time you heard a Christian mention Judgment Day? These days everyone goes straight to heaven and there is no need for the risky business of being judged.) The problem is that the Christian, for all practical purposes, is no different from anyone else. Nietzsche states: "The Buddhist does not act like the non-Buddhist; the Christian acts like all the world and has a Christianity of ceremonies and moods."[8] Nietzsche asks:

> Where has the last feeling of decency and self respect gone, when our even our statesmen . . . Anti-Christians through and through in their deeds, still call themselves Christians today and attend communion? . . . Whom then does Christianity negate?"[9]

Very few, I think, is his implied answer.

If Nietzsche is correct, Christianity has become little more than a religion that requires us to adopt a certain posture. As practiced, it is no longer provides ideals worth adopting. It does little to distinguish us from others, and it does not call upon us to strive for self-perfection. The problem is not unique to Christianity. It occurs whenever we try to define ourselves negatively or easily. Seeing myself as a conservative (or an environmentalist) when all this requires of me is a ritualistic condemnation of liberals (or sports utility vehicles) is equally problematic. These standards are barely worth having as defining features of ourselves. They provide no positive ideal to strive for; they do not distinguish us from many others (although we will exaggerate the numbers) and they demand nothing from us. It is like giving up tequila for lent. No matter how much I might

---

[8] Nietzsche, *The Will to Power* (New York: Random House, 1968), Section 191.
[9] Nietzsche, *The Anti-Christ* (New York: Penguin Classics, 1990), Section 38.

moan about the difficulty I have imposed upon myself, there is no real sacrifice and I am no different from those for whom lent is irrelevant.

Similar things can be said about the prevalence of tattoos and piercings in society today. Masses of people are trying to assert their individuality by doing what everyone else is doing, in a slightly different way, in a slightly different place. It is as if there is a great migration of rings, baubles, and graffiti across the collective body of U.S. citizens. It is like shouting, "Look, I am different *too!*" But these are feeble attempts at establishing individuality because they are culturally chosen. And yet we hear it said that "This is who I am, who I *really* am!"

Call Me Bronco

Contrast this with Phil, strutting into the movie theater, dressed in full cowboy garb. "Call me Bronco," he says, when his date addresses him as Phil. Phil is expressing something important about himself (at the very least, a good sense of humor and the strength to make the best of a strange situation), and in so doing, his individuality is expressed as well. There is no pretense that the cowboy outfit expresses his individuality because he *really* belongs in such an outfit. The clothes are not the person, and the point of the scene is clearly not that Phil has found his true self. He certainly is not truly Bronco, yet his individuality is established by rejecting cultural norms and imposing himself and his self created ideal (for the evening at least) on the world. He is strong enough to embrace his (terrible? absurd? soul crushing?) situation and still thrive and laugh.

Embracing eternal return involves a self-assertion, which is consciously without any metaphysical justification. Nietzsche doesn't need to claim that *in fact* there are endless recurring cycles in the universe and we shouldn't look for something to *force* us to embrace this life. Insofar as we believe in some transcendent value, and insofar as this belief is supported by looking about for a comfortable consensus, we are hardly better off than if we were always looking forward to eternal happiness. We have adopted a culturally determined way of dealing with life's problems, and are looking away from this world rather than towards it.

This is why Phil as Bronco wonderfully illustrates Nietzsche's point. Nietzsche claims that "[a] man's maturity consists in having found again the seriousness one had as a child, at play."[10] What could he mean? A child at play is very serious, despite the fact that he or she is well aware that it is all a game. This knowledge does nothing to diminish the seriousness or importance of the game, the imposition of oneself onto the world by creating rules and goals is sufficient to imbue the world with meaning, purpose, and value. When we take ourselves too seriously, especially when negatively oriented towards something or someone, we cease being a child at play. We lose sight of how our perspective, the values we have created and endorsed, have played a part in creating what is before us. We are in a sense complicit in creating the terrible event. Nietzsche's alternative to Christianity, then, involves "self expression without metaphysical justification." It avoids culturally predetermined ways of living and metaphysical crutches. It involves a freely embraced ideal, an ideal embraced without any pretense of metaphysical necessity, and this ideal must be also be demanding, otherwise it will not serve to distinguish us from others.

Nietzsche is not romanticizing life. He is not claiming that "life is what you make it" if that means that adopting a cheery disposition will make everything good in your life. He states that:

> we must beware of superficiality and get to the bottom of the matter, resisting all sentimental weakness: life itself is essentially appropriation, injury, overpowering of what is alien and weaker; suppression, hardness, imposition of one's own forms, incorporation and at the least, at its mildest, exploitation - but why should one always use those words in which a slanderous intent has been imprinted for the ages?[11]

Rita is mistaken when she claims, "It *all* depends on how you see it", for there are burdens in this life. Nietzsche's point is that we can incorporate the bad into our life as a necessary aspect of who we are, and affirm it all.

In closing I want to mention the Greek myth of Sisyphus. Sisyphus's situation is much like Phil's. Sisyphus disrespected

---

[10] *Beyond Good and Evil*, Section 94.
[11] *Beyond Good and Evil*, Section 259.

the gods and they punished him by condemning him to roll a stone up a mountain, at which point the stone would roll back down the hill and he would have to do it again. Camus, in reflecting upon Sisyphus's situation, wrote:

> I leave Sisyphus at the foot of the mountain. One always finds one's burden again. But Sisyphus teaches the higher fidelity that negates the gods and raises rocks. He too concludes that all is well. This universe henceforth without a master seems to him neither sterile nor futile. Each atom of that stone, each mineral flake of that night-filled mountain, in itself forms a world. The struggle itself towards the heights is enough to fill a man's heart. One must imagine Sisyphus happy.[12]

Why must one imagine Sisyphus happy? Our lives too are cyclical. Phil's life prior to going to Punxsutawney was not all that different from the strange events of Groundhog Day, and our lives are not all that different from his. Whether we like it or not we find ourselves reliving the same day over and over again. For some of us this cycle will be measured in semesters and school years and we will find ourselves once again giving our "First Day Lecture." For others the cycle involves work weeks and grumbling about Monday morning. In either case, the cycles of life are unavoidable. Will the knowledge that you will relive the same day over and over again drive you mad and drag you down? Will you seek to comfort yourself by telling yourself that it will end someday? Or will it compel you to choose some way to integrate yourself—including your past, present and future—into something worthwhile?

---

[12] Albert Camus, *The Myth of Sisyphus and Other Essays* (New York: Vintage, 1991), p. 123.

To Think About

1. How would you describe or explain Phil and his behavior through the course of *Groundhog Day?* When does he change? Why does he change?

2. How different is Phil's situation from ours?

3. Would you live differently if you knew you would live forever? Would you live differently if you knew there was no heaven?

4. Suppose on your deathbed someone were to ask you: "Would you do it all over again?" If you answered, "Yes," wouldn't this tell us all we needed to know about the meaningfullness of your life?

To Read Next

Friedrich Nietzsche. *The Gay Science*. New York: Vintage, 1989.

Friedrich Nietzsche. *Thus Spoke Zarathustra*. New York: Penguin, 1976. The idea of eternal return can be found in both these works.

Friedrich Nietzsche. *The Genealogy of Morals*. New York: Vintage, 1999.

Friedrich Nietzsche. *Twilight of the Idols and The Antichrist*. New York: Penguin Classics, 1990. Nietzsche's critique of Christian morality can be found in both these works.

Walter Kaufmann. *Nietzsche: Philosopher, Psychologist, Antichrist*. Princeton: Princeton University Press, 1980. A sympathetic discussion of Nietzsche's ideas.

You Mean We Have to Say Something about Ourselves?

DAVID BAGGETT is Assistant Professor of Philosophy at King's College in Wilkes-Barre, Pennsylvania. He is co-editor (with Shawn Klein) of *Harry Potter and Philosophy: If Aristotle Ran Hogwarts,* working on a book on the Euthyphro Dilemma with Jerry Walls, and slated to co-edit *Alfred Hitchcock and Philosophy* (with Bill Drumin). He used to do a lot of work in ethics, but hasn't done an ethical thing in years. Because he thinks he's solved the mystery of life with the essay in this volume, Dave's expecting early tenure. Obviously he's mistaken.

MICHAEL BAUR is Associate Professor of Philosophy at Fordham University, and very often looks like he just woke up. His two main areas of research are German Idealism and the philosophy of law; he is translator of Johann Gottlieb Fichte's *Foundations of Natural Right* (Cambridge University Press, 2000). He has published journal articles on Kant, Fichte, Hegel, Aquinas, Lonergan, Adorno, Habermas, Rawls, Heidegger, and Gadamer—even though he does not remember writing any of those articles. He does not have any tattoos, he thinks his wife is perfect, and much of the time he just wants to eat potato chips.

SHAI BIDERMAN is a Ph.D. candidate in Philosophy at Boston University. He's interested in contemporary continental philosophy, the relationship between philosophy and culture, and ethics. Shai has written on the notion of reasonability in the TV series *Seinfeld*, and on the relationship between law and desire in Jim Jarmusch's *Down by Law*. He spends his free time reading obituaries, and quarrelling with lampposts. As for the meaning of life, he claims it starts with a G, has four syllables and might attack you if given the chance.

KIMBERLY A. BLESSING is Assistant Professor of Philosophy at Buffalo State College. She is happy to have returned to her hometown of Buffalo, New York, where, she claims, weathermen simply re-run footage from the Blizzard of '77. Her areas of interest began with Descartes and his "missing ethical theory." Early in her career, she ambitiously set out to become *the* expert on all subjects about which Descartes had nothing to say. Unfortunately, nobody seemed interested in anything she had to say about that about which Descartes said nothing.

MARK T. CONARD is Assistant Professor of Philosophy at Marymount Manhattan College in New York City. He's the co-editor of *The Simpsons and Philosophy*, and *Woody Allen and Philosophy*, both published by Open Court, and is the editor of the forthcoming *The Philosophy of Film Noir* (University Press of Kentucky). In addition, he's the author of the novels *Dark as Night*, and *Williams Bucket* (forthcoming), both published by UglyTown. After spending most of his adult life in Philadelphia, he now lives in New York with his cat, Mona, and a fifteen-year-old case of chronic insomnia. Besides possessing the usual vices, he's invented a few interesting ones of his own.

NIR EISIKOVITS is an attorney and a Ph.D. candidate in Philosophy at Boston University. He is interested in legal and political philosophy, as well as in the philosophy of international relations (because it sounds cool). Nir has published on the role of luck in criminal law, and on conceptions of personal identity found in different areas of the law. He's looking for a new hobby, having recently given up chasing ambulances, and has asked to be woken up if anyone figures out the meaning of life.

STEVEN FESMIRE teaches philosophy and heads the Environmental Studies department at Green Mountain College—Vermont's environmental liberal arts college. That is, when he's not gardening, hiking, camping, cross-country skiing, or traveling with his partner Heather Keith. He is the author of *John Dewey and Moral Imagination: Pragmatism in Ethics*, published in 2003 by Indiana University Press.

REBECCA HANRAHAN is an assistant professor of philosophy at Whitman College. She received her A.B. from Smith College and her M.A. and Ph.D. from the University of North Carolina at Chapel Hill. When asked to write a short but witty description of herself, she found herself in a bit of a bind. As a feminist, she is contractually obligated to never be witty. So, she decided to play it straight here (no pun intended). Her research interests include epistemology, feminism, and environmental ethics. When asked what the meaning of life is, her usual response is—why would you want life to have meaning?

GEORGE T. HOLE is Distinguished Teaching Professor at Buffalo State College. His most recent publication is "Pragmatic Platonism: Skillful Means for Everyday Enlightenment," in *Teaching Philosophy*, 27:1 (March 2004), where he discusses more fully his incorporation of experiments in doing philosophy. He has a practice in philosophical counseling. He was recently unanimously elected to the Sports Hall of Fame at the University of Rochester for his record achievements in football and track.

HEATHER KEITH, in spite of being a genuine flatlander from Nebraska, enjoys living and working in the mountains of Vermont, where her passions include skiing, snowshoeing, hiking, mountain biking, festival-going, and leaf-peeping. In the off season, she teaches philosophy at Lyndon State College in Vermont's beautiful Northeast Kingdom. Her research interests include American philosophy, Asian studies, and ethics.

WALTER OTT is Assistant Professor of Philosophy at East Tennessee State University, where he also directs the undergraduate honors in philosophy program. His work focuses mainly on the history of philosophy, especially early modern empiricism. Recent work includes *Locke's Philosophy of Language* (Cambridge University Press, 2003) and "The Cartesian Context of Berkeley's Attack on Abstraction," forthcoming in the *Pacific Philosophical Quarterly*. He lives with his dog Helga, who divides her time between napping and committing minor acts of civil disobedience.

ERIC REITAN is an Assistant Professor of Philosophy at Oklahoma State University, where he strives faithfully to live out the roles of teacher, scholar, husband, father, dog-owner, amateur violinist, and award-winning novelist (the last without success). While he is often tempted to believe that the meaning of life is found in earning tenure, he devotes considerable time and energy to writing philosophical articles aimed at convincing himself otherwise. Ironically, this effort seems to be helping him in his tenure bid.

JONATHAN J. SANFORD is Assistant Professor of Philosophy at Franciscan University of Steubenville. His publications include *Categories: Historical and Systematic Essays* (as co-editor and co-contributor, 2004), and "Scheler *versus* Scheler: The Case for a Better Ontology of the Person," *American Catholic Philosophical Quarterly* (forthcoming). He has contributed articles to volumes in Open Court's Popular Culture and Philosophy series. Though Sanford would like to point out that the phrase 'meaning of life' is ambiguous, he would also like to make the *non sequitur* that it (not the ambiguity) has much to do with playing with your children.

ANTHONY C. SCIGLITANO, JR. resides in Jersey City and teaches Catholic Theology in the Religious Studies Department at Seton Hall University. He is currently writing a book on Catholic theology as it relates to Judaism. When asked about the meaning of life, he pauses dramatically, makes a serious face, and with due gravity informs the student that she will not find it in *The Da Vinci Code*. Most of the ideas in his chapter are not original to Anthony—in fact, he is highly suspicious of Originality; the arrangement, relation, and application of the ideas are, however, his fault alone. He dedicates this essay to his parents, Jeanine and Tony, who know well the drama and beauty of this life.

MICHAEL SILBERSTEIN is Associate Professor of Philosophy at Elizabethtown College and an adjunct at the University of Maryland where he is also a faculty member in the Foundations of Physics Program and a Fellow on the Committee for Philosophy and the Sciences. He has published and delivered papers on both philosophy of science and philosophy of mind. His primary research interests are philosophy of physics and philosophy of cognitive neuroscience. His most recent book is *The Blackwell Guide to Philosophy of Science* (co-edited with Peter Machamer), published in 2002; he is currently working on a book entitled *The Whole Story: Emergence, Reduction and Explanation Across the Disciplines.* And because he is eclectic to the point of being schizoid, he also does work in philosophy and film and is currently working on a book entitled *Illuminating Images: Philosophy, Film and Interpretation.* He lives in Pennsylvania Dutch country where scrapple is the meaning of life and all foot massages are Platonic.

JIM SPENCE teaches at Bowling Green State University in Ohio. He has also taught at Louisiana State University in Baton Rouge (great blues!) and The University of Tennessee at Knoxville (great mountains!) and a number of other places. His area of interest is moral philosophy. He wonders about when we should hold someone responsible for the consequences of their actions, whether or not their intentions really matter, and sometimes, actually, quite often, he wonders about Nietzsche. He usually teaches ethics-related courses and has recently taught courses in business ethics, bioethics, and the morality of war.

KEVIN L. STOEHR is professor of humanities at Boston University. He has edited *Film and Knowledge* (McFarland, 2002) and is the co-author of *Jung's Psychology as a Spiritual Practice and Way of Life* (University Press of America, 2002). When asked by students about the meaning of life, he simply tells them to get some rest and then prepare well for the *final examination.*

PAUL J. TUDICO is lecturer in the Department of Philosophy and Humanities at East Tennessee State University where he teaches courses in critical thinking and the meaning of life. His interests include ethical theory, political philosophy, and a dog named Hobbes. He confidently asserts that he knows the meaning of life, but feels that revealing the answer would be bad for business.

JERRY L. WALLS is professor of philosophy of religion at Asbury Theological Seminary in Wilmore, Kentucky. Among his top five favorite movies are *Casablanca* and *Hoosiers*. He has contributed chapters to volumes in Open Court's Popular Culture and Philosophy series and is co-editor (with Greg Bassham) of the forthcoming volume *The Chronicles of Narnia and Philosophy*. He has also written *Heaven: The Logic of Eternal Joy* (Oxford University Press) and *Hell: the Logic of Damnation* (Notre Dame University Press). He would like to see a movie where Jay and Silent Bob visit heaven and hell.

WILLIE YOUNG is an assistant professor of theology at King's College, in Wilkes-Barre, Pennsylvania. He has published articles in *New Blackfriars, Literature and Theology*, and *Modern Theology*, as well as contributing to *Baseball and Philosophy* (2004), edited by Eric Bronson. Like Red, he feels free when having a bottle of suds on the roof with his friends. For him, the meaning of life is in compassionate communities of friends, devoted to the life of the mind and creative expression. He hopes to get to Zihuatanejo someday.

JOHN ZAVODNY teaches at a *very* small environmental school in Maine called Unity College. In addition to philosophy classes on everything from introduction to philosophy to eastern thought and postmodernism, he teaches song writing and an introduction to education course. He is currently working with education students to conduct research on his *Perspectives on Environment* course, where students learn about environmental issues by researching, writing, directing, and performing a play. As far as the meaning of life goes . . . whatever it is, I'm sure we can do better.

Index